FATS WALLER

Courtesy of Michael Lipskin.

FATS WALLER

by
Maurice Waller
and
Anthony Calabrese

Foreword by Michael Lipskin

SCHIRMER BOOKS
A Division of Macmillan Publishing Co., Inc.
NEW YORK

Schirmer Books
A Division of Macmillan Publishing Co., Inc.
866 Third Avenue, New York, N.Y. 10022

Collier Macmillan Canada, Ltd.

Schirmer Books Paperback Edition 1979

Library of Congress Catalog Card Number: 77-5208

Printed in the United States of America

Casebound printing number

  2 3 4 5 6 7 8 9 10
Paperback printing number

1 2 3 4 5 6 7 8 9 10

Library of Congress Cataloging in Publication Data

Waller, Maurice.
   Fats Waller.

   Includes index.
   1. Waller, Fats, 1904-1943. 2. Jazz musicians--
United States--Biography. I. Calabrese, Anthony,
joint author.
ML417.W15W3   785.4'2'0924 (B)   77-5208
ISBN 0-02-872730-4
ISBN 0-02-872710-X pbk.

To my mother, Anita.
—from Maurice

For Rosemary, who nurtured, encouraged, tolerated, and believed when no one else did. And for Christopher.
—from Tony

Contents

Foreword by Michael Lipskin **ix**

Acknowledgments **xix**

1 1864–1904
The Background of the Waller Family **1**

2 1914–1919
Fats Discovers Harlem Nightlife **11**

3 1919
The Death of Fats' Mother **17**

4 1920–1922
Fats Meets James P. Johnson and Willie The Lion Smith **25**

5 1922–1924
Fats Marries Edith **35**

6 1923–1924
Fats and the Music Publishers **49**

7 1924–1926
Fats Meets His Second Wife and Captain Maines **55**

8 1927–1928
Fats Writes *Keep Shufflin'* **69**

9 1928–1929
Fats Writes *Load of Coal* **81**

10 1930–1931
Fats Becomes a Recording Regular for RCA **93**

11 1932–1933
    Fats Goes to Work for WLW **105**

12 1934–1936
    Fats Makes It to the Top as a Composer
    and Recording Artist **123**

13 1937–1943
    Buster Shepherd Remembers
    the Good and the Bad Times **141**

14 1940–1943
    Fats at His Peak as a Recording Artist and Songwriter **149**

15 Maurice Remembers His Father **163**

16 1943
    The Death of Fats **175**

    Recording Dates and Personnel **185**

    Fats Waller's Published Songs **209**

    Fats Waller's Unpublished Songs **213**

    Fats Waller's Piano Rolls **217**

    Song Arrangements **219**

    Index **231**

Foreword

There is a growing interest in America's cultural heritage—witness for example the numerous film revivals, pictorial social histories, and expansive record reissues. So today, over thirty years after his death, there is a renewed interest in Thomas "Fats" Waller and his contributions.

Fats Waller excelled in many ways. He was a jazz piano stylist with a touch that influenced the course of the pop and jazz keyboard, a composer of hit songs and Broadway musicals, and an energetic performer capable of bringing happiness to thousands during the mid Depression and early World War II years as they listened to his hundreds of recordings, heard him on network radio, or had the special pleasure of seeing him live with his band "Rhythm."

In 1937, for example, Fats' "I'm Going to Sit Right Down and Write Myself a Letter" would be playing on countless phonographs in both black and white neighborhoods. At the same time, Fletcher Henderson, Benny Goodman, and Louis Armstrong might be playing his "Ain't Misbehavin'" or "Black and Blue." Several publishers would be submitting his latest material to big bands on the road, to record companies, and at remote radio pickups.

Fats Waller's story is unique in that he was able to function both as a popular entertainer and, more privately, as a superb pianist and keyboard composer. Normally, the creativity of a musical artist is directly proportional to the amount of time spent alone. But Fats could, and did, write hit songs and complicated piano pieces, and simultaneously capture an ever-increasing share of public adulation and attention.

Until recently, Fats Waller's piano playing was largely overshadowed by the tools of his success, the singing and writing of pop hits. He was always considered to be a fine jazzman, but was dismissed by many critics with a few short paragraphs that often cited his obvious contributions as a sort of historical footnote. Part of the reason for this oversight was the rapid evolution of jazz that took attention away from the past, focusing on what was topically considered new and "daring." But then, jazz historians traditionally have been biased against artists who have "made it" commercially.

Since stylistic changes in jazz are becoming much more subtle with the disappearance of schools of musical leaders and followers, individualists have come to have much less influence on each other. There is now the necessary breathing room to appreciate a past that includes Fats Waller and his very sophisticated approach to music—music that employs the kind of full voicing and harmonics that few others could approach in richness. The ability to combine tremendous energy with contrasting delicacy and total control was a Waller trademark that his many imitators, both white and black, were unable to duplicate.

This individual creativity is all the more impressive considering its early placement in the history of jazz. Further, Fats and his genius teacher, James P. Johnson, were operating within a more structured musical framework. Today the performer has only to state the simple melody, or "head," and thereafter may improvise with harmonic and rhythmic abandon. In the twenties and thirties, however, the variations and improvisations had to take both the specific chord progressions and the melodic line into account.

In spite of Fats' clowning, heavy drinking, and public image as a happy-go-lucky entertainer, he was capable of an intellectual understanding of the importance of music, and of his role as a black musician. In all his work there was an underlying seriousness and self-respect for what he was doing. If a song he had to sing was banal, he would work out an ingenious parody of the syrupy lyrics, always having the last word at the end. He also refused to portray the stereotyped Negro of the 1930s. In his Hollywood film appearances he insisted on script changes so as not to be put in an ethnically degrading role. If an announcer on a network broadcast would get carried away with adjectives about the hot "colored" sound from Harlem, Fats would retaliate by playing the wrong song—to the horror of the house band, which frantically would try to adjust to the rearranged order of things.

As soon as he could command it, Fats had written into his contracts that he would not have to perform if the promoter did not furnish a tuned Steinway grand piano; and that he would not be required to play boogie woogie, the aborted version of Midwest piano often requested by swing-era fans. The few times recorded that he did acquiesce on the latter point demonstrate his excellent boogie bass, as if to say "I can play this, but prefer not to."

The Fats Waller story is not just one of contrast between public entertainer and serious pianist-composer, but also that of a prodigy. Fats started playing piano as soon as he discovered what it was—when he was six years old, in a neighbor's apartment. He quit high school to work as a movie-theatre organist accompanying the silents, and recorded his first piano solos for Okeh Records when he was eighteen. His first work was published when he was nineteen, and by twenty-five he had highly original piano solos on discs, and was in demand as an accompanist for blues singers.

Listening to this nineteen-year-old accompany Sara Martin, the singer on Okeh, one is amazed at the ability to play newly learned material behind the singer, never getting in the way, always perfectly synchronized with her voice. Even then he demonstrated hints of that clean touch and inventiveness along specific musical guidelines as he subtly bent rules of composition. In no small way was this ability due to the influence of Harlem stride piano and James P. Johnson, the man who brought the style to its creative peak.

"Stride" is a word coined in the early fifties to describe the extremely full jazz piano idiom in which the left hand alternates between single notes, or tenth intervals in the lower portion of the instrument, and chords toward middle C. The left-hand movement takes on a striding appearance, playing both the rhythmic and harmonic structure at the same time, almost trying to be in two places at once. The right hand is thus free to work out melodic improvisations. This musical language developed and was identified with the maturation of Harlem as a cultural center for black America before World War II.

In 1923, when a young Duke Ellington first arrived in New York, he called Harlem "the world's most glamorous atmosphere. Why it's just like the *Arabian Nights.*" Ellington was more than correct, as this small northern section of New York's Manhattan Island was the hub where musicians ended up after leaving New Orleans, Chicago, or St. Louis. The area fostered not only stride piano, but the first big-band jazz units that eventually led to the swing era, and finally bebop.

As Harlem developed, at first middle-class Negro society moved there, and a proper music followed. By 1910 there were enough musicians uptown to form the Clef Club, a booking agency that provided the prejazz orchestras for high society, the show functions of the Castles, and the Ziegfeld Follies. The piano was then the main source of home and saloon entertainment in the United States, and every bar had one. Correspondingly, there appeared a growing number of keyboard "professors," ragtime kids or ticklers as they were called, traveling from city to city and bar to bar. Often they were accompanied by a retinue of "ladies of the evening" who supplemented the musicians' limited income.

From Baltimore to the Jungles, one could hear such colorful

characters as Willie "Egghead" Sewell, "One Leg" Willie Joseph, Walter Gould, Jack "The Bear" Wilson (immortalized by Duke Ellington in a big-band piece of the same name), Richard "Abba Labba" McLean, Freddy "Harmony King" Bryant, William Turk, Fats Harris, and Jess "Old Man" Pickett. As Harlem grew, these pre–World War I musicians slowly migrated to New York, playing a version of ragtime that differed from the slower Midwest sound of Scott Joplin and Tom Turpin. Their music reflected a cosmopolitan exposure, and rather than play specific pieces they used a variety of material that included popular songs of the day and classical themes. Theirs was a faster ragtime that also combined the rhythms of the Southern Baptist church dance known as the ring shout (referred to in James P. Johnson's "Carolina Shout").

When they reached the Northeast, a group of younger pianists that included Eubie Blake, Luckey Roberts, Stephen "Beetle" Henderson, Leroy Tibbs, Willie "The Lion" Smith, and James P. Johnson followed the "professors" around. At the same time, an influx of Southerners and West Indians into Harlem slowly changed the atmosphere of the area from staid middle class to a vibrancy exploding within a set of city blocks featuring a variety of cabarets and nightclubs.

This then became the center of performance and music development where the younger men could expand their ideas and professionalism. Unlike the older pianists, they were very much interested in their music, and did not engage in pimping. They worked more steadily at jobs that gradually demanded reading sheet music and the ability to transpose songs on sight to accompany singers.

After hours the young men would meet, and try to outplay each other. These "cutting contests," in which musicians tried to prove technical superiority over one another, happened throughout jazz history. Sometimes whole bands battled all night. With stride, though, the sound literally went nonstop for hours as one pianist took over from another. Beetle, for instance, would begin a pop tune and play as long as his creative juices would flow. Luckey Roberts, standing by, would then slide in alongside him and, at the end of a chorus, relieve Beetle's hands, one at a time. Luckey would play for as long as he cared, and then Willie The Lion would replace him in the same fashion. Finally the dean, James P. Johnson, would sit in, and in this manner a single tune would last for perhaps a hundred choruses, with seemingly infinite variations.

During the 1920s Cliff Jackson, Donald Lambert, Duke Ellington, Willie Gant, and other younger pianists like Fats Waller entered the cutting contests. As testimony to James P.'s superiority, they often used one of his compositions as the basis of a contest, each performer trying to equal the master on "Harlem Strut" or "Carolina Shout." The nightclub job requirements, and the fine honing of cutting contests, helped evolve Harlem stride into an anachronistically mature idiom unequaled in either variety or subtlety of technique until decades later.

By 1919 it was evident that James P. Johnson was the master and leader of the uptown piano. He could play faster than the others, transpose with a singular facility, and improvise with an inventiveness that didn't stop. Born in New Brunswick, New Jersey, in 1894, Jimmy moved to San Juan Hill while in his teens. As the young Fats would a decade later, James P. played piano day and night as a child. First learning by ear, he sharpened his technique by "woodshedding" (playing in all keys) the rags of the older men. Later he taught himself Bach and Chopin. By the time he was twenty-five he had commercial player-piano rolls on the market, and his "Caprice Rag," "Carolina Shout," "Harlem Strut," and "Mama and Papa Blues" were a part of the repertoire of many other pianists.

James P. remained a musician's musician even though he had pop success on Broadway, recorded beautiful sides with Bessie Smith, and wrote the hit theme of the 1920s, "Charleston." During the Depression he spent most of his time at home in St. Albans, New York, writing serious symphonic works, some of which were performed at the Brooklyn Academy and Carnegie Hall.

Some twenty-odd years since Johnson's death in 1955 we are just beginning to properly evaluate this man's immense influence on everyone from George Gershwin and Fats Waller to Duke Ellington (many early Ellington band pieces are orchestrated by James P. Johnson) and Thelonius Monk.

The story of Fats and James P. would make a book in itself. No student and teacher in jazz were ever closer. Shortly after the death of Fats' mother, James P. took Fats under his wing and painstakingly taught him basic technique, the concept of composition and improvisation, and, of course, the language of stride. Here was a generosity and devotion to music that left a strong, lifelong mark on Fats. Without Johnson, jazz piano's course would have been altered; further, Waller's sound would have been totally different.

While James P. was teaching Fats, Harlem was witnessing the birth of "race" records discs recorded by black talent for the black audience. Although the first supposed jazz record, "Livery Stable Blues" by the Original Dixieland Jass Band, had been released by the Victor Talking Machine Company in 1917, it was a white version of the poetic New Orleans music that was being created in the ghettos throughout the South and Midwest.

Then there were almost no black records, and the only significant ethnic outlet then was through piano player rolls. Eubie Blake, Luckey Roberts, and James P. had all cut rolls by 1916, but the final sound was mechanical, not conducive to displaying the subtle rhythmic and technical differences. For this reason their piano-roll product was distributed in the same manner as that of George Gershwin, Jimmy Durante, Felix Arntd, and Max Kortlander. Young Ellington and Waller studied their masters' styles and techniques by slowing the rolls down and placing their fingers in the depressed keys as the piano played.

In any case, Harlem was host to an ever-increasing number of blues singers, dancers, and instrumentalists, all making the new "hot" music in the uptown nightspots. One songwriter from Georgia, Perry Bradford, had some blues songs, and vainly attempted to get the downtown record companies interested in his material. Ralph Peer, the recording director for Okeh, was finally interested after hearing Mamie Smith, a singer then working in Harlem, sing Bradford's "Crazy Blues." In 1920 an Okeh recording session was arranged, with Willie The Lion conducting the house band from the Club Orient. They cut "That Thing Called Love," "You Can't Keep a Good Man Down," "Crazy Blues" and "It's Right Here for You," all with Mamie Smith as featured vocalist. Okeh released the first two sides without much reaction, probably because they contained more of a novelty than a blues feeling. But when they issued "Crazy Blues" someone had the idea of making sure the Harlem record stores would play the disc.

As uptown people went to work one morning they were astounded to hear, coming out of stores, the sound of one of their own, singing the blues with a band that was definitely from the neighborhood. The response was fantastic, and Okeh, happily surprised, sold hundreds of thousands of this first blues record in black areas throughout the United States. This episode was important because it proved to the music businessmen that there was money to be made in black music, today called R and B or "Soul." Subsequently Okeh, Columbia, Vocalion, Perfect, and other record labels of the 1920s turned out thousands of blues and jazz discs made by the talent of Harlem. W. C. Handy even started a firm uptown, called Black Swan, but eventually had to sell out to Paramount Records, a Midwest company. Finally, Eubie Blake, James P., and others were sought out to accompany blues singers and even cut their own featured solos. Basically, this was how the young Waller was given the opportunity to record, too.

Technically, the method of recording bears little resemblance to the complicated 16- and 24-track systems of today. Long before magnetic tape was invented, wax was used as the medium. A pizza-shaped "platter" revolved on a heavy turntable as a stylus cut a groove corresponding to the sound played. The artist had to get the performance correct all the way through, or be required to do another "take" on a completely new wax platter, from start to finish. There was no editing possible, and the result was monophonic. If the session director liked the wax, it would be sent to a plant for processing; and what they played was what you got. With few exceptions, pop and race records were available as ten-inch, 78-rpm discs that allowed slightly more than an average of three minutes' playing time. Interestingly, the duration of most pop 45-rpm issues and single selections on LPs remain within this time limit, even today when this is no longer necessary.

This digression into recording history is appropriate, since Fats Waller cut his first solos in 1922 and made records every year—except 1932—until his death. By 1934 the pianist's audience was large enough to convince RCA Victor to sign him to an exclusive contract, furthering his recording activity from then on. The following narrative is filled with references to his work in this area.

Since much of the material was written immediately before the recording session, and because he and the band were on the road for months at a time, they often had to learn selections in the studio. Fats' method of preparation was summed up during a radio interview conducted by Eddie "Rochester" Anderson. Anderson asked him when he had time to rehearse, and he replied "We rehearse on the job the following evening, at the public's expense."

The session director or the artist and repertoire (A&R) man would discuss songs to be cut. Often, his interest in certain material was as financial as it was musical. Publishers would heavily promote the songs they owned, by tie-ins with movies, on radio, and at live engagements, and so the A&R man had a better chance at a hit with their help. And the A&R man would not infrequently be rewarded with a portion of the publishing income for himself.

After the songs had been decided, Fats would announce to the band which order the solos would be in, and they would learn the material by ear. Occasionally a comic routine would be created. Working diligently, they would complete as many as twelve sides in one day. (Nowadays, pop artists take many weeks, sometimes months, to complete one L.P.) Spontaneity was omnipresent, as was Fats' effervescent humor—which, to the chagrin of the RCA executives, often made use of double entendre. Parody was the Waller reaction to the banal material he was asked to record. Before the bridge of his 1937 "Spring Cleaning (Getting Ready for Love)," the pianist yells "No, lady, we can't haul your ashes for fifty cents. That's bad business." Before his piano solo on the 1936 "Christopher Columbus," he says "Since the crew was making merry, Mary got up and went home." And on one of his best-sellers from the same year, "It's a Sin to Tell a Lie," he warns, "If you break my heart I'll break your jaw and then I'll die."

Jazz critics attacked Waller and Victor for the material he recorded. Had he not been successful commercially, and had he not been pressured to record songs that caused him to invent satire, we would have been left with far fewer joyous records by the Rhythm—and much less humor.

A Harlem stride offshoot was songwriting. More than any other jazz idiom, this force somehow was applicable to manuscript. Luckey Roberts, Willie The Lion Smith, James P. Johnson, and Fats Waller all saw Tin Pan Alley as both a means for easy cash and a vehicle for further success. Fats' "Wildcat Blues" was published in 1923, and he continued writing until his death. The list of copyrighted songs at the end of this book attests to his prolificacy, highlighted by such tunes as "Honey Suckle Rose," "Ain't Misbehavin'," "Stealin' Apples," and "Blue Turning Grey Over You."

Because there were so many melodies in his head, Fats often would give away much of what he created to down-and-out friends with hard-luck stories. He even set up his sidekick Buddy Allen in a publishing company, handing him a pile of manuscripts. And he would sell a potential hit, outright, for quick cash, and then watch it become a best-seller, with another man credited as writer.

During the twenties Fats and his legendary lyricist, Andy Razaf, would work on tunes whenever they needed money. (Razaf was so facile that Eubie Blake claimed all he had to do was play a new melody twice and "Andy would hand me the completed words." This may be an overstatement, but the fluid prose of Razaf's hundreds of hits with different melodists attests to his ability.)

After the writing was done, the duo would ride the subway down to the Brill Building at Forty-ninth Street and Broadway, where most of the publishers maintained offices. Always looking for new songs, the publishers would furnish a piano, some booze, and rapt attention. Fats and Andy often would meet George Gershwin, Vincent Youmans, or Irving Berlin in the piano rooms of such firms as Santly—Joy, Shapiro—Bernstein, Leo Feist, Mills Music, and Joe Davis. During the Depression both Fats and James P. were on steady retainer to write.

For years, publishers would give false statements to songwriters—especially Harlemites. Record companies often paid no royalties to unsuspecting artists; and one large firm actually made new acts sign an agreement waiving the total writer's share of income due them on a record of their own composition. Fats and Andy were forced to live by their wits as well as their writing ability.

Like most artists, Fats possessed a very complicated personality. On the surface there was the sense of humor that pervaded any situation, be it in a private party, hotel room, or concert hall. His humor always managed to get a laugh. But, on another level, it subtly pointed out the basic contradictions and deceits that he saw around him every day. There was the rampant sensualist, with tall tales of how many steaks, hamburgers, pies he could eat at one sitting. And there were the women who wanted Fats, whom Fats had trouble resisting. Above all, there was the tremendous drinking that the man could do, and did for too many years. His gargantuan capacity for life was in many ways responsible for his premature death.

Occasionally, when the party stopped, there appeared a sadness, increasingly apparent on the later slow-tempo compositions cut at private sessions, on his *London Suite,* and in his last Associated Program Service transcriptions. Conjecture as to specific reasons for this disparity is pointless, but conflicts in his upbringing appeared early. Fats' father, a Baptist deacon, rejected the young Waller's music, Fats' moral support coming from his mother, whose death, in Fats' fifteenth year, was a tremendous blow to him. In those times, before mass black consciousness, Negro families frowned upon jazz, and certainly did not like their children playing a music that they felt demonstrated the worst aspects of their society.

Although he took pride in what he did, and had a healthy attitude toward his music, in some small way Fats never got over the feeling that what he was contributing was not an end in itself; that his real artistic success would lie in the creation of "serious" or "classical" music. Like James P. and the highly individual Willie The Lion, Fats admired the "serious" tradition. The Lion's own wonderful compositions referred constantly to impressionists of the late nineteenth century, and this influence rubbed off on Fats. Consequently, Fats never quite appreciated the fact that his own contributions were different but equal in value. But it is the rare artist who has a proper perspective on his place in history.

What Fats and those around him did was create a beautiful and whole music, on both an extended intellectual level and a sensual level, many years before there was anything approaching equal opportunity for formal education, the end of segregation that would allow proper exposure to the tools of Western tradition, or the existence of a collective black ego.

Michael Lipskin

Acknowledgments

We would like to acknowledge the help and information supplied by the following people: Naomi Waller Washington, Buster Shepherd, Donna Waller, Al Casey, Harry Beardsley, Don George, Bennie Martini, James Powers, Richard Savitsky, Jay Anson, Joe Allegro, Rosemary Peters, Lou Capone, Glen Wesson, Ed Kirkeby, the staffs of the Lincoln Center Library, the *New York Times* "morgue," and ASCAP index, and the many members of ASCAP who came forward to tell us amusing anecdotes about Fats. Credit for a sensitive and perceptive editing job goes to David Aronson.

Our special thanks go to Michael Lipskin, for clarifying many details of fact and chronology and for editing the list of recording dates. His expert advice greatly contributed to the authenticity of this book.

Maurice Waller
Anthony Calabrese

An early shot of Fats at the keyboard.

Chapter 1

1864-1904

The Background of the Waller Family

Born in rural Virginia a few years after the Civil War, Edward Martin Waller and Adeline Lockett were raised in poverty. They grew up on nearby farms and saw each other frequently, meeting every Sunday at the local church. As they grew older, Edward and Adeline would meet more frequently and, as youngsters do, they would talk about their individual futures. Not surprisingly, they eventually started talking about their future together.

One thing Edward saw in their future was leaving the Bermuda Hundred district of Virginia. Edward had always been an individual with great determination, convinced that he could overcome any obstacle in his path. As a child, he had been afflicted with a stammer that would leave him frustrated, stamping his foot, after every failed attempt to communicate. But with great effort the young boy developed a slower speech pattern, and with great patience he cured himself of his speech impediment. Edward saw the obstacles to a black man's earning a living in the rural South and decided that his luck would be better in the fast-growing industrial cities of the North.

But what attracted Edward most to the North was that there, unlike in the South, every child could attend school. And Edward saw education as the only means for a black child to escape a life of poverty. Adeline had her doubts about moving to the evil North, but she did want to raise a family with greater opportunities than offered in the Bermuda Hundred.

In 1888 Edward left for New York. His experience handling horses on the farm back in Virginia helped him land a job as a stable boy. Two months later he returned to Virginia and married Adeline. Edward and

Adeline Waller packed their few belongings and took the train back to New York. They were sixteen years old.

My grandparents were among that wave of blacks adventurous enough to leave the South for the promise of jobs, better housing, and an education for their children in the North. When those rural blacks emigrated to the large industrial complexes, they brought with them their customs and their churches. In New York the black communities were downtown on the fringes of Greenwich Village and north of Forty-second Street, in the area that is now Lincoln Center. My grandparents looked for a place to live and they chose Waverly Place in Greenwich Village because they found an old friend there: the Abyssinian Baptist Church.

As a young girl from rural Virginia, Adeline was overwhelmed by the city and she turned to the one place where she knew she'd be safe, the church. It became the center of my grandparents' world. It was their bulwark against the devil and they spent most of their time participating in the social and religious affairs of the church. That slow speech pattern that Edward had developed as part of his self-cure for stammering had given him an air of solemnity and dignity. The church saw these qualities, and soon Edward, with his deep rich voice, was asked to preach on the street corners. In later years as my uncles and aunts were born, the whole family stood on street corners, singing hymns and preaching the gospel. Everyone played some sort of instrument and joined in the singing.

Of Adeline's eleven children only five survived childhood. Charles A. Waller was the first, born in September 1890, and died as an infant. Edward Lawrence, Uncle Larry, was born in 1892. He was followed by Uncle Robert, or William Robert, in 1893. In 1895 Alfred Winslow was born, but died in 1905. Ruth Adeline was born in 1902 and she also died in 1905. May Naomi, Aunt Naomi, was born in 1903, followed by my father, Thomas, born on May 21, 1904. In 1906 and 1907 Esther and Samuel were born, both dying during infancy, and in 1909 an unnamed boy died in childbirth. On July 25, 1910 the last child was born, Edith Salome.

Watching six of her children die took a heavy toll on Adeline, and she spent many hours in church, seeking consolation. Perhaps Edward was able to forget his grief by throwing himself into his work. In any event the Waller family prospered financially during those years. Edward had saved enough money to buy a wagon and team of horses and had begun his own trucking business. It was a modest enterprise, but it provided the family with a comfortable living. They weren't rich, not by any means, but when the church moved uptown, the Wallers were able to follow it.

When the church relocated to Eighth Avenue and Fortieth Street, our family settled on West Sixty-third Street, then a thriving black community.

At the turn of the century Harlem was a rural, uptown area that had become the hub of a building boom. Many developers and speculators felt that white families would jump at the opportunity to move to Harlem and escape the clamor and filth of the downtown business district. But the developers overlooked the poor transportation facilities and thus the new houses went begging for occupants. Philip Payton, a black real-estate operator, convinced the developers that he could rent the buildings and keep them rented. Desperate to get some return on their investment, the developers and speculators gave Payton a chance to prove himself. The real-estate operator induced black institutions to move to Harlem. The Wallers were among the many black families who moved there, following the Abyssinian Baptist Church. After trying a few apartments they finally settled at 107 West 134th Street. (Years later I was born just around the corner.)

Adeline Waller had ideas of her own on how to raise children and those ideas were put into practice. The apartment at 107 West 134th Street was chosen because it was adjacent to a school house. Grandma didn't want her brood to linger on the streets where they could be physically hurt or tempted by the evils of the devil. She watched over the children with the attention of a clucking mother hen. Adeline was determined that her five surviving children would grow to adulthood.

Confined to the house, the children made the apartment their playground. And as they were a lively bunch, every room swarmed with the kids' antics. Young Thomas was one of the more mischievous members of the clan and he was ably assisted by his equally mischievous sister Naomi. Aunt Naomi was a tyrant and she wanted to run the house or at least rule the kids in it. Naomi weighed two hundred pounds at an early age and she knew how to throw her weight around. She was known all over the neighborhood as Little Jack Johnson. Naomi loved to scrap and could whip any boy her age. When Dad began to seriously play the piano, Aunt Naomi always fought his battles so he wouldn't hurt his hands.

Dad and Naomi always managed to get into trouble together, but only he was able to get away with it. Naomi used to tell me that her brother knew how to exploit Grandma's greatest strength and weakness, religion. When it was inevitable that he was about to get a good licking, Dad would start to sing hymns loudly or fall to his knees praying for forgiveness. Grandma would be deeply touched by his penitence and so his punishment was light.

One rainy afternoon Thomas was giving Naomi a "ride" on the piano stool by spinning the seat around. Then he decided to give the baby, Edith, a ride too. Naomi held Edith in her arms as Thomas spun the piano stool faster and faster until the seat came off and the girls tumbled to the floor. Baby Edith was unhurt but she began to scream and cry, which, of course, brought their mother charging into the parlor. She spied both girls on the floor, snatched the baby up, and placed her in the crib. Then she tore her belt off and headed straight for Naomi. Thomas couldn't have been responsible because he was sitting off in a corner singing a hymn. Between yelps, Naomi was able to communicate that she had not been alone in the crime. As my aunt was to later tell the story, Thomas rolled his big innocent eyes up to the heavens and claimed, "That naughty devil, he made me do it." (He was years ahead of Flip Wilson and Geraldine.) He still hadn't escaped punishment, so he added the coup de grace: "Don't you think we ought to pray?" Grandma obliged his pious request and they both knelt on the parlor floor and prayed.

From the time he was a child, Dad could charm anyone, and poor Adeline was a pushover. But one thing always puzzled me. Why didn't Naomi catch on and save herself a lot of wear and tear?

Thomas and Naomi were given the chore of doing the family's grocery shopping. At the store one Saturday afternoon, Naomi spied a beautiful woman, heavily made up and dressed to match. Coming from a household where beautiful clothes were forbidden by cost and makeup was forbidden by the mother, Naomi was impressed by this exotic woman, who was a call girl. After a while the woman was joined by an equally beautifully dressed man whose diamond pinky ring further caught Naomi's attention. Smiling, the woman said, "Hello, pimp." The woman took the man's arm and they left the store. They were the most magnificent people Naomi had ever seen and the neatly dressed slim man reminded her of her father. Remembering how the man grinned broadly when the woman called him a pimp, Naomi repeated the word over and over to herself.

When they got home Naomi rushed to tell her mother all about the beautiful lady and well-dressed man she saw in the store, but Adeline was too occupied with her chores to really listen. Early that evening when Edward came home from work, Naomi ran to meet him at the door as she usually did. She regarded her father as a beautifully dressed man, both handsome and elegant, and thought it a compliment when she greeted him, "Hello pimp."

Edward stopped, took off his hat, and slowly walked into the apartment.

"What did you say?"

"Hello pimp!" she greeted him eagerly.

Her father waited as Naomi told him all about the beautiful woman and the elegant man in the grocery store. Edward was flattered that Naomi felt that he too was elegant and well dressed but he explained that she should never use *that* word again. Naomi was lucky that her father was a patient man, but even luckier that her brother wasn't in the room to further test that patience.

By the time he was six, Thomas was beginning to like music as much as mischief. Like the rest of his brothers and sisters, he would accompany Edward and Adeline to the street-corner missions. Thomas would do his share, playing the harmonium, his little fingers stretching to form basic chords. One of his great desires in life was to learn enough music so that he could accompany Adeline's sweet, steady voice singing hymns for the passers-by.

In those preradio, prephonograph days the parlor upright was the main source of entertainment in America. But in Harlem, the instruments also served an economic purpose. If you had problems making ends meet, you'd hire a few good pianists, buy some beer and chitlins, and throw a "rent party."

These parties were offshoots of the church-social-and-box-lunch affairs. At the church functions the congregations used to mix food, a Sunday outing, and good music together to raise money for the church reparations or to pay the minister's salary.

The custom moved up North with the black Baptists, and when they moved to Harlem, the parties left the church and moved into the apartments of anyone hard pressed for the month's rent. People paid a dollar to eat, drink, and listen to some good jazz or stride. Those parties kept a lot of poor Harlem families from being evicted from their homes.

The Wallers' upstairs neighbor had a piano for such occasions, and on a visit to her apartment, one day, six-year-old Thomas spied the idle instrument. He asked politely if he could play it, and was soon exploring the keyboard. Several times a week he'd venture up the stairs to play the nice lady's piano.

When he was alone, downstairs in his own apartment, the boy would take two chairs, place them together, and pretend they were a piano. He'd kneel in front of his silent instrument and send his fingers over the imaginary keyboard.

My father told me that one day his older brother (Uncle Bob to me) saw him in front of the makeshift piano and watched him for a while.

"Do you want to play the piano?" Uncle Bob asked. Dad told him all about the lady upstairs and his efforts to learn the keyboard. Uncle Bob thought it would be a good idea if the family purchased a piano so that his younger brother could take lessons and become a real pianist. Edward and Adeline agreed that it was a fine idea, but with seven mouths to feed there just wasn't enough money to buy a piano. Uncle Bob was so impressed with Dad's efforts that he took the problem to Pat Bolling, Adeline's step-brother. Dad had no idea of any of these machinations, and the only piano he expected to see was the one upstairs. But one afternoon when he came home, there it was—a brand new, shiny black upright with the famous Horace Waters' action. Dad sat down and played all afternoon and for several days no one could pry him from the old Waters. At first, Adeline couldn't scrape the money together for piano lessons, but she was determined. The only problem was that she was determined that Naomi, not Dad, was going to have the lessons, and grow up to be the concert pianist. Luckily for Dad, Edward had something to say. Gradually having given up the idea of his son becoming a minister, Edward saw a future for the boy as a classical pianist. A compromise was agreed upon. Naomi would have lessons and Dad would go along to keep out of trouble—and also take lessons.

Miss Perry, a lively and patient old woman, was the neighborhood piano teacher. Aunt Naomi was never really interested in the lessons and couldn't wait for them to end. Dad was also impatient, but for a totally different reason. Miss Perry's approach was scales and exercises. "I don't want to play scales, I want to play music," he would protest. But the pleas had no effect on Miss Perry. So the boy tried another ploy.

He would ask her to play one of the popular songs of the day and she often would. He'd stare at her fingers, trying to memorize every movement of her hands. Sometimes he would have her play the pieces several times through. Afterward he'd race home and sit at his own piano, playing the piece exactly as he had heard it. Adeline, hearing him one afternoon, was astonished at his prowess and asked where he had learned the piece.

"I remembered it."

Shortly after that the lessons stopped: Miss Perry believed that Adeline was throwing good money away, since my father didn't want to practice the lessons as taught. For a very long time Dad learned by ear. He listened, watched, and imitated. He would go anywhere someone had a piano. Adeline knew of his activities and cautioned him, "Go out, but come back before your father comes home."

The obvious place to hear music was the church and Dad would go there frequently, listening to the choir practicing hymns for Sunday services. After the choir finished, he'd cajole one of his young playmates to pump for him and he'd play the multileveled keyboards, filling the empty church with music.

Playing the organ in church, watching Miss Perry, or just living in Harlem and listening to the sounds all around him were a great influence on the young boy, but by the time he was old enough to enter Public School 89, he was ready for a more structured education. Miss Corlias, an understanding, sympathetic woman, taught music at PS 89 and soon discovered his natural ability. Miss Corlias taught him to read music and convinced him to study the violin and the bass. These studies improved his ear and his ability to read music, thus aiding his piano playing.

The school orchestra boasted several prominent musicians, one of whom, the violinist, was Edgar Sampson, who later would write "Stompin' at the Savoy."

Miss Corlias felt dad wasn't quite ready to play in the orchestra but she did have a position of importance for him. He would be allowed to play the march music for the students to file in and out of school assemblies. What an opportunity . . . a full house! With an audience in front of him there was no way that Dad could play it straight. As soon as the first student would come walking through the auditorium doors Dad would break into a syncopated or driving beat that would quickly have the kids clapping their hands and stamping their feet. It was love. Dad would mug a funny face and roll his eyes, and the audience in PS 89 loved him right back, the same way they would years later in Carnegie Hall or the Apollo.

News of these piano concerts inevitably reached his parents and Edward wasn't especially happy about it. Music was fine, as long as it was used to glorify the name of God. Thomas' efforts were not discouraged, but that was because Adeline was pleased by his natural abilities. Edward was willing to stand quiet in the background but he wanted to be convinced of his son's talents and ability.

One morning Miss Corlias informed Thomas that he should go off to rehearsal. He was the new pianist for the school orchestra. As soon as school was over for the day he rushed home to tell his parents the good news. Edward had finally received that affirmation he was waiting for. His son's talents had been "officially" recognized. Twenty years had passed since he had come North so that his children might receive a good education, and for Thomas Wright Waller that education meant exposure to the best music. Edward purchased two balcony seats and took PS 89's new pianist to Carnegie Hall to hear Ignace Paderewski. For weeks and weeks the boy could only talk about that piano recital. The great Paderewski had left his mark.

Those early years were happy ones for Dad. In the summer the Waller household attended church services and would then go off for a Sunday picnic in Central Park. On rare occasions the family would journey to Coney Island in faraway Brooklyn, where they enjoyed the beach, the amusements, and each other. Dad loved Coney Island and in later years whenever we were in New York during the summer we'd go there frequently. He'd take us to Luna Park and we'd ride the roller coaster hour after hour. He never outgrew his love for the beach and the rides—and the hot dogs.

When he was a boy, his mother's food certainly filled his frame amply. Thomas Waller, like all the Waller children, was *big*. As a man, my father stood six feet tall and weighed nearly three hundred pounds. There's no doubt that Adeline's cooking gave him a good start. One Sunday afternoon, Thomas was running several errands before the family left for their picnic in the park. Adeline answered a knock at the door and found one of the neighborhood boys standing there.

"Is Fats home?" he asked.

Of course Adeline had never heard of anyone named Fats, so she told the boy he was at the wrong apartment.

Naomi overheard the scene and told her mother that she thought the young man wanted Thomas. Adeline hated the new name given to her son, but there wasn't much she could do about it. Naomi, eager to even the score with her brother, picked up on the name and from that day, Thomas was Fats Waller.

James P. Johnson, father of Harlem Stride piano and teacher of the sixteen-year-old prodigy Fats Waller. *Courtesy of Michael Lipskin.*

Chapter 2

1914-1919

Fats Discovers Harlem Nightlife

Things were beginning to change in the Waller family. Adeline had developed diabetes and her strength began to fail. In the best of health, taking care of the large family had been demanding, but with the illness it was an impossibility. The children would have to take on greater responsibility and the family would have to move to a new apartment where there would be fewer steps for Adeline to climb. The new apartment was equipped with a piano, so the Waters that my Uncle Bob had worked so hard to obtain was given to the Pentecostal Church. Young Fats had hoped that the new piano would be a player type so that he could sit and learn the fingering for new songs and material. He was disappointed. But it was a minor disappointment.

The whole family was excited about the move to 134th Street and Lenox Avenue, the heart of growing Harlem. "We were so proud of our new place," Dad told me many years later, "that I went out and got a bucket and a brush and I painted 'Waller' in large letters right on the top step of the stoop." "Waller" was on that doorstep until the building was torn down.

Naomi, Fats, and the other children assumed their new responsibilities. Naomi's childhood wish was fulfilled: she became the unquestioned boss of the house. Fats found an after-school job as a delivery boy for Eckert's Delicatessen, earning a very respectable seventy-five cents a week. He'd deliver groceries, sandwiches, hog maws, and chitlins to all parts of Harlem. One day, on the way to someone's apartment with a bagfull of groceries, he was followed by a group of white punks. They taunted him, called him names, and then attacked him. He struggled with them for several minutes and when it appeared as if he was about to free himself, one of the boys stabbed him. The wound wasn't serious but that first terrible exposure to racism was never forgotten.

If the children had to assume more responsibility due to Adeline's illness, they also were given more freedom. But the stabbing incident brought back a greater degree of parental control over the family. Adeline made sure that the children returned home immediately after they finished work, and Edward, now a deacon in the church, reinstituted the family's daily prayer readings. Adeline kept a tight rein on the children as far as her health would permit, but the advent of World War I, and a growing Harlem limited that control.

The war touched the Waller family and left unhealable scars. Uncle Larry was of draft age when the war broke out and Adeline's health suffered further when he was inducted. A few weeks after Uncle Larry was shipped overseas he became separated from his unit and was listed among the missing in action. The news was a crushing blow to the entire family. Adeline's health worsened and she spent all of her time praying for her son's safe return. The household was overjoyed when Larry was found and returned to his unit, but Adeline lived under great tension until the war ended.

Harlem, after World War I, was no longer an isolated farm community. It was becoming part of the metropolis, and blacks were rapidly encroaching upon the neighboring Jewish, Irish, and Italian communities. Small clubs and bars were springing up, offering live entertainment that had an anarchic ragtime—blues sound based on the pop songs of the day. The heart of Harlem was Lenox Avenue, and Lenox Avenue was the home of the Wallers.

Dad was discovering the streets, and they throbbed with excitement and music. It was here that he first heard black spirituals played with a wild syncopation, and the blues, new rhythms that thrilled him. One afternoon Edward heard his son playing a very bluesy "Praise God from Whom All Blessings Flow" at the church organ. The response to that impromptu session was a good thrashing. Like many people, Deacon Edward regarded this new musical form, jazz, as the devil's own music. And that incident ended Edward's last dying hope that his son Thomas Wright Waller would be a minister. Years later, Dad told Murray Schumach, a reporter for the New York Times, "[My father] wanted me to mess around in the church but I found my level in cabarets. I was born in Harlem, right in the middle of it, and here I remain, happy as the day I was born."

And Harlem was beginning to jump. New clubs sprang up every day in cellars and store fronts. Luckey Roberts, James P. Johnson, Flournoy Miller, and other black entertainers were headlining on Broadway and Lenox Avenue. Dad was surrounded and assaulted everywhere by music. He became obsessed with it and decided that he had to make music his life. But he was still hampered by his limited ability to read music, poor technique, and sloppy fingering. He had to study but lacked the funds.

Dad told me that when he first approached his father, he sounded more like Fats than Thomas. After one year of high school at De Witt Clinton, Dad felt he was wasting his time because, "there wasn't any rhythm in algebra." Edward was not very impressed with that argument, so Fats shifted gears and went into his "Thomas, the good son" routine. Thomas reminded the deacon that Adolph Waller, Edward's father, was a violinist well known throughout Virginia. If music was good enough for Edward's father, wasn't it good enough for his son? Thomas won the battle, and Fats won the war. He would be allowed to quit school so that he could earn enough money to pay for his piano lessons.

In the summer of 1918 Fats and Naomi found jobs working for a jewel-box manufacturer downtown. The owner of the factory was one of Edward's trucking clients, imposed upon to hire the two youngsters. Dad worked as a polisher, shining the outer rims of the jewel boxes. He hated the job because even if he was earning a little money for his lessons, he couldn't play the piano while he was polishing. Eventually he found something of an outlet at the Trinity Church in lower Manhattan. The church, which was the burial place of many famous American Revolutionary heroes, was a few blocks away from the factory. Dad and Naomi soon became friends with the church's elderly sexton, who was impressed with Dad's enthusiasm for music, and he consented to let Dad use the church's piano. Every noon hour he and Naomi would spend their lunch at the famous church playing the piano. Several times they were late back to work and the boss lashed them with stern warnings. The extended lunches continued and the factory owner complained to his trucker. Edward, never enthralled with his son's chosen profession, felt that punctuality was more important than an hour at the keyboard. A family row ensued, and Dad wound up quitting the factory to seek another job that would allow him the time to spend with his music.

Connie and George Immerman owned a thriving, prosperous delicatessen in the heart of Harlem. Immerman's was always known for its fine food but since the beginning of Prohibition it was also known for it's bootleg liquor and beer. Dad took on a job as delivery boy, earning a weekly salary and good tips from the customers, who liked their liquor more than they respected the Volstead Act.

The delivery boys carried the bottles in paper bags and picnic hampers and, understandably, the Immerman brothers were concerned about being caught by the law. At fourteen, Dad was already larger than most full-grown men. He suggested that he stash the bottles under the baggy clothing he used to wear. Why not? A quart here or a quart there would hardly show on that body. A few weeks later there was a bust.

"One day the cops were making a routine search of the place," he told me. "I had some bags to deliver and some bottles under my coat. The cops searched all the other boys, but only asked me for my name and address. That's it. They never suspected a thing. I walked out of there with all the booze. They didn't know a thing!"

Immerman's gave him the time to study music, which meant visiting the local cabarets and absorbing every sound he heard. His behavior was bothering Edward, who disapproved of the late hours, the job at Immerman's—and jazz. The arguments' rate and intensity were a constant strain on all, and eventually one afternoon Dad didn't return home. My grandparents were frantic and the whole family began a search of all the places they knew he haunted. When they were unable to find him Adeline began praying.

The next morning Dad visited Mrs. Lamont Johnson, a good friend of my grandparents. He told her that he had been thrown out of the house by his father, who was ashamed of him and didn't want him anymore. Mrs. Johnson permitted the boy to stay at her home but she had a pretty good idea as to what was really going on. Later that day she told Adeline, who asked her friend to send him home immediately. By the time Mrs. Johnson returned to her apartment, Dad was gone.

That same afternoon Edward spotted his son on 135th Street just off the corner of Fifth Avenue. They spoke quietly and Edward convinced him to come home. Edward preferred not to give his children any physical punishment, but he felt that his son had gone too far this time. Dad suffered a far greater pain when he learned that his absence had so effected Adeline that she had had a diabetic relapse, confining her to bed for some days. He promised to behave better, but in Harlem, surrounded by nightclubs and music, that would be an impossible task.

The private Fats at work without an audience. *Courtesy of Frank Driggs.*

Chapter 3

1919

The Death of Fats' Mother

Life now had a regular routine: practice every morning on the piano; afternoons at Immerman's making the daily deliveries; and nights haunting the cabarets. He loved jazz but he couldn't play it, so he watched the men who could: Russell Brooks, older brother of his classmate Wilson; Willie "The Lion" Smith; and James P. Johnson, who was soon to become the acknowledged leader of the Harlem stride-piano sound. Dad wasn't old enough to gain admittance to the clubs but he made every effort to watch and listen. Johnson, Smith, and Brooks were his three favorites and he'd go anywhere they were to study them.

One afternoon, a few hours before he had to go off to Immerman's, he stuck his head into Adeline's bedroom. Her illness now kept her permanently bedridden.

"I'm worried about you, Thomas," she told him. "Worried because your're a lone wolf and you don't understand people." He tried to reassure her that he was capable of caring for himself, but she had something important to say and she cut him off.

"I know Naomi, Larry, and Bob can all take care of themselves. They don't want much out of life so they won't expect too much. But you, Thomas, you want more so you're going to face harder times than the others."

His efforts to comfort her were silenced.

"Thomas, I'm not going to be here to help you with your problems. I'm not going to be here too much longer and you need special help."

He was devastated. He had always regarded his parents as a permanent fixture in his life, and at fifteen he just wasn't ready for his mother to tell him she was dying. Adeline asked him to pray with her and he knelt beside the bed. Afterward he went into the parlor and played her favorite hymn until she fell asleep. Grief stricken, he needed consolation. The boy turned to the only refuge he knew outside his home: the street.

Every day on his way to Immerman's he passed the Lincoln Theatre. The Lincoln, on 135th Street, was a former nickelodeon turned "modern" movie theatre. He became curious about the large theatre and ventured in. In Edward and Adeline's house, anything they knew nothing about was the devil's own work. Motion pictures were lumped into that general category and for Dad to buy a ticket was like tempting fate.

Like the majority of movie houses in 1919, the Lincoln had both a piano and organ to accompany the silent movies and the stage shows on its program. The scores accompanying those silent films demanded that the pit pianist be able to play classical as well as contemporary music. In large theatres like the Lincoln it was necessary to have both a pianist and an organist. And the Lincoln had quite an organ. The instrument had been purchased around 1915 or so for about ten thousand dollars, and in 1915 that many dollars could buy a lot of music.

Those big houses in Harlem drew all the finest black stage talent of the day. Incredible musicians would be working in the pit, playing Tom Turpin's or James Scott's newest music. The shows would be full of headliners on the weekends and it was not unusual to see a famous white composer, band leader, or talent agent in the audience, looking for new material or talent. George Gershwin and Irving Berlin spent many hours in Harlem theatres admiring the talents of Eubie Blake, Freddy Bryant, or One Leg Willie Smith.

But a fifteen-year-old Fats Waller had never seen any of these acts. The only thing he knew about the Lincoln was that it was one of those places his parents had forbidden him to enter. He took his seat in the rococo theatre and waited. The movie left only a slight impression on him but he was fascinated by Miss Mazie Mullins, the pianist who accompanied the silent film. He was overwhelmed by her vast knowledge of music and her ability to adapt any piece of music to the situation on the screen by changing tempo, rhythm, or harmonies. He moved down closer to Miss Mullins to watch and listen, and sat through the film staring at her flying fingers. After the film he was ready to leave but a young man sat down at the enormous pipe organ so Dad stayed where he was. He listened and watched as the organist accompanied the stage acts, played the interlude, and led the sing along. Edward Waller had been wrong. The Lincoln Theatre wasn't the house of the devil, it was heaven.

The Lincoln became a new part of the boy's daily routine. He would buy a ticket every day, take a seat near the pit, and watch and listen. Afterward he'd race home and try to play what Mazie Mullins had performed. He spent most of his efforts working on the variations, taking a selection and changing the tempo, rhythm, or harmony. Eventually Mazie Mullins noticed the enormous kid in the front row. How could she miss a two hundred-pound boy who always wore shorts or knickers and stared at her with big frog's eyes?

"One day," Dad told me, "she asked my name and I told her. She asked me what I was doing there every day. I told her and I laid it on thick. She told me I could sit in the pit with her so I could watch more closely." It was the beginning of a friendship and an education. He sat next to her day after day, observing and asking questions. After each session he'd spend hours at his own piano putting to use the new musical knowledge he had acquired. Mazie became fond of her eager pupil and a strong rapport grew between them. It wasn't too long before Dad started plotting as to how he might get to play the Lincoln's piano. Miss Mazie worked long hours without any rest, and like anyone else she needed a little time every now and then for herself.

"I told her, 'Miss Mazie, you should take a little break. I'll take over the piano for you.' I was a real killer, so she finally gave in." It became a custom. Dad would con her, off she'd go and he'd play for five or ten minutes. The next recipient of Dad's "kindness" was the organist. No one could say no to the big kid in shorts, and one afternoon the organist allowed him to play the intermission music.

"That was the biggest thrill of my life . . . playing a ten thousand dollar organ." After a pause, Dad looked at me and said, "It's still the biggest thrill of my life."

Marie Downes, the owner of the Lincoln, also noticed the big boy in the baggy pants hanging around the pit. She meant to ask Mazie about him but it skipped her mind. And then the boy started playing for Miss Mazie whenever she needed a break. Mrs. Downes decided to reprimand her pianist. After all, her customers weren't coming to the Lincoln to hear some eager kid take his piano lessons. But there was something different about the boy's playing. It was naive, but there was some intangible spark of originality about it. And the audience always responded enthusiastically. As long as her audience was happy, the owner decided, she would say nothing.

As the boy's talents developed, Miss Mazie grew prouder and prouder of her young protégé. And when the opportunity came, Mazie showed Dad just how confident of his ability she really was. The regular organist was ill with influenza and Mrs. Downes was frantically looking for a replacement. Why didn't he, Fats, ask for the job? Dad ran to Mrs. Downes' office and badgered her until she agreed to give him a chance at it. Everything went well on his first attempt and he was hired to replace the organist for ten days. He had got his first paying job as a professional musician.

Even though Marie Downes had hired him she always stood in the back of the theatre to be sure he performed well. She was aware of his limited musical education and repertory but he absolutely amazed her with his uncanny talent for absorbing music.

"You know," he said, "at the end of those ten days I had learned more music than in all the time before I started. Of course my school pals were a big help, too.

"I was playing a Saturday matinee. . . the intermission, and I was almost finished. Someone in the balcony shouted 'Make it rock, Fats!' In a couple of minutes some other guys were shouting the same thing— 'Make it rock, Fats! Make it rock!' I looked around and saw some of the kids I went to school with."

A big devilish grin spread across his face and he let loose, improvising intricate rhythms, raising the audience to its feet. When they screamed for more, the stand-in organist gleefully responded to further shouts and screams from the balconies. None of which was missed by Marie Downes.

"At the end of the ten days, Mrs. Downes was so grateful she gave me a permanent free pass and I could go into the pit whenever I wanted to."

Reuben Harris, a local drummer, heard Dad play at the Lincoln and sought him out. Harris had a gig to play a block party in the Bronx and he needed a pianist. Would Fats be interested? Yes. Rather than face another battle with his parents, still unreconciled to a musical career for their son, he kept the next few days' rehearsals a secret from them.

The group played in an open lot on the corner of Brook Avenue and 165th Street and they brought the place to life. Crowds of people hung out of the tenement windows, listening to the good sounds coming from the street below. Fats went into his usual act, mugging like a giant bullfrog and rolling his eyes at every pretty girl who passed by.

Dad really hadn't developed an interest in women yet, but that night an attractive young girl caught his eye. After asking around to learn her name, he kept calling her from the piano until she came to see what the jolly fat pianist in short pants wanted. Edith Hatchett was flattered that this young man, who had won the adulation of the crowd, wanted to talk to her. They spent the night chatting and Dad asked if he could see her again. She agreed and a long courtship began. It certainly wasn't a very sophisticated romance. Dad's "older woman" was only born several months before he was. And Dad was just fifteen.

He asked Adeline if it would be all right to bring Edith for dinner. The answer was an enthusiastic yes. Adeline wanted a first-hand look at this young woman who had successfully turned her son's head. Edith turned out to be the perfect girl for Edward and Adeline: modest, and well schooled in the Bible and religion. Adeline was especially impressed with her level-headedness and asked her to visit frequently. Edith Hatchett was soon part of the Waller family.

Dad now added regular visits to Edith to his routine. Although awed by his prowess and the adulation of the crowd, she was trying to get him to learn a trade. She might have succeeded if the organist at the Lincoln hadn't left for a better-paying job. Dad was hired immediately, earning twenty-three dollars a week—a fantastic sum in 1919. His new job meant he had less and less time to spend with Edith, but music was more important to him than companionship.

When the word spread through Harlem that Fats Waller was the regular organist at the Lincoln, the youngsters flocked to the theatre—which was exactly what Mrs. Downes had hoped for. Once again his classmates stomped and shouted at him to "make it rock." He'd raise his eyebrows and mug as his fingers slid over the keys. Dad became aware he could make the crowd laugh with a raised eyebrow or a funny face, and this was all the encouragement he needed. He told me he delighted in those Saturday matinees and wished his parents would come to the theatre to hear him play.

But that was a wish never to be fulfilled. At first Edward was appalled that his son, the son he had hoped would be a minister, was playing music in the devil's temple. But Fats Waller was the talk of Lenox Avenue and everywhere Edward went he heard his son spoken of in glowing terms. Reluctantly he acknowledged his son's ability. Soon that reluctance turned to enthusiasm, but Edward still wouldn't go to the Lincoln to see him. Adeline, who had always encouraged him, even against Edward's wishes, was especially proud of him and let everyone in Harlem know it.

If Edward took pride in his son's ability and reputation, he still found it difficult to regard music as a serious career. And there was no defending the late nights or patronizing the night spots in Harlem. He was torn by his religious teachings and paternal pride. Religion prevailed. Father and son fought incessantly and Dad wanted to leave home to be on his own. This only increased the frequency and intensity of their quarrels and Adeline usually had to intercede to restore peace. But the effort eventually proved to be too great a strain for her.

After one momentous row sometime in 1920, Adeline was left quite seriously ill. Dad was very concerned about his mother's failing health and tried to behave himself. He spent what free time he had at her bedside, praying with her.

Late in the afternoon of November 8, 1920 Adeline suffered a massive stroke. There was no one in the house and she was unable to call for a doctor. By the time Naomi arrived home, Adeline was dying. All the family could do was sit and wait. Two days later Adeline Waller, forty-eight years old, was dead. She had always been the center of the family, holding everyone together with her love.

Shocked by the suddenness and finality of events, Edward plunged into a state of shock, barely able to communicate with anyone for months. Larry and Robert had married and left home. Fats and Naomi were in their middle teens, capable of taking care of themselves, but ten-year-old Edith needed a mother. So once again, as she had been during Adeline's more serious bouts with diabetes, Edith was sent down South to live with relatives.

My father was overwhelmed by his mother's death. She had been his defender, encouraging his goals even when they conflicted with her ideals or made life difficult between herself and Edward. She had instilled in her son Thomas a deep religious belief and equally strong belief in himself. But the only thing he felt in those days after Adeline's death was an intense sorrow. Walking around the apartment, he spied the old upright piano in the parlor, and grew sadder as he thought about the many times he sat there, accompanying his mother as she sang hymns. He never touched it again.

Dapper Willie "The Lion" Smith in his latter years. Fats was introduced to "The Lion" in 1920 by James P. Johnson. *Courtesy of Michael Lipskin.*

Chapter 4

1920-1922

Fats Meets James P. Johnson and Willie The Lion Smith

By 1920 the emergence of black music was beginning to revolutionize the sounds coming from Tin Pan Alley. As is the case with all revolutions, this "new" music was a long time coming, and its roots could be traced back over many years.

Before the turn of the century, black pianists were playing ragtime, a blend of European classical-traditional form and the African syncopation that had survived through the years via minstrel music and the cake walk.

Tom Turpin, James Scott, and Scott Joplin were the first to write published pieces of the new music. Joplin had the first ragtime hit, "Maple Leaf Rag" (and his music has since again achieved popularity through the revival of his "The Entertainer," on records and as the theme for the film *The Sting*). He was born in Texarkana, Texas, in 1869. Although he received some formal musical training, like most black musicians he was unable to find a place in the white world of serious music. Ragtime was considered unsavory around the turn of the century, so the music and its writer-performers were relegated to the honky tonks and whorehouses.

The sound moved East, and by the beginning of World War I, a dialect of improvised rag had developed on the pianos in black neighborhoods predating Harlem. Played by such men as Freddy Bryant, "Abba Labba," One Leg Willie Smith, and Eubie Blake, the music developed into a jazz piano style now referred to as Harlem stride piano.

Willie The Lion Smith, an acknowledged master of stride, described it as an extension of ragtime, referring to it as "Eastern ragtime." In stride the left hand, playing the bass line and chords, is as important as the right hand, playing the melody. Thus the stronger the left hand, the richer the sound of the stride.

Willie The Lion explained to me several times how stride came about. "I played a 'shout' and a shout is a stride. Shouts came about because of the Baptist Church and the way black folks sang or 'shouted' their hymns. They sang them a special way and you played them a special way, emphasizing the basic beat to keep everybody together." That produced the flavor and inspiration for stride.

In 1920 three black pianists, Russell Brooks, James P. Johnson, and Willie The Lion, among others were playing stride, the new form of piano, and Fats Waller's association with these three men began with a chance meeting with Russell Brooks. Russell told the story to anyone who'd listen and he must have entertained me with it a dozen times.

"I was playing for a dance in a tent on Lenox Avenue and 140th Street, just a few blocks from where Fats lived," he told me. Russell was playing one of those ten-cents-a-head dances, featuring a local favorite pianist. Dad knew Russell and had at least a casual speaking acquaintance with him because Russell's younger brother, Wilson, had been a classmate and very good friend of his.

"I saw someone pull aside the tent flap and sneak in. It was Fats. He came in and strolled right up to the bandstand." Fats sat next to the piano to watch Russell play and talk shop. Russell had heard him play many times at the Lincoln and advised him to add shouts and rags to his repertoire if he was going to make his mark as a pianist. Fats said that he wanted to play the new music but his fingers just got all tangled up when he tried. Of course, he would certainly appreciate it if *someone* could give him a few lessons. Russell knew what the young Fats was hinting at, but Brooks was not a piano teacher. However, he did have a friend who might be able to help. Russell vaguely promised that some time in the even vaguer future he'd introduce Fats to James P. Johnson. The elated Fats thanked him and bounded off the stage.

"I watched Fats run for the exit along the edge of the dance floor. He caught his foot in one of the ropes that held up the tent and he fell against some other ropes. Then he pulled the whole tent down around all of us. Once he got himself free I yelled at him. 'Hey Fats, why don't you untangle your feet while you're at it.'" The two musicians went their separate ways, and nothing more was said about the half-arranged lessons.

A few months later, Russell's brother, Wilson, came home one night to find Fats camped on his doorstep. Following a particularly heated argument with his father, Fats had decided to leave home. This time for good. Wilson invited him to spend the night on the sofa.

The next morning Wilson's surprised parents found a sleeping Fats in the parlor and went directly to their son's room to learn who he was and what he was doing there. Wilson explained and Mrs. Brooks immediately softened. "After all, the boy just lost his mother." During breakfast Mrs. Brooks asked him a lot of questions, but mostly she wanted to know why he left home. This woman had a son who was a professional musician, whom she had nurtured and encouraged, and she had no difficulty empathizing with the runaway. Russell had recently married and there was a room for Fats in the Brooks' house if he'd like to move in and live with them.

Mrs. Brooks took it upon herself to discuss the situation with Edward, trying to make him understand what a talent his son had and how important it was to encourage him. Edward finally consented and agreed that if Fats wanted to live away from home it might be best for everyone. Edward considered the Brooks family a good, religious group and they lived nearby, so he was mollified to some extent.

Fats was ecstatic. At the age of sixteen he finally felt truly liberated and the Brooks family had a player piano, something he had longed for all of his life. They also had a collection of piano rolls featuring James P. Johnson and Luckey Roberts. Those rolls were played for hours, the boy running his fingers over the keyboard until he memorized complete passages.

The technique for learning from piano rolls was simple enough. He'd pump the piano until a new passage was played and then he'd fit his hands to each chord trying to assimilate it. He would then release the locking mechanism and practice the chord by himself, without the aid of the piano roll. Once comfortable with the fingering, he would play the piece through until coming to another difficult section, at which point he would go back to mimicking the piano roll.

"One morning I came to see my mom," Russell told me. "I didn't know Fats had moved in but I heard the piano upstairs and I was surprised to see him sitting there. He was teaching himself with a piano roll. He was kind of embarrassed. Fats was practicing James P. Johnson's "Carolina Shout" and I remembered our conversation about James P."

A few weeks later Russell ran into Johnson on the street. "I asked him if he knew Fats Waller, the kid who played the organ at the Lincoln. He knew who Fats was, but didn't know him personally. I told James P. that Fats wanted to meet him real bad and that he wanted to play just like him. I asked him to listen to Fats and maybe help him a little. I kept telling James P. how much Fats wanted to play like him and eventually he agreed to see him."

James P. Johnson, the man who brought the stride-piano style to its creative height, was born in New Brunswick, New Jersey in 1894. His mother, like Adeline, played and sang and she was his first teacher. But unlike Adeline Waller, Mrs. Johnson loved black music and encouraged her son to play it. James P. was given formal lessons at the age of nine by an Italian teacher who emphasized scales and playing them properly. His mother often took him to the local black dances, known as promenades or cotillions, and it was there he first heard ragtime and cake walks. Black music was a part of James P. Johnson's heritage and he was intelligent enough to assimilate it into his style.

When James P. was a teenager his family moved from New Brunswick and settled on West Sixty-third Street, or San Juan Hill, as it was known in those days. He began to play and learn in the local spots where the great pianists of his time, "Abba Labba," Eubie Blake, and Luckey Roberts, helped him to grasp and master ragtime and stride. Eubie relates that, even as a teenager, James P. was able to listen to Blake's piano pieces and quickly copy them, playing them in different keys, at a faster tempo than Blake could himself. James P. married and moved with his bride to Harlem, where he became a regular participant at rent shouts and the star attraction at Barron's, a Harlem night spot. By 1920 he had already written "Carolina Shout," among other rags, and had won a substantial reputation as a composer.

Fats was beside himself with anticipation, waiting for the meeting with the great James P. Johnson. In spite of the job at the Lincoln, Fats was forever low on funds, or trash, as he would say. He didn't have any decent clothing to wear, so he always wore short pants or knickers, which, more often than not, were worn through. His patched shirts resembled quiltwork and his shoes were always worn down and scuffed. He was more than a little self-conscious about meeting the notoriously elegant James P. Johnson.

I've heard the story of that encounter between my father and James P. hundreds of times from both of them, and from Russell Brooks.

"The first thing I noticed," Dad told me, "was that Jimmy had *two* pianos, a baby grand and an upright. I never played on a baby grand before." He sat in the parlor in awe of the man, his home, and his pianos, waiting for James P. to make his appearance. Johnson was only twenty-six, a mere ten years older than Dad, and already had a vast reputation.

After about ten minutes James P. came into the room. He said hello to Russell and then asked, "Is this Fats?"

"I'm Fats," came the nervous answer.

"Well, sit down, Fats." He tried to make the boy comfortable and then he got rid of Russell. He ordered Fats to the upright and told him to play . . . and Fats played all afternoon.

"At first James P. didn't say much. He just let me play. Then he'd tell me to do this, or try that, and I did. Before I knew it, he was sitting on a stool next to me, making that piano rock. He'd play trills and strong bass figurations. He taught me more in an afternoon than I had learned in ten years."

But what most surprised the student was that James P. kept on emphasizing the importance of scales, pointing out that the root of Fats' difficulties was his inability to move adeptly through those same rudiments that Miss Perry had stressed ten years earlier. Miss Perry's instructions were one thing, but James P. Johnson's were like the law of God. Scales were now accepted as a necessary building block, and they were to be mastered.

Around six o'clock Lil Johnson interrupted the lesson to remind her husband it was supper time. Dad was invited to dinner and to spend the evening with the Johnsons.

"You're going to spend some time where it'll do you the most good."

"You mean Leroy's?!"

"I didn't mean church."

For the first time Fats was able to get into Leroy's to watch one of his favorite idols without sneaking in.

Leroy's was a popular club owned and operated by Leroy Wilkins, whose brother, Barron Wilkins, was the proprietor of the equally popular Barron's. Both places were known for their good music and the white trade, who followed them when they moved from downtown. Leroy's was a family affair for the Johnsons, James P. playing the piano and Lil working as a dancer. Dad always said that James P. made him feel like a prince that night. He was introduced to all the musicians in the band and to the performers. Someone in the band fetched a chair for him and he spent the night at James P.'s side. Jimmy gave him some pointers, instructing him to watch for certain passages or to listen to particular progressions.

James P. had not forgotten the kindness shown him by Luckey Roberts, and he felt the best way to pay back his debt was to take Dad under his wing. The boy was now spending almost as much time in the Johnson house as he was with the Brooks family. Lil Johnson became yet another second mother to him. She made sure that he left Leroy's early enough every night so that he would get enough sleep. She even bought the boy his first pair of long pants so that he wouldn't be embarrassed by his shorts at the night club.

A lot of the great pianists "traveled" at night to listen to each other or to sit in on an impromptu jam session. Fats would listen as they talked about music and the keen competition at last night's rent shout. He was yearning to go to one of these gatherings and he constantly asked James P. to take him to one, but Jimmy didn't feel he was ready.

The daily routine continued: learning fingering by mimicking the piano rolls, lessons and evenings with James P., and working at the Lincoln. And the patrons at the Lincoln enjoyed a steadily growing repertoire, every night including more and more tricks, rhythms, and progressions picked up from James P.

Eventually the teacher decided that it was time to take his student to the rent parties, where he could meet the city's leading pianists as well as the Broadway crowd who would come uptown. It wasn't un-usual to meet bandleader Paul Whiteman or George Gershwin at one of these functions. Gershwin came to listen to this new black music and then successfully married it to white popular and musical revue sound. He loved good music and he'd go anywhere to listen to it. He and Dad became very close friends and he was a frequent visitor to our home. George always spoke fondly of those rent-party days. "I loved to watch your father eat. I would sit there and feed him and encourage him to drink more. I was determined to see him fall flat on his face, but no matter how much he ate or drank, nothing ever happened."

These musical gatherings were known as parties, rent shouts, rent socials, parlor socials, or Saturday-night functions. It didn't matter what you called them, they all meant the same thing: someone was low on funds and had decided to throw a party to help make ends meet. Rent parties weren't limited to Harlem. In fact, in every black ghetto where rent money was hard to come by Saturday-night functions would occur. In New York, stride pianists performed, while in Chicago Jimmy Yancey, Jimmy Blythe, and others played boogie woogie.

The only problem was making sure that enough people attended the affairs. First you told the local numbers runner that you were planning to have a rent shout. He went to nearly every household in Harlem as practically every black family played the numbers. It was a cheap and effective method of advertising. (In later years hawkers sold tickets to rent shouts on the street. The makeshift tickets usually fea-tured the name of the pianist. My father was overjoyed the first time he saw his name printed on the back of one of these cards. In Harlem, every serious pianist knew how important the rent shout was.)

The next ingredient for a successful shout was two or three out-standing pianists. These men, like James P., Willie The Lion, Stephen Henderson, and Corky Williams received three to five dollars a night, plus tips and all they could eat and drink. And for Fats Waller, those fringe benefits were quite an incentive.

The admission at the door would pay for the musicians, and would vary according to their popularity. The apartment owner would make his rent by selling the drink and food. This was during the height of Prohibition and the hooch was usually rotgut whiskey or bathtub gin. But it wasn't the food or liquor that attracted crowds to a social, it was the music and the fierce competition that existed between the pianists. That's what you paid your two bits for, to see James P. outdo Willie The Lion, or Luckey Roberts cut up Eubie Blake. This was exuberant music, shouts, and stride. People came to have a good time and they didn't want to hear the blues. The men who played this music were garish extroverts who led the revolution in black music. It wasn't unusual for one of these parties to last all through the night and once the competition got going, two pianists would battle for hours on end. Each would try to outdo the other with dazzling rhythms, new harmonies, or new tunes. Constant improvisation and variation were demanded, leading to many changes and the maturation of jazz piano style.

If you wanted to make it as a rent-party pianist you had to take on all competitors, and to do so successfully you had to have new material all the time. The only place to get new material was to write it yourself and put together the complicated arrangements that showed you off. The competition usually started off with someone demonstrating an intricate arrangement of his newest work. His opponent would then do the same when *his* turn came. The music would develop into an intricate weave as the pianists would borrow from each other, working out variations, and combining the two pieces.

James P. Johnson had written very difficult piano pieces, such as "Caprice Rag," "Harlem Strut," and his recorded hit "Carolina Shout." These were the weapons he used to put others to shame. But everyone had his specialty, a "signature," that he pulled out when he was falling behind. Those parties must have jumped when the competition got heavy. Tape recorders were still a future invention, so no record exists of the improvisation those parties produced.

(Interestingly, the crowds came to hear piano playing and the only musician who sang while he played was a wiry man, Corky Williams, who specialized in bawdy tunes like "The Boy in the Boat.")

James P. saw to it that Dad met all the greats: Luckey Roberts, Eubie Blake, Willie Gant, Stephen Henderson ("The Beetle"), and two younger men who had only recently come up North from Washington, D.C., Cliff Jackson and Duke Ellington. They all had their

31

own signatures, and they all had their influence on Fats Waller. But the one man he wanted to meet eluded him: Willie The Lion Smith.

Willie The Lion was really William Henry Joseph Bonaparte Bertholoff Smith, part black and part Mohawk Indian. William Bertholoff was born in Goshen, New York, a rural community not far from the Catskill Mountain resorts. His parents then moved to Newark, New Jersey, and settled in a predominantly Jewish neighborhood. Willie learned to speak Yiddish on the streets of Newark and attended Yeshiva to keep out of trouble. (If he wanted to impress you, he'd burst out into Yiddish and talk for hours.) He then went on to Howard University, where he studied music. He enlisted in the army at the outbreak of World War I and served with the 350th Field Artillery in France. He volunteered to be part of a team firing cannon on the front lines and his bravery earned him the title "The Lion." Somewhere along the line he adopted the "Smith" and Willie The Lion Smith emerged.

Willie was a unique man and I deeply loved and admired him. He was known for his light touch at the piano, but he could play a raucous stride beat with the best of them. The Lion loved impressionist compositions and would often refer to Ravel or Debussy. He could swing the classics, and his own compositions, "Echo of Spring," "Morning Air," "Rippling Waters," and "Sneakaway," were unique extensions of Harlem piano. They impressed Fats Waller immensely. Willie was an iconoclast and fiercely independent, always wanting his way and when he couldn't have it, he'd just walk out. He skipped out of many an important gig but the owners of the clubs were more than eager to have him back.

Willie was a sharp dresser, always wearing expensive suits. His trademark was his derby, perched ever so precariously on his head in a rakish way, and a large cigar. Dad blatantly copied The Lion, dressing and acting just like him. And in later life Willie would often sit at the piano and tell the audience, "My good friend, Fats Waller, used to sing this song . . ." and then he'd do his impression of my father.

Willie was known for his notorious temper and his insistence that a piano be in perfect condition before he'd sit to play it. Frequently at rent shouts the piano was out of tune, missing a string or perhaps having a key that stuck, and Willie would refuse to play. If he were forced to perform, he would demolish the poor instrument with fortissimos that actually snapped the strings. I loved him, but he was a moody guy and if he were in a bad mood, it was best to be in another room. Willie must have been in a horrendous mood the night he first met my father.

The Lion was holding court at Leroy's with a small band to back him up. James P. and Willie frequently followed each other into Leroy's or Barron's and they were good friends and drinking buddies. Aware of what a natty and dapper individual The Lion was, James P. had ordered Fats that night to wear his long pants. They went to Leroy's and walked up to the bandstand where Willie was sitting and drinking.

James P. greeted his friend, who first grunted and then, staring, asked "Who the hell's the punk kid with you?"

"Fats Waller."

"Fats Waller . . . he looks more like Filthy Waller. You can't bring no punk kid in here lookin' like that. Get his pants pressed and buy him a new shirt. This here's a high class joint."

"I'm takin' Fats around town . . . meetin' people. Tryin' to help him along. He plays a good piano, man. Let him play something for you. He plays some of my stuff really good."

"I can't be bothered listenin' to some punk kid," The Lion said, turning away as if to dismiss them both.

"Just sit and listen and *don't* worry," James P. whispered to Dad.

Willie and the band went about their business entertaining the customers and when the set was completed the musicians went off for a break. The Lion got up and walked over to a nearby table where he joined some friends, drinking and talking.

"Get up there and play," James P. told Dad, whose response was instant paralysis. James P. just urged him on, waving his hands. Dad sat on the stool and looked to The Lion, who was laughing and drinking and totally ignoring him.

"Play!" James P. insisted. Dad's fingers hesitated and then he hit the keys, playing for all he was worth. He finished with a flourish and turned to Jimmy and Willie.

"Nice goin', kid," James P. said encouragingly, but The Lion was still gossiping with his cronies.

Slowly Willie worked his way back to the bandstand, quietly stepped up and eased his way to the piano. "That wasn't bad, kid," he said as he took his place at the piano. ("I wanted the kid to play," Willie told me years later, "but I couldn't let on that I'd listen to some punk kid in a beggar's costume." And the kid in the beggar's costume was taken in by Willie's act.) Dad was so thrilled that he couldn't force a "thank you" out of his throat.

Fats Waller had met another idol and the idol was pleased.

Fats talking to the keys. *Courtesy of Frank Driggs.*

Chapter 5

1922-1924

Fats Marries Edith

In six months the kid in shorts, who had pulled down the tent on top of Russell Brooks, had befriended the latter, been "adopted" by his family, taken on as the protégé of James P. Johnson, and had impressed The Lion. His "foster mother," Mrs. Brooks, expressed her happiness and encouraged him, but she wasn't Adeline. Lil and James P. voiced their joy over Fats' triumphs, but a void remained unfilled. He rarely communicated with Edward, who still failed to see any worth in his son's career. Fats was seventeen and he was lonely.

The more he sunk into his loneliness, the more he reflected on how Adeline would have been able to share in his daily progress and give him some warmth. Edith Hatchett, like Adeline, was from a deeply religious background, and, like Adeline, she had always shown satisfaction in Fats' accomplishments. He decided to see her.

They spent the next few weeks discussing one thing and the next, getting to know each other again. He discussed his growing abilities with rags and shouts and she listened attentively. Edith encouraged him and shared in his victories. Dad asked her to marry him, and much to his surprise and delight, she accepted. Her parents didn't quite approve of piano playing as a profession, but he was from a religious family and so they gave their blessing. As he was still a minor, Fats needed the consent of his father to marry in the state of New York. In the short time since his wife had died, Edward had become an old man. They had only a brief conversation, Edward posing no objections to the marriage, but even in the few minutes he was in the house, Fats could see that without Naomi, Edward would fall apart.

Three days later, bride and groom were married in City Hall by a municipal clerk. Two strangers served as best man and maid of honor. Even with the steady job at the Lincoln, there wasn't enough money to furnish an apartment, so the young couple moved in with Edith's parents on Brook Avenue in the Bronx. It was meant to be a temporary convenience but it would turn into a permanent inconvenience for everyone.

During the first weeks of their marriage Dad departed from his regular routine. Lessons with James P. were kept to a minimum and the nightly tours of the cabarets and rent parties were temporarily postponed. It appeared, at least to Edith and her parents, that the young man was getting "that music thing" out of his system once and for all. It was not a logical assumption.[1]

Of course, the Lincoln job continued. One of the vaudeville groups playing there was Liza and Her Shufflin' Six. Liza's act was about to go on tour, up and down the Northeast,[2] when their regular accompanist became too ill to go on tour. Liza was impressed enough with the playing of the Lincoln's organist to ask him if he'd like to work on the black vaudeville circuit for a while as a replacement organist. Marie Downes was consulted and agreed to allow her organist accompany the group. James P. and Lil thought it was a great idea. The only people not consulted were Edith and her parents. And running up and down the coast was not what the Hatchetts considered responsible behavior for a newly married husband. In any event, Fats Waller was on the road.

During their fourth week on tour, the group was laying up in Boston for an extended engagement. Dad found a furnished room in one of those theatrical boarding houses downtown. Another tenant there was an acquaintance and fellow pianist, William Basie. Basie was in Boston accompanying an act at the Mutual Burlesque. They ran into each other the first day Dad was there and agreed to meet later that afternoon to talk.

Dad was trying his hand at writing music and he wanted someone he trusted to hear his stuff before he played it for James P. Johnson. He was pleased when his friend told him he liked the song.

"It's got words. Wanna hear them?"

"Sure," Basie said.

Dad then sang the lewd words to Corky Williams' "The Boy in the Boat." He told Basie that he could never get it published with those words and so he planned to leave it as a piano solo. Dad called it

---

[1] I should mention, at this point, that what little I know about that first marriage is from conversations with family friends. I never knew of Edith until after my father's death.

[2] The tour was arranged by the Theatre Owner's Booking Association (then nicknamed Tough on Brown Acts). This circuit provided sometime employment for artists such as Bessie Smith, Ethel Waters, and the team of Eubie Blake and Noble Sissle. TOBA was identified with discrimination because of the shabby accommodations it arranged for its performers, and its notoriously faulty payments.

"Boston Blues" in honor of the city where the two musicians were both appearing.

Now it was Bill Basie's turn to make a request. He was always a shy man and it wasn't easy for him to ask a favor of anyone. Slowly he explained that he had heard Dad play the organ several times at the Lincoln and he was impressed with Dad's ability.

"Fats, when you have the time, I'd like to have a lesson on that organ," Bill finally said.

"Sure," Dad answered, "I'll be back in New York in two weeks. Stop up at the theatre." They shook hands and went off to work.

A few weeks later, Bill Basie showed up for his first lesson at the Lincoln. They would meet several times a week and the Count proved to be a very fast pupil. Before long, Basie was taking long solos and Dad was taking breaks just as Mazie Mullins had some years before. But because of Basie's shyness, he would never play while his teacher was still in the theatre.

One night Bill was playing the organ when he spotted a pair of size thirteens sticking out from under the red curtain. It was Dad, who hadn't left the theatre because he wanted to check on the progress of his pupil. Dad told his friend that he rocked that organ as well as anyone and soon Bill added the instrument to his repertoire. Those lessons helped solidify a friendship that endured many years.

But as far as the Hatchetts were concerned, Bill Basie was just one more worthless musician. The road trip had convinced the Hatchetts that Fats Waller had best find himself another career. Pressure from the in-laws continued until Fats and Edith moved into their own apartment in Harlem. Away from her family, Edith tried to understand her husband's profession and tolerate his friends. Life grew less tense and soon she announced that she was pregnant.

Excitedly, Dad ran to James P. and told him he was going to be a father. He also told Jimmy he needed to make extra money. James P. decided that the man to see was Raymond "Lippy" Boyette. A former pianist himself, Boyette now booked the musicians for the rent shouts. He told James P. that he had never heard of Fats Waller.

"He's gonna kill 'em. You'll see," said James P. enthusiastically.

"I'll see what I can do," Boyette answered.

A few days later James P. brought the good news that there was a gig to play with Corky Williams and Russell Brooks. James P. apologized that he couldn't make his student's debut because he was already booked that night for another party.

Corky Williams and Dad met at Russell Brooks' place before heading for the party. Russell remembered giving some last minute instructions before they left for the party at Lenox and 141st Street.

"Take it easy, Fats," Russell cautioned. "You can't rock a joint by tryin' too hard. Go easy at first."

They met Lippy Boyette at the front of the building and he ushered them up the stairs to the party. On the third floor he knocked softly at one of the doors and the group was admitted. Lippy introduced the three pianists for the night and the function started. Corky led off with his rollicking piano and bawdy songs while the other two pianists retired to the bar.

Russell took over from Corky and began to play "Carolina Shout," the same rag he was playing the night Dad knocked over the tent. Lippy was anxious about the ability of his third pianist, but Russell had to have a break. Boyette gave Dad a tense nod.

Russell told me the story of that first rent party:

"I was finishing up when Fats appeared on my left, nudging me over. I reminded him of what I said before we came in the building—about takin' it easy—and he just nodded and sat down.

"Fats began to vamp in the same key I had been playin', F sharp. I was surprised because it was a difficult key. Corky and I looked at each other, shocked. A few months before that he could only play in C or G, the two simplest keys. He stopped his vamping and swung into one of his own tunes ["Boston Blues"]. Everyone in the place recognized the meter, which was like a limerick, and every cat in the joint was singing "The Boy in the Boat." Lippy was glowing, telling anyone who would listen that Fats Waller was his 'personal discovery.'"

Dad segued into another song and this time he started to let go. He spread those chubby fingers and played tenths in the bass, just like James P. had shown him.

"I turned to Corky," Russell told me, "and I said maybe I should take lessons from James P. I never saw anyone improve so much in such a short time. I couldn't believe this was the same Fats Waller who slept on the sofa in my mother's parlor and practiced fingering on the player piano."

For the rest of the night Dad kept the place jumping and the crowd wouldn't let him stop. He was a sensation and Lippy promised to book him as often as possible. Dad was excited, knowing that the extra money would help with the baby coming; and he thought Edith would be happy, but her reaction was far from enthusiastic.

Edith Waller was never really cut out to be the wife of a musician. The insecurity that musicians accepted as dues to be paid, was driving her crazy. She never adjusted to the late hours or the instant crowds in the house. At five in the morning Fats would appear with a legion of comrades demanding breakfast and something stronger than orange juice. By the time Edith was coming to life, the sun was rising and her husband would be ready to fall into bed. He'd sleep until noon, dress, eat breakfast, and then rush off to his job at the Lincoln. Most nights of the week there would be a party to play, and on those days he'd rush home, wolf down his supper, and take off for someone's apartment. Days off were spent with James P. or other musicians trying to write some new tunes.

Edith was coming to her wit's end. She had done everything that her upbringing had promised would bring her a happy family. She was religious. She had married and was going to become a mother. But she was lonely, nervous, and wanted to spend her time with a husband who had normal hours like other men. Edith's parents suggested that she wait until the baby was born, and then use the child as a means to discourage nights out at rent parties and all that drinking.

Edith wanted a nice steady job for her husband, and it was just that sort of work that Willie The Lion was getting tired of. He had been playing at Leroy's for several months, and that was long enough for The Lion. In his customary fashion, he just walked out, and Harry Pyle, the manager of Leroy's, was in trouble: he needed an immediate replacement for the next night's show. He approached James P., but Jimmy had to turn him down, because he was about to leave for a road trip. But Jimmy's friend, Fats Waller, might be available—if Pyle was interested. Harry Pyle didn't care who the pianist was as long as he was at Leroy's that night for the first show.

James P. rushed to Dad's Harlem digs and banged on the door until someone came to answer it. Finally Fats Waller, in his underwear and rubbing sleep from his eyes, opened the door.

"You want to work at Leroy's?" Ten minutes later, shaved and nattily dressed, Fats Waller was ready to go. There was one problem, however. The work he had done with Liza and Her Shufflin' Six just wasn't the same thing as working with club singers or a floor show. Jimmy offered to spend the afternoon coaching his friend. James P. then phoned up the Lincoln to tell them that his friend was too ill to work that day's shift.

All afternoon Jimmy and Lil helped Dad with the finer points of accompaniment. Working solo or with a band, a pianist is usually the lead and can let loose whenever he wants, but when accompanying a performer, it's very important to lay back. Establishing a steady beat, and sticking to it, is more important than vamping. James P. taught Dad the basic principals. Lil would dance and Jimmy would accompany her as Dad watched. Then the student would give it a try. Then after a while they practiced accompanying Lil as she sang. In a matter of hours James P. and Lil were convinced that the new pianist would be just fine at Leroy's.

Dad had dinner with the Johnsons and then they all left for the club. My father already knew all the boys in the band: Tommy Benford on drums, Leroy Parker on violin, Dope Andrew on trombone, Addie Major on cornet, and Ernest Elliot on clarinet.

James P. sat at a ringside table to watch his protégé play his first really big job. As soon as the music started a surprise visitor walked in. Willie The Lion had come by to see how his replacement was doing.

"Why d'ya push the punk kid? He's gonna take your place. He sounds like you playing up there," Willie told James P.

"There's something about that kid. He's like family and lives music. That's why I've been teaching him everything I know."

"Well, you taught the punk, all right. Just listen to him. He's got a few tricks of his own, too." The place was rocking and everyone was pleased. Especially Harry Pyle.

The Lion was right about those few tricks. The Waller style was evolving and some of its earliest characteristics were beginning to show. Dad had stretched his fingers and he was now playing sustained tenths in the bass. He would then hit the chord crisply with his left hand on the after-beat while his right hand kept playing the melody clearly. The tenth voicings and heavy afterbeat were to remain a distinct feature of the Waller style.

Edith was in the last months of her pregnancy while her husband was playing at Leroy's. And even though Fats was a tremendous success at the club, Edith was hoping for a more stable life. She went into the hospital to give birth just as the Leroy's gig was ending. She had thought that the arrival of the child would keep the new father at home, but she was sadly mistaken. Thomas Waller Jr. was born in the Spring of 1921. Instead of spending more time at home, Fats intensified his efforts as a bread winner.

Until his contract expired at Leroy's, Fats was working there nights, and at the Lincoln during the day. Willie The Lion, when he wasn't otherwise occupied, regularly attended Leroy's. He and the younger pianist were becoming close friends. The independent, cagey, Lion was warming up to the "punk" kid and this annoyed Edith all the more. When the contract at Leroy's expired, it was back to the shouts again, and nearly every night Dad was out playing somewhere with Russell Brooks and Corky Williams. The Lion tagged along frequently, offering playing tips to Dad. The four musicians would regularly show up at three or four in the morning, and Edith could stand it no longer.

She told her husband that the drinking and partying were driving her mad. She was a good Baptist and she couldn't tolerate his behavior. The insecurity of not knowing where the next job would come from was too much for her to take. Edith demanded that he quit music and learn a decent trade.

Dad decided that Edith would be consoled if he brought home more money. He confided in Russell Brooks that if he didn't start to make more money than he was pulling in from his job at the Lincoln, his marriage might be finished. Russell told him that Corky Williams was in Asbury Park for the summer and suggested that maybe Corky could fix him up with a good-paying gig for the tourist season. A letter was sent to Corky, the wife and baby packed off to the in-law's apartment, and Dad headed across the Hudson River for New Jersey.

Corky played piano at night but during the day he worked as a soda jerk at his mother's place, the Clef Ice Cream Parlor. He arranged a place for Dad to stay and a job at Scotty's Bar and Cabaret, a popular night spot that featured swinging music. Pop did a double take when he saw the sign reading FATS WALLER—NEW YORK PIANO SEN-SATION. Although he was pleased with the billing and happy that he was making better money, he couldn't fight off the feeling that he was still, after all, in *New Jersey*. His attitude changed when he started to meet the other fine musicians doing the summer circuit. He was soon jamming every night with Corky and Bill Basie, another summer refugee. Pop received valuable tips from Corky and his playing improved over the summer.

Dad returned home anxious to see his wife and baby but his reception was cold. Edith rehashed her grievances and threatened to divorce him if he didn't give up music and find a respectable profession. Once again he figured that he could console his wife if he made some more money. So he let out the word again that he was looking for work, work that paid well.

The Lion was working at the Capitol, a large, popular Harlem club. He arranged for Dad to follow him as a soloist and to pick up extra work playing with the house band. A short tour with a burlesque show followed. Nothing was available following that gig, but he was unworried because there was always his job at the Lincoln.

This time when he returned home he found Edith reinforced by her father. They demanded that he take up a decent trade—carpentry. Fats refused. The battle that followed brought irrevocable changes in both Edith and Dad. She was resigned to her fate as a musician's wife, but she demanded that her husband show her and the child more attention. He appealed to her that she try to understand his way of life, that she join him at the cabarets and rent parties. But that was too much for her to contend with. She had been strictly raised a Baptist and it was too late in her life to change. She wanted him to be with her and the child. He countered that the only way to do that was for her to be there at the clubs. There was no solution and they both knew it. Dad gave up at this point. Home soon became a place to sleep and eat breakfast. The parties became more frequent and the drinking got heavier.

The only thing that remained constant in his life was his steady job at the Lincoln. He soon learned, much to his surprise, that while he was on tour Marie Downes had sold the theatre to Leo Brecher and Frank Schiffman. These entrepreneurs had previously purchased the Lafayette Theatre. Schiffman realized the larger Lafayette with its Seventh Avenue location was a better theatre for vaudeville and stage attractions. He decided to turn the Lincoln into a straight movie house and the Lafayette into a showcase for black entertainment.

Dad wasted no time getting down to Frank Schiffman's office, trying to get his old job back. He had nothing to worry about, however. Schiffman was aware of Dad's popularity and his Saturday following, and he was astute enough to know that Fats Waller's presence at the Lafayette would help insure the theatre's success as a black vaudeville house. He offered a salary of fifty dollars a week. Dad quickly accepted. This was 1921 and fifty dollars was quite a sum, but what Schiffman didn't realize was that he could have hired Dad for nothing if he had shown him the enormous Robert Morton organ at the Lafayette. It was the first grand organ in Harlem.

Extra money wasn't going to stop Fats Waller from playing the rent parties whenever he could. He was earning a "good time Charlie" reputation and he loved every minute of it. At these parties he was constantly running into two people: Clarence Williams and Buddy Allen. The short, talkative Allen owned a small music shop on 135th Street and he spent the majority of his time around pianists, representing some of them with the downtown music publishers. Allen idolized my father and was sure to be at every rent party he played.

Clarence Williams and Dad were fast becoming very close friends. In early 1922 Williams had started his own music-publishing company and he invited Dad to come down to his office. My father was frequently there, learning everything he could about Tin Pan Alley, centered around the Brill Building at 1619 Broadway. He would play his tunes for Williams but wasn't interested in having his material published. In fact he hadn't bothered to write most of his material down. With the increasing pressure at home, the only thing he was interested in was the endless round of parties.

"Do you wanna stay in Harlem all your life?" his friend asked.

"Don't worry about me. I can take care of myself."

Williams considered Dad a potentially gifted composer, and promised he would publish the material if dad would put it on paper.

Clarence Williams was something of an agent as well as a publisher, and his activities brought him in contact with the people at Okeh Records. His wife, Eva Taylor, was one of their recording artists and Clarence himself frequently wrote tunes or played piano for the company. He wanted to get his pal, Fats, involved with Okeh Records, confident that he would make a fine recording artist. Okeh was quite a phenomenon and had made a tremendous impact in the two years it had been in business.

A core of knowledgeable executives had made the company a viable enterprise in a very short time. A former music publisher, Fred Hager, in charge of AR (artists and repertoire), decided what and who appeared on the label. Ralph Peer, also a publisher, directed sessions and promoted the records around the country.

Okeh had purchased "You Can't Keep a Good Man Down," written by Perry Bradford, for Sophie Tucker to record but she was unavailable because of an exclusive contract with the Aeolian label. Perry Bradford suggested the song be cut by Mamie Smith. It was unheard of for a black performer to make a recording when Peer and Hager brought Miss Smith into the studio in February of 1920. The record sold very well, as did her next recording, "Crazy Blues." Peer became aware that her recordings sold especially well in the South, predominantly in black areas. Hager and Peer decided to go into the black music market and surrounded themselves with outstanding black talent, including Perry Bradford and Clarence Williams.

Williams convinced Hager and his partner to record "Sugar Blues" with Sara Martin, a black singer from Louisville, Kentucky. Hager auditioned her and was enthusiastic about the session. While Clarence was rehearsing and polishing Miss Martin, he persuaded Hager to allow Dad to play the actual date, telling the AR man that this Fats Waller had a special feeling for the piano and he would be a valuable asset to the recording. When Hager agreed Clarence made a phone call to the Lafayette Theatre.

"I don't need the cash right now and I *don't* want to accompany anyone." Clarence was persistent, however, and demanded his friend appear. Finally Pop agreed to do the session.

Sara Martin, Fred Hager, Ralph Peer, and Clarence Williams were all at the studio promptly, ready to cut the record, but the pianist was nowhere to be seen. They waited for a long time but still no Fats. Everyone began to pressure Clarence to do the accompaniment, but he spoke so glowingly of his friend's ability, that they decided to wait a little longer. When half of the morning was gone, Hager told Clarence that they couldn't wait any longer. "Sugar Blues" was cut with Clarence Williams playing the piano.

That record launched Sara Martin as a prominent blues singer and it sold a lot of copies. It also launched Clarence Williams as an accompanist for such greats as Ethel Waters and Bessie Smith.

The errant Mr. Waller was given a second chance to accompany Sara on her next recording, a month later. But when he failed to show for that gig, Hager decided to stop wasting nickels phoning the Lafayette, and to stick with Clarence as his regular pianist.

James P. and Willie The Lion may have helped Fats Waller become a better pianist, but Clarence Williams made the effort to help Dad organize his life. Clarence was one of the first black publishers in New York, and, by nature, a good organizer. He was very helpful in representing Harlem talent, and getting uptown artists work for the downtown record companies. Vexed by Fats' behavior, he gave him a vicious tongue-lashing, attacking his cavalier attitude and life style. He seemed unconcerned about his career and, apparently, all he was interested in were good friends and good times. His attitude toward money was that all that was needed was enough for the rent, food, and booze. Clarence became my father's unofficial manager, helped to shape his career and gave him purpose and direction. Many people in the music industry claim that Clarence Williams would set up Dad's gigs and then travel to the Bronx in the morning to make sure he would show up.

Clarence was deeply troubled by Dad's marital problems and he tried several times to be a peacemaker. He tried to make dad understand his responsibilities as a husband and father and how his partying was destroying the marriage. Clarence talked with Edith, emphasizing how important it was to support and encourage her husband and to try to be involved in his life, even if only on a superficial level. Knowing that Dad and Edith respected W. C. Handy, the famous jazz trumpeter, Clarence even had Handy try to reason with them—to no avail.

Twice Clarence had imposed on Fred Hager to use Dad to accompany Sara Martin on a record and twice Hager had been let down. Clarence knew he'd have to take another tactic if there was going to be a third recording session. He ushered Hager to the Lafayette Theatre on a Saturday afternoon so he could hear Dad play in front of his audience. Hager was convinced.

Ralph Peer had heard a song, "Muscle Shoals Blues," that had been recorded by a white band with little success and Peer was convinced it could be a hit with the black community if it were recorded by a black performer. He brought the tune to Fred Hager, who im-

mediately recommended that Fats Waller record it. Clarence was terrified that there would be a repeat performance of the first two sessions, so he had a long talk with his friend. It was fine to be a star in
Harlem, Clarence cajoled, but making it on Broadway was the big
time, and if Fats took advantage of this opportunity. . . .

This time, the musician showed up promptly for the date. He
looked over the sheet music, made some pencil notes and signaled
Peer that he was ready. The record was cut and Hager and Clarence
sighed in relief. Peer came out of the recording booth, satisfied with the
take, and suggested that they cut something for the flip side. No one
had expected to cut two sides that morning, so there were no charts
prepared. Dad lit up a cigarette and gave the matter a few moments
thought. "This is gonna be the 'Birmingham Blues.' " The pianist
began to improvise a tune. Peer was a very happy man. In two takes
they had cut both sides of a record, not a very common feat. He was
so impressed with the new pianist's abilities, that he asked Hager to
use him as frequently as possible.

It was already late October, but by the end of 1922 Dad recorded
"Tain't Nobody's Bizness if I do," "You Got Everything a Sweet
Mama Needs but Me," "Momma's Got the Blues," and "Last Go
'round Blues" accompanying Sara Martin's vocal; and accompanying
the Sara Martin–Clarence Williams duets on "I'm Cert'nly Gonna See
'bout That," and "Squabblin' Blues."

Thomas Jr. was almost two years old, and eating more food every
day. James P., impressed with his student's successes on the shout
circuit and recording studios, had a plan for Dad to earn more money
to feed the wife and baby. Jimmy was picking up extra cash by recording piano rolls. He got fifty dollars for every roll he cut, and as he was
going on the road for a while, he figured Fats could take his place.

Piano rolls were a flourishing business and had been for quite
some time. The player piano was the first popular form of musical
entertainment through mechanical reproduction. Classical pieces, Tin
Pan Alley hits, novelties, and black ragtime were all available in piano-
roll form. It was an early outlet for the black musician to display his
talent. By 1916 Eubie Blake, Luckey Roberts, and James P. had rolls
in hundreds of music stores.

The two leading piano-roll companies in the twenties were Aeolian
and QRS (Quality Reigns Supreme). The latter was a subsidiary of the
Melville Clark Piano Company, which manufactured player pianos.
James P. told Dad that working for QRS was a good job because the
company's owners, Max Kortlander and J. Lawrence Cook, were
pianists themselves, and appreciated the talent of their black artists,
like Luckey Roberts and, of course, James P. Johnson.

Jimmy brought Dad to the office at Walnut and East 135th Street to see Kortlander and Cook, who were both pleased to meet James P.'s replacement. Cook had attended the Lincoln Theatre several times and was already impressed with Dad. He promised a recording date as soon as they could find an appropriate selection.

The tune selected was "Got to Cool My Doggies Now" written by Clarence Williams. Clarence, who wrote "Gulf Coast Blues," "I Ain't Gonna Give Nobody None of This Jelly Roll," and "Baby Won't You Please Come Home?" was born in New Orleans. He migrated to Chicago and then to New York, where he became a writer and publisher of "race music." To augment his income he toured the TOBA as a performer and one of the theatres he performed in was the Lincoln, where he first met Fats Waller. After the shows he would sit and chat about music with Dad for hours. They respected and admired each other and Dad was pleased that he was going to cut his friend's tune.

The recording date was set in March 1923. When Dad arrived he was fascinated by the process. A special Melville piano was fitted out so a roll of paper, the master, could be threaded into the piano mechanism. Dad would play the song and Cook would listen to the tempo and duration.

As the pianist touched the keys, a vacuum pump set eighty-eight steel fingers in motion, corresponding to the notes played. These fingers made carbon impressions on the master roll. The impressions were punched out manually by a technician. The master was then played through a player piano to check for errors. At QRS J. Lawrence Cook was the master editor. He not only corrected mistakes, but would often add melody lines, employing a "third hand," by changing the holes and covering others. After the roll was considered perfect, a series of *additional* holes were perforated in the master to simulate the sustaining notes. (The vacuum pump which set up the carbon impressions was unable to make these impressions for sustained notes, and so the additional holes.)

Everyone was happy with the recording session, and Dad was so proud of his work that he kept a copy of the roll in his pocket. This was a habit he maintained throughout his association with QRS. He always carried his most recent effort.

Fats hamming it up. *Courtesy of Frank Driggs.*

Chapter 6

1923-1924

Fats and the Music Publishers

Clarence was enthusiastic about his friend's success, and continued to urge Fats to write down some of his own material. Since Williams had heard the "Birmingham Blues" improvisation he was quite sure that Dad had a special ability as a composer. Strangely, Dad didn't give in to Clarence until after he had started doing the piano rolls. Perhaps he decided to try his hand at composing because he was going through a dry period at Okeh.

In any event, one day in the early summer of 1923 Fats showed up in Clarence Williams' office and said that he was ready to give it a try. Clarence was surprised but he suggested they get right to it. They went over the tunes and Clarence started writing lyrics for them, the first of which to be published was "Wildcat Blues." It was cut by Okeh Records during that summer by Clarence's studio group, the Blue Five, which included that great New Orleans soprano saxophonist, Sidney Bechet.

Clarence enjoyed Dad's parody of "The Boy in the Boat," so he decided to write a lyric for it. Eva Taylor, his wife, has frequently claimed that the original intention was to parody "Kiss Me Again," a Victor Herbert hit. The end result turned out to be "Squeeze Me," which proved to be a sleeper. Over the years it has been recorded many times by jazz musicians because its structure lends freely to improvisation.

The two men wrote well over seventy songs together in a period of less than five years. Most of these compositions were never recorded or published. In the late fifties they were sold to Decca Records[1] as part of the Clarence Williams collection.

---

[1] In 1947 I found a small carton in our garage. When I opened it I found dozens of unpublished manuscripts that my father had written in collaboration with Williams, Andy Razaf, Spencer Williams, and many other lyricists. The songs are now being catalogued.

The collaboration was by-and-large a successful one, but Dad still saw himself as primarily a pianist. He was getting to be very confident, in fact a bit overbearing, about his playing ability. When he heard the Roosevelt Theatre was having a contest that gave a cash prize he was quick to enter. Boasting that he was the youngest player there, he won easily, playing James P.'s "Carolina Shout." But then, how many of the other contestants were coached by the composer of their selection?

After the contest, a lean twenty-eight-year-old man chased after Dad outside the theatre. He congratulated him and suggested they have a cup of coffee together. The young man possessed an infectious personality and one cup stretched to several cups of coffee. The casual conversation grew into a pact to write songs together. The young man was a poet and lyricist, Andy Razaf.

Andy chose the name Razaf because no one could pronounce his real name, Andrea Menentania Razafinkeriefo. His mother, whose maiden name was Waller, was the daughter of the Madagascarian consul to the United States in 1895. When Madagascar was occupied by the French the consul and his pregnant daughter settled in Washington, where Andy was born that winter.

Andy was a firebrand, and as a youth poetry was the outlet for his boundless energy. He decided that he would make his career as a lyricist, and was so determined to do so that when money was short he operated an elevator at night so that he could write during the day. He once went as far as promoting one of his songs from the rear of a truck where he had a piano. He had written a song for the famous Fifteenth Infantry Regiment. As the song was about those black soldiers who fought during World War I, Andy sold the sheet music from the back of a truck to the black people of Harlem. Andy's hard work and diligence eventually helped him sell his song, "Baltimore" to the producers of "The Passing Show of 1917," the Shuberts' version of the Ziegfeld Follies.

Andy Razaf came along at the right time in Fats Waller's life and in very many ways their relationship was like a marriage. As helpful as Clarence Williams was, Andy was even more energetic and determined. Perhaps that little bit extra determination was enough to convince Dad that if he put in the effort of a serious composer, Andy would certainly work just as hard as a serious lyricist. During their years together Andy's methodic planning and discipline served as a necessary balance for his partner's instability.

In those days many music publishers would pay songwriters an advance but "neglected" to pay royalties. Andy and Dad knew that this was going on so they developed their own counterstrategy. The two of them would hit the Brill Building, and make the rounds. They'd approach one publisher and Dad would play while Andy sang. The tune probably would be purchased for twenty-five to fifty dollars. Then they'd play a second version of the song to a rival publisher, and that might result in a sale as well. They would spend the rest of the day going from publisher to publisher, selling the same song over and over again.

If the publishers suspected some chicanery on the part of the composer and lyricist, they were still willing to take their chances. Even in the twenties, fifty dollars was a very cheap price for a potential hit record. And if a publisher thought he could buy a song for fifty cents, he'd try. Once Andy was so infuriated with what he considered an outrageously low offer for one of their compositions that he tore up the score rather than sell it too cheaply.

It was an unwritten law in the industry that the first to publish a piece owned all the rights on it. Once the Razaf—Waller team became famous, publishers went into something of a frenzy, trying to dig up material they had bought and subsequently filed away. Andy and Dad were able to continue their multiple-sales tactics long after they were found out because the publishers knew that even if they weren't the first to buy they might be the first to print.

By 1923 James P., Willie The Lion, Eva Taylor, Clarence Williams, and Andy had replaced Edith and Thomas Jr. as Dad's family. Edith sought and won a divorce. The settlement was thirty-five dollars per week for child support and alimony. Dad agreed to pay, but from the very first installment the money came in late, and rarely was it the correct amount.

Free from a marriage he no longer wanted, he found an apartment in Harlem and began living at an even faster pace. Dad was still playing at the Lafayette, working with James P. or Willie The Lion, and composing. And Clarence Williams saw to it that there was plenty of new activities. Clarence, who had formed the Blue Five and handled the keyboard assignments on recording dates, used my father as the group's pianist whenever they played theatres. Clarence saw radio as a way of promoting his own material and eagerly agreed to performing on the new media. Dad played for one of these live broadcasts, originating from the Fox Terminal Theatre (Newark) and sent out over the wires of a local New Jersey station.

Dad also used this period to increase his circle of musical friends. Don Redman, a striving arranger and saxophonist, met my father at the Lafayette and spent many afternoons shooting the bull with him. The two men formed a very close bond. Don introduced Dad to Fletcher Henderson, a bandleader who was becoming a major force in popular music.

Fletcher came North from Atlanta in 1920 and went to work for Pace and Handy Music. When Pace left the publishing business to form the Black Swan Label he took Fletcher along to be an accompanist and recorded him backing up Ethel Waters on "Down Home Blues" and many other "race" sides.

Pace, who saw the financial potential in black artists and records, formed and managed a company of black singers, musicians, and dancers known as the Black Swan Troubadours. On one of the group's tours to New Orleans, Henderson spotted a young, remarkable jazz trumpeter named Louis Armstrong, hired him, and brought him to New York.

In 1921 Fletcher formed a band of his own, with Don Redman and Coleman Hawkins in the reed section. Henderson's approach to jazz was unorthodox because of his training in classical music. Usually jazz combos used sketch arrangements from which the ensemble played together at the beginning and final sections of a musical piece. Most of the piece would be devoted to improvisation, with block chords and rhythm as the unifying force. Henderson's band was before its time in both the caliber of its soloists and the group's arrangements. Larger than the traditional quintet or sextet, Fletcher's group included a reed section that provided riffs under the melodic line and improvisation. With recordings for Vocalion, Columbia, and Perfect labels, and long club engagements, this preswing era group was the first of its kind to be a success.

In 1923 Charley Burgess hired Fletcher and his group to play Roseland and the engagement lasted nearly eight years. One night the Henderson Band was moonlighting at Harlem's famous Savoy Ballroom after a full session at Roseland. Don Redman suggested that Fletcher allow Fats Waller to sit in for a couple of sets and Henderson readily agreed. It was the beginning of a long association. At another moonlighting session at the Hoofer's Club, Dad met Louis Armstrong. Clarence Williams saw how well the two musicians worked with each other, so he occasionally would use Satchmo and Fats with the Blue Five on the live radio broadcasts.

There was a lot of jamming and songwriting in those days but the money wasn't coming in fast enough to keep up with Dad's life style. He was beginning to pick up a habit that he would live to regret: selling his material—for whatever he could get—when he needed some trash. Bud Allen used to tell the story that one day Dad cornered J. Lawrence Cook in Bud's store and offered to sell him a handful of manuscripts for ten dollars. Cook gave Dad the ten dollars and told him to keep the manuscripts. He then took Dad by the hand, led him over to one of the nearby counters, and pointed to the QRS piano rolls. Holding one of the rolls in front of Dad's face he said: "See the name Fats Waller? That name's worth more than a few dollars." Unfortunately the effect of that lesson only lasted about as long as the ten dollars.

If Dad still hadn't learned the true value of his composing ability, at least Andy was able to convince him that he had quite an asset in his voice. The team kept on going to the Brill Building to sell their material and Andy kept on doing the singing, but he constantly argued that if Dad sang the material his buoyant personality would increase their sales.

Dad wanted no part of it, and said so. "You write 'em, man. You should sing 'em."

But Andy persisted and eventually Dad gave in.[2] As things turned out, they sold twice as many numbers and Fats Waller became a singer.

---

[2] Willie The Lion also claimed responsibility for encouraging Dad to sing.

In bad times as well as good, Fats' abundance of energy and high spirits attracted a continuous stream of admirers. *Courtesy of Michael Lipskin.*

Chapter 7

1924-1926

Fats Meets His Second Wife and Captain Maines

By 1924 Fats Waller was known throughout all of Harlem's music scene. He was something of a star on the rent-party circuit, and was known for his piano rolls, recordings, and radio broadcasts. But he was only enjoying his fame in Harlem, and that meant that he had to continue working at the Lincoln and Lafayette Theatres.

Next door to the Lafayette, the Shuffle Inn had fallen on bad days. The owners asked the Immerman brothers to come into the business and pull the club back to its feet. In a very short time the revamped Connie's Inn became a very popular club. And naturally enough, Fats Waller began spending a lot of time there, floating in after he finished playing at the theatre. He was never on the regular payroll but he was constantly playing requests or intermission music at the baby grand, rehearsing new acts, or writing some incidental music to pick up some extra cash.

Because of the club's popularity many white musicians and show people started to drift in from downtown. One of those patrons, Captain George H. Maines, had made quite a name for himself as a press agent. He was exactly the type of man with the influence and friends to catapult an entertainer into national prominence.

For some time Captain Maines and his wife were fascinated by my father and his antics at the baby grand and they frequently requested songs just to watch him. One night they invited him to the apartment of a friend on the fashionable West End Avenue. The apartment featured an organ and a piano and Dad entertained them for hours. Maines was convinced my father was a man of tremendous ability both as a composer and performer.

It wasn't uncommon for the wealthy white people to bring the latest hot performers of Harlem into their homes. Socialites, who could afford the best whiskey Canada could offer, threw lavish parties and competed just as vigorously for the top Harlem acts as the speakeasies and clubs did. During those Prohibition years Dad played quite often in Park Avenue penthouses or luxurious Long Island estates. Bill "Bojangles" Robinson was the top black attraction of the day, and, as his favorite accompanist, Dad spent many evenings playing the "upper crust" circuit. At the Schwab mansion on Riverside Drive Dad would sometimes work at the same party as Willie The Lion or James P.

Captain Maines began to search for the right outlet for Dad. He introduced him to many famous people and rekindled his old friendship with Irving Berlin, who hadn't seen him since the rent-party days in Harlem. Berlin, who couldn't read music very well, had a specially constructed piano that shifted all key signatures to F sharp. Dad sat at that piano in Irving's office and played wild improvisational passages and when he finished he would turn to Berlin and ask what was the name of the tune.

Berlin rarely recognized the music and that made his guest rock with laughter because he had been improvising Berlin's current hit. He'd then play it straight so Irving would recognize it, and once again burst into intricate improvisational patterns.

Maines also saw to it that his client had steady employment. He pressured Nils T. Granlund to have Pop appear as a soloist on radio station WHN. One afternoon Maines ran into Bert Lewis, the master of ceremonies of the Kentucky Club on West Fifty-second Street just off of Seventh Avenue. The press agent began promoting and soon Lewis promised an audition. They arrived at an empty club and Dad sat down at the piano. Playing in front of an empty house, Dad felt stiff even knocking out his favorite rags and shouts. He knew that what he was missing was some sort of a feeling of audience participation so he started trading off-color jokes back and forth with Lewis, and after a few minutes of this everyone was having a high time. The management of the Kentucky Club was duly impressed and they wanted to book Dad into the spot.

But the resident band at the Kentucky Club was led by Duke Ellington and he had his own reputation as a pianist to guard. Ellington, who had met Dad in Washington and knew of his abilities, approached Maines and pointedly told him that he wouldn't permit Fats Waller to play with his band. The club management, Maines, and Bert Lewis reached a compromise with the Duke that Dad would work as Bert's accompanist and as a soloist with some kind of gimmick that would differentiate him from Ellington. Maines soon converted Harlem's Fats Waller into Ali-Baba, the Egyptian Wonder, replete with jeweled turban. Bert Lewis was just as big a clown as Dad and my father's fondest memory of the Kentucky Club was an encounter he had with Bert on Seventh Avenue.

"It was between shows," Dad used to tell it, "and I stepped outside to get a refill. I was in a hurry so I went onto the street in my Arab costume. Just off Seventh Avenue, I ran into good old Bert, who was also looking for a place to get a refill. We started to shalom and bow to each other like two big potentates from the Middle East. Pretty soon everybody on the street was stopping to watch us. Well, after a while we couldn't keep it up any longer. Bert threw his arms around my shoulders and we started laughing like hell."

Dad loved any kind of shtick and he used all kinds of costumes and gimmicks in his act. His favorite was the Hawaiian bit. As soon as the house lights dimmed, the band started playing a hula. Out slithered Fats from between the two giant folds of the house curtains. He would grab one end of the curtain and wrap it around his large, portly frame like an enormous hula skirt, roll his eyes suggestively, and begin the funniest, lewdest dance ever seen. Then he would undulate those huge hips and sashay from side to side, finally making it over to the piano, where he would stare at the stool for a long moment.

"Hmmm, how am I gonna put all of me on that little thing?" he'd ask, as he cautiously lowered himself onto the stool. Then he'd look down and shout, "Hey, Fats, are you all there?" It was a little bit of hokum that always brought the house down.

The combination of Ellington's band, Bert Lewis' singing and patter, and the great Ali-Baba added up to marvelous entertainment, but Captain Maines wanted to highlight his client in a bigger house. The Broadway publicist turned to an old friend, theatre orchestra leader Hugo Reisenfeld, and convinced him to book the entire Kentucky Club show into his New Amsterdam Theatre on its dark night (most legitimate theatres are closed one night a week). The cast members' names were prominently displayed on the theatre marquee and at the top of the bill wasn't "Ali-Baba—The Egyptian Wonder," but "Fats Waller and His Songs." It was quite a thrill to see his name on a placard in Asbury Park, New Jersey, but Dad told me that he never forgot the incomparable sensation of seeing his name in lights over a Broadway theatre. The show, which played only on the theatre's dark nights, ran successfully for nearly two months.

In his personal life, my father was one of those people who liked everything regulated and regular and he should have been disciplined in his professional life, but the opposite was the case. He had an extremely chaotic life as a musician, late for rehearsals, erratic, and undependable, and was often—unfairly—accused of not being serious about his music. No matter how unreliable he was regarding appearances at sessions or concerts, he was always devoted to his music, as his recordings and prolific writing prove.

In 1924 Dad was deep into his daily schedule, playing at the Lafayette or Lincoln, hanging around at Connie's Inn, working rent parties, and playing record dates. Clarence Williams' band, using the name of the Jamaica Jazzers, cut two sides on Okeh with Dad on piano and Clarence Todd and Williams on kazoos. The records were "You Don't Know My Mind Blues" and "West Indies Blues." During the same period Dad cut some more piano rolls, including "The Clearing House Blues," "Do It Mr. So and So," and "Eighteenth Street Strut." The daily regimen of songwriting sessions continued with his favorite collaborators, Andy Razaf, Clarence Williams, Spencer Williams, and a new one, J. C. Johnson.

Johnson's first name was James, but because of the potential confusion with James P. Johnson, he used his initials. Originally from Chicago, early in life J. C. dedicated himself to learning the piano with the same enthusiasm Andy Razaf devoted to his lyrics. Like Razaf he worked at any job, including shining shoes on street corners, to earn the money to pay for his piano lessons and to finance his career as a musician. J. C. knew New York was where it was all happening, he migrated to the city sometime around 1915 or 1916. As soon as he heard the piano masters playing the Harlem scene he decided it was foolish to pretend he was in their class, so he turned to songwriting. In 1918 he had his first song (the title is uncertain) published, and in 1923 he met Dad and began collaborating with him.

All of Dad's work, and the help of George Maines were actually bringing in enough money to pay expenses and put something in the bank, a totally new experience for Fats Waller. But in spite of his relative affluence and his agreement to pay alimony and take care of child support, Dad was falling farther and farther into arrears. After numerous appeals to her ex-husband Edith finally turned to the courts. She needed the money badly and the judge agreed that a man making a decent living had no excuse to deprive his child of food and clothing.

Dad never disputed the judge's decision, but he couldn't forgive Edith for bringing an outsider (the judge) into what he considered a family matter. Why shouldn't Edith's father take care of her and the child? (In those days financial responsibility was not one of Fats Waller's stronger assets.) In any event, Dad applied inverse logic to the judge's edict. If a man making a decent living had a responsibility to pay his debts, then, went the Waller proposition, a man making little or no money had little or no responsibility to pay his debts. The solution:

earn less money. But neither Edith nor the law agreed with Dad's mathematics, and what developed was a running contest between my father and the process server.

The stories of Dad's efforts to elude Edith and the law are well known. Almost every one of his cronies had a favorite Fats Waller drinking and/or alimony story, some of which were just too fantastic to be true. For example, Spencer Williams and Ken Macomber, who was to later work as an arranger for the Waller band of the thirties, two men who were not prone to spinning tall tales, used to tell a whopper.

A judge, tired of Dad's regular visits to family court, decided to teach him a lesson by sentencing him to a little time in jail. Dad was sent off to the Raymond Street jail in Brooklyn and bail was set at an astronomical five hundred dollars. Spencer, Razaf, Clarence Williams, and Perry Bradford fanned through Harlem trying to raise the bail bond anywhere they could. Spencer and Andy even went so far as to sell some of their material for instant cash. Once they were able to make bail they raced to Brooklyn to spring their buddy. However, their friend, the indomitable Fats Waller, wasn't too happy to see them.

He sat in the cell with a wealthy, middle-aged companion, smoking a fat cigar and sipping good scotch. In the corner of the cell sat a brand new, white upright piano. He asked his cellmate to excuse him for a moment and motioned to Spencer and Andy to join him in a neutral corner. "Save your money, fellas. I've decided to serve my full sentence."

Confused, his friends demanded an explanation. Dad's cellmate was a millionaire who claimed that he'd rather spend time in jail than pay his wife "blood money" and Dad was learning from his example. Besides, the man was able to get anything he wanted from the easily bribed guards. Here in the jail they had plenty of good whiskey, steaks every day, and the piano that the millionaire had brought in so he could hear Fats Waller play. Pop remained in jail a few days more, and then, bored with his lack of activity, begged his friend to free him.

Frank Schiffman also had a favorite "Fats Waller and the law" story. Frank would often sit in the back of the dark Lafayette, listening to Dad practicing on the enormous organ. This particular afternoon, Frank was occupied with some other business and not paying attention to what was happening on stage. He became aware that the music had ceased, and stopping to investigate, Frank spotted a man in the front of the theatre.

"I'm looking for Thomas Waller," the man said when he saw the theatre owner.

"He was just playing the console," Schiffman replied.

"Well, he's gone now," the stranger said.

"Can I help you?"

The visitor was a process server with a court order for nonpayment of support to serve. Schiffman shrugged and invited the stranger to wait for Mr. Waller. The process server stayed about twenty minutes and then left. Shortly after, Dad reappeared at the console as if nothing had happened. Frank went back to his work and didn't ask about the stranger until the rehearsal session was over. The explanation was simple enough.

"I saw that piece of paper in his hands and decided to get goin' while the goin' was good!"

A bachelor again, Fats began to pursue women with the same zeal with which he would satiate his appetite for good food or liquor. He was an enormously sense-oriented person, and he made a career out of satisfying his senses. I have to attest that he never gave up those habits, even after he remarried. When my brother and I were growing up, whenever Pop was in New York he would proudly take us around town to show us off. Occasionally these trips would take us to a home of a lady in Queens or Harlem. As I grew older I became aware that these ladies fell into two categories: those who had ornate pianos, newly purchased, and those who had no pianos. Those women who were instrumentless were friends from the old neighborhood and those who owned instruments were ladies Dad showed a more recent interest in. He'd always caution me not to mention these visits to my mother, and I never did.

Shortly after his divorce from Edith, Pop began frequenting the many houses of prostitution that sprang up in Harlem in the waning years of Prohibition. When it became obvious that liquor would be legalized once again, the racketeers began to search for a new source of income that would be as profitable as hooch and the speakeasy. The mob turned to prostitution and opened plush parlors all over Harlem that featured good drinks, attractive women, and the top entertainers of the day. *Everyone,* including my father, played at these establishments. Some of the houses and the madames even became celebrated in song. One of these places, the popular Daisy Chain, was later honored by Count Basie in his famous recording, "Swinging at the Daisy Chain." The madame who ran the establishment was Hazel Valentine, for whom Dad wrote and recorded his "Valentine Stomp." In later years, when Mayor La Guardia and District Attorney Thomas E. Dewey began to crack down on the houses, Hazel Valentine found herself in financial trouble and several times Dad helped her out by paying off either the rent or the cops.

Pop used to boast that the Daisy Chain was "heaven on earth for a poor sinner like me." The parlor contained a grand piano and plenty of good gin and that's where Fats held court, drinking, playing, and always surrounded by some of the off-duty physiotherapists. Katharine Handy Lewis, daughter of the famous composer, told me that her brother always said, "If Fats Waller were locked in a room at the Daisy Chain with a bottle and several cuties, he'd certainly come up with the most beautiful music written this side of heaven."

Dad was quite a killer-diller, as he would say, but soon he began to take notice of one particular girl. He'd occasionally go to Mother Shepherd's place (a boarding house—barber shop—luncheonette—grocery store), and there he noticed a shy, pretty girl with large liquid eyes. Mother Shepherd's enterprise was around the corner from his apartment and just down the block from where Naomi and Edward Waller lived. Dad never spoke to the sixteen-year-old girl and she never took notice of him, but he tried to go to Mother Shepherd's as often as possible, hoping to get to know the young girl. One day during his frequent visits to the luncheonette, he decided to visit Naomi and Edward to bury the hatchet.

Having followed his son's career on records and radio, Edward now had a different attitude about music as a profession, and he was truly happy to see his prodigal son. Their reconciliation was a permanent one and the two men were never at odds again. (Dad's strained relationship with his father deeply affected his relationship with my brother and myself. Like most fathers, Pop was a disciplinarian, but he never forgot how painful it was to have a parent oppose his desires. He always encouraged us in whatever we were interested in. When I became interested in horses as a ten-year-old he made certain I had my own pony and riding lessons, and he came to watch me on that pony as often as possible. And when he learned about my curiosity for music he was beside himself with joy, and I was given lessons in classical piano. We shared an uncommon bond from that day on.)

In 1925 Fats Waller was trying to do everything. Captain Maines tried to impose some direction on Dad's career, but with that first taste of success in his mouth, discipline wasn't all that attractive. One place Dad was applying himself was in the record business. He was in great demand as an accompanist, and most of the recordings he made in the midtwenties were in this capacity. He backed up Alberta Hunter, Anna Jones, and Hazel Meyers on several dates. Perry Bradford, who had formed his own group, called the Jazz Phools, had a recording date for Vocalion and he asked Pop and James P. to play duo pianos. Louis Armstrong and Don Redman were also part of that group, famous for their recording of "Lucy Long" and "I Ain't Gonna Play No Second Fiddle."

Satchmo had grown tired of the stringent confinement of Henderson's "arranged jazz" and he decided to leave for Chicago to form his own band. Louis enjoyed both Dad's company and music, so he invited him to come out some time and join the group. Dad was willing so he packed his bags and got on the train. As was his custom, Dad always tried to work as many gigs as possible, so he managed a booking in the Hotel Sherman. (The following story, told often by my father, has been verified by Katharine Handy Lewis, and by Frank Serpe, a film executive who heard it from Frank Costello.).

Dad was playing solo piano at the Hotel Sherman, not very far from East Cicero, the home of Chicago's "second mayor," Al Capone. Every night Dad rocked the joint with his dazzling playing, funny stories, mugging, and risqué patter. He was immensely happy with the gig. Soon he began to notice a bunch of mugs in black ties and wide-lapeled suits coming to listen to him nightly, but thought nothing of it. Then, one night these gentlemen leaped up from their seats, pulled out machine guns, and told everyone to be as still as possible as they searched the audience for a "friend." Satisfied that they had found their acquaintance, they told the rest of the audience, a rather large group of people, to get into the men's room. Dad was the first in and had to be persuaded to come out after the police had arrived.

A few nights later Dad noticed the same thugs sitting in the first row and he remembered what had happened the last time they paid the Hotel Sherman a visit. He was nervous during the performance, and by the time he slipped out to get something to eat he was relieved that there hadn't been another incident. Suddenly someone shoved a revolver into his paunchy stomach and ordered him into a car. He did what he was told. The gunman ordered the driver to take them to East Cicero, and Dad began to sweat it out. What were the possibilities? Had he crossed a mobster unknowingly? Had he said something during the first incident when he should have kept his mouth shut? Was Edith getting her ultimate revenge for his desertion? Pop prayed as hard as he knew how, but a sinking feeling gripped his heart.

It only took the shiny black limousine a little while to make it to its destination. The car pulled up in front of what appeared to be a hotel or fancy saloon. It was the headquarters of Al Capone. Dad's four escorts shoved him through the front door and then through a crowd of people, led him to a piano, and told him to play. It was a surprise birthday party. Capone, who had heard Dad play at the hotel, was delighted when he saw the present the boys brought him sitting at the piano. Frightened, Dad began to pound the keyboard with something less than his usual gusto, but when he saw the enthusiastic response from Scarface and his buddies, he really began to swing it. In fact he swung it so hard, Capone kept him there several days, shoving hundred-dollar bills into his pocket whenever he played a request, and filling his glass with vintage champagne whenever Dad (frequently) emptied it. After the birthday party was over, three days later, the mugs returned him to Chicago several thousand dollars richer. Dad always said the incident stood out in his mind because it was the first time he ever drank champagne.

Happy to get back to the safe streets of Harlem after that Chicago gig, he returned to his regular job as house organist for the Lafayette and the Lincoln, his security blanket with seats. One Saturday after-noon, just before the matinee started, he spotted Anita Rutherford, the pretty granddaughter of Mother Shepherd, coming into the theatre with a boyfriend. Dad followed her, trying to catch her attention. She took her seat and then looked around to see if there was anyone nearby she might know. She spied Dad, who waved to her as if they were old friends. The funny, fat boy looked familiar to her but she didn't quite know where she had seen him before. Later, during the performance, he waved to her from the large organ console. She waved back, and he gave her what must have been a winning smile because she stopped to talk to him for a moment when the movie was over.

He reminded her that they were schoolmates from public school (even if he quit school when she was only ten), and that he frequently came to Mother Shepherd's for this or that. He asked to take her out, but she frowned and told him that she was only allowed to go out with one boy at a time and if they *did* go out together he'd have to pick her up at her parents' apartment and meet her mother and father. Dad readily agreed. A short while later they were seeing each other steadily. Pop told her about his father and his late mother, about his struggles to become a musician. He introduced her to some of his closest friends.

During the courtship with Edith Dad poured his heart out to her to help overcome his deep emotions related to the death of his mother. This time he was pouring his heart out, too, but he was doing it for a different emotional reason. Anita soon found herself becoming emo-tionally involved with the young man. She started asking questions, attempting to understand the different facets of the man's character. She wanted him to correct his very erratic alimony payments. When he asked Anita to be his wife she answered that she needed some time to consider the proposal because she wanted to be married for the rest of her life.

Anita went to see Captain Maines. She questioned him about Dad's financial situation and his potential to earn a living to support a family. He told her that he felt Fats Waller had a fantastic future as a musician and composer if he could get a little direction and purpose to his life. Maines suggested that Anita could be just the reason Dad needed to pull himself together. She thanked him but still wanted a little more time to consider marriage. Dad had no choice but to agree.

Captain Maines realized that little Anita Rutherford was the best possible thing that could happen to Fats Waller. She was a sensible, intelligent woman who wanted her future husband to do well for himself and his family. Maines told Pop that Anita truly loved him and that she wanted the marriage but was apprehensive about Dad's attitude. Pop told the Captain that he was sincere and wanted this marriage to be permanent. After Maines' matchmaking Fats Waller and Anita Rutherford were married in 1926.

Captain Maines was certainly right that the marriage would straighten out Dad. Fats Waller was a different man after he married Anita Rutherford. He still partied and stayed out late with his buddies, but he applied himself with a new vigor to his work. And he was moving with some real direction now. He was ready to apply himself to new projects, and, as luck would have it, those projects were already in the making.

By 1921 vaudeville veterans Eubie Blake and Noble Sissle, who had already written hits for Vernon and Irene Castle and Sophie Tucker, felt that it was time to attempt a full-scale musical about blacks, written and produced by blacks. The cast included the comic team of Flournoy Miller and Aubrey Lyles and Gertrude Saunders as the lead female singer.

Shuffle Along appeared doomed from its inception. Few people thought that the musical would have a prayer on Broadway. The producers emptied their pockets, backing the show, and then started to borrow here and connive there from friends and relatives. Money was just barely scraped together to pay for the transportation down to the Howard Theatre in Washington, and for the next two weeks, there and in both Baltimore and Philadelphia, survival was a day-to-day proposition dependent upon that night's receipts. A number of racial incidents made those weeks even more unpleasant. Having experienced that sort of a pre-Broadway run, everyone expected the worst when they opened in borrowed costumes at Daley's Sixty-third Street Theatre. But the audience lit up like a Christmas tree with the first bars of "I'm Just Wild about Harry." The show was a smash.

With backers eagerly knocking at their door, the producers wasted no time in reeling off a series of hit shows, including *Dinah, Chocolate Dandies,* and *Running Wild.* James P. Johnson wrote the score for the latter, and in so doing was probably responsible for introducing the Charleston to New York. In any event, the race was on. Everyone in town was looking for black shows to back and composers to write the scores.

Early in 1926 Frank Schiffman (who had earlier enjoyed some success with a few fully staged reviews scored by James P.) asked Dad and Spencer Williams to write the score for a revue to be staged at the Lafayette. The show was worked around some of the local vaudeville stars and staged by Leonard Harper. Clarence Williams liked the material well enough to publish it, which was lucky for Dad, because *Tan Topics* contained his first legitimate hit, "Señorita Mine."

Schiffman was satisfied with the show's four-week run at the theatre and the modest profits from another month or so on the black theatre circuit, so he commissioned Dad to write the score for a second revue. But Spencer, Dad's partner, had been offered a job writing for Josephine Baker, the star of *Chocolate Dandies*. She was off for Paris and the Champs Elysees Theatre to open *Revue Negre*. Spencer had written the score and was now hired to go along with the troupe. Dad said goodbye to his friend and settled down to the task of a new score.

The producers of the new show had decided to pattern it after Lew Leslie's smash, *Blackbirds*. They even went so far as to christen the effort *Junior Blackbirds*. But without a star like Florence Mills, *Junior Blackbirds* failed to live up to its model's success.

Writing the two revues certainly demanded a strict discipline, and Fats was becoming a more serious composer every day. And working on *Junior Blackbirds* without the help of a partner, he was made all the more aware of his deficiencies. On George Gershwin's recommendation, he began to study counterpoint and advanced harmony with Leopold Godowsky. Impressed with his former student's diligence, James P. soon turned to Godowsky's tutelage.

In the early fall Fletcher Henderson asked Dad to play piano and write arrangements for his band. Working with Ken Macomber, Henderson's principle arranger, was an added incentive. Instead of rent parties it was now trips to Roseland. Fletch soon included "Keep a Song in Your Soul" and "Stealin' Apples" in his repertoire. One of the regular patrons at Roseland and a big Fats Waller fan was the King of Jazz, Paul Whiteman. (Dad would later write "The Whiteman Stomp" for the famous bandleader.) On November 23, 1926 Fletcher and his band, which included Dad on piano, Don Redman on alto sax, and Coleman Hawkins on tenor sax, cut "The Chant" and "Henderson Stomp" for Columbia Records.

Ralph Peer, who owned the Southern Music Publishing Company, had moved to the Victor Talking Machine Company as AR director of race and hillbilly records for the Victor label. Ralph wanted Fats Waller,

Jelly Roll Morton, Fletcher Henderson, and other black talent to record for the label and wasted no time contacting them.

Victor's home office was in Camden, New Jersey, not far from Philadelphia. In Camden they pressed records, built phonographs (Victrolas), and did much of their recording in a church they had purchased. Naturally, the church had an organ, and that was just perfect for Dad. On November 17, 1926 Fats Waller recorded his first record as a soloist, his slow tango-tempo version of W. C. Handy's jazz classic, "St. Louis Blues," and, on the flip side, his own composition, "Lenox Avenue Blues." The record was not a hit in 1926, but it has since become a priceless collector's item.

By the end of the year George Maines, and everyone else around him, knew that Fats Waller was going to be a star. And not just in Harlem.

The composer of *Keep Shufflin'* entertaining a radio audience.
Courtesy of Michael Lipskin.

Chapter 8

1927-1928

Fats Writes *Keep Shufflin'*

Ralph Peer was pleased enough with the November sessions to ask Dad, in early January, to make another trip down to Camden. Peer had always considered Dad to be one of the country's finest organists and was eager to have him do more work on the church's instrument. Captain Maines tried to take advantage of the situation and press Victor into an exclusive contract, but the company wasn't ready to commit itself. Even without the exclusive contract, Pop was thrilled at the opportunity to record on what he considered his first instrument. (He always looked at the piano as sort of a second choice to the organ.) He had begun playing the organ when he used to sneak into the Trinity Church (after Adam Clayton Powell, Jr., the reverend's son, showed him how to force open the basement window) and, as a teenager, for church services. Perhaps it was through this religious background that he first developed his reverence for the great classical composers.[1]

On January 14, 1927, under Ralph Peer's capable supervision, Dad made the Victor's pipe organ jump as he cut "Soothin' Syrup Stomp," "Sloppy Water Blues," "Loveless Love," "The Rusty Pail," and "Messin' around with the Blues." Peer was with my father back in the Camden studio February 16 for another session to cut "Stompin' the Bug," and "Hog Maw Stomp." A wonderful piano solo, "Blue Black Bottom," was also recorded that day but remained unissued until Victor's Vintage series was released. Dad was pleased with the

---

[1] In the *Yearbook of Swing,* Charles Smith reported that Dad recorded several Bach fugues and Rimsky-Korsakov's "Flight of the Bumble Bee" on the pipe organ for Victor, but the records were never issued. Dad acknowledged this as fact, but he told me that he was never told why the records were shelved. I have heard from several sources that when one of the company's top classical performers heard the pieces played with the Waller swing, he demanded that the masters be buried.

sessions, even if Victor dropped the "Fats" from his name, listing the organist as Thomas Waller.

Captain Maines was delighted over Victor's interest in Dad, it being a very convenient vehicle to bring him national prominence. When Fletcher Henderson decided to take his band on a tour of college campuses, Captain Maines urged Dad to accept Fletcher's invitation to go along as the group's pianist. Bringing jazz to the college campuses was something of a novel inspiration. But Fletcher had correctly gauged student interest. The band, with Pop at his mugging best, packed them in at the fraternity houses at Yale, Harvard, and Princeton.

Fats Waller's life on the rent-shout circuit was over. And he was now a family man. On September 10, 1927, Maurice Thomas Waller was born. Captain Maines, who was by now a cross between agent and family member, was arranging jobs so as to provide the best financial security. Dad was eager to take up bandleader Erskine Tate's offer to play with his group in the Vendome Theatre in Chicago. Dad's old buddy, Louis Armstrong, was in the band, and gigging with Satchmo was an added incentive. But before the Chicago trip Maines urged Dad to do two more recording sessions to put some more money in the bank.

On April 27, 1927, Fats Waller was at the Columbia studios, playing piano for the Henderson Orchestra. One of the cuts was his own composition, "The Whiteman Stomp." (As in the previous Henderson recordings Don Redman and Coleman Hawkins were sidemen.) On May 20 it was over to the Victor recording studio. Peer had decided to record each of the day's selections twice, once with Alberta Hunter doing a vocal and once as an instrumental. Peer had Victor issue all of the cuts, with and without Hunter singing, both proving to be good sellers. The songs were "Sugar" and "Beale Street Blues."

That same day Peer had an inspired idea. Victor had signed a cornet player named Thomas Morris who led a group called the Hot Babies. The group was essentially a "pickup" band, Morris, the leader, being the only permanent member. The composition of the group being as fluid as it was, Peer decided to have Dad play hot organ and piano with Thomas Morris' Hot Babies. This was the first time an organ was used with a jazz group. The sound they produced that afternoon and in subsequent sessions was unique and vital, some of the best jazz ever recorded. The May 20 cuts were the "Fats Waller Stomp," "Won't You Take Me Home," and "Savannah Blues."

With Captain Maines satisfied that the bank account was solvent, Anita began packing the bags (and me) for the trip. The Waller family was going to stay with Tate and his wife, Lil Hardin. Chicago was always one of Dad's favorite cities, and he was looking forward to this trip.

Tate and his orchestra had been playing continually at the Vendome since 1918 and his group was a particular favorite in the Windy City. At various times he used guest stars such as Earl "Fatha" Hines, Buster Bailey, and Louis Armstrong. The orchestra played the background music for the films and put on a spectacular show at intermission, which featured a no-holds-barred jam session. The job was very much to Dad's liking, being reunited with his friend Satchmo and ripping up the audience with his work on the organ.

For many years the Carroll Dickerson Band had played at the Sunset Cafe, with Satchmo as a member of the group. When Dickerson decided to call it quits, Louis formed his own band, which included Earl Fatha Hines on piano. It was a late-night gig so Satchmo could work it in with Vendome job. The band featured duo pianos (but the name of the second pianist is unknown to me). Whenever Dad could get over to the Sunset, the second pianist would yield his stool and a fine jam session would begin. I was only one year old then and I've always regretted never hearing my father cut up with Satchmo and Earl.

My mother always said that period in Chicago was one of the happiest times in Dad's life. He was overjoyed to have her and me with him and jubilant about her being pregnant again. Pop was being paid well by the Tate Orchestra and he liked the work and the men. Royalties were coming in from Victor on his recordings and compositions and it seemed to be an ideal time for him. However, Dad was on the road, and when he was on the road he suffered from an almost incurable disease: partial amnesia, directly blotting out all memory of alimony. Naturally enough, Edith was tired of nonsupport, so she tied up his salary and royalty checks and then had an arrest warrant issued. Dad was unceremoniously arrested and hauled off to New York to face the wrath of family court.

The police escorted him back to New York before he could make any arrangements for our safety and financial needs. Dad was filled with rage, and he was heartsick and humiliated when Mom had to wire her mother for help.

Expecting the worst, he asked his father to come along, the logic being that if the judge issued a stiff jail sentence, Edward would follow his son's instructions, arranging for the care of my mother and me. With these preparations considered, Dad was shocked to be let off with a stern lecture. Pop threw his arms around his father and they joyfully marched out of the court room.

With the law off his back, Dad started sending out feelers for extra work. (Even with his royalty payments, the job at the Lafayette was needed occasionally. In those days very few artists were able to live off their writing and recording money.) Dad was determined to pay back his mother-in-law, and it had taken quite a lot of money to get Mom and me out of Chicago, and then to keep the family going until after the court appearance.

Help came from an unexpected corner. Miller and Lyles were planning to work another show and they had heavy financing. Their backer wanted his money spent on the best costumes, sets, director, and songwriting team available. The first man approached was James P. Johnson, who was interested but already had committed himself to write another show. Miller and Lyles convinced James P. to write half of the score and James P. convinced them to hire the Waller–Razaf team to write the other half of the score. During the preproduction period and rehearsals of the show, Dad became very friendly with the man who was bankrolling the show, Arnold Rothstein.

Few men had done more to promote organized crime than Rothstein, and yet he never directly did anything illegal himself. Due to his uncanny business sense, Rothstein was nicknamed "the Brain" by his good friend Damon Runyon. It was generally believed that Sky Masterson, of Runyon's *Guys and Dolls,* was based on Rothstein. He was a gambler, horse fancier, nightclub owner, expert pool player, bootlegger, gang organizer, and the man generally regarded as the fixer behind the Chicago Black Sox scandal of 1919.

Rothstein made a fortune in rum running from the first day of Prohibition and laundered his money in many legitimate business enterprises, including a real estate company, the largest insurance company in New York, and a bail-bonding business. If you had an interesting idea, you proposed it to A.R. and he would lend you the money . . . if you pledged your life as collateral. He gave you the cash you required after you purchased a life insurance policy from his company for double the amount you borrowed. If you lived and paid him off, he made a neat profit on the policy. If you were killed during the course of business, Rothstein, who was the beneficiary on your policy, collected double. (And if you failed to pay back your loan, double indemnity was very likely.)

Anne Nicholas had written a play that had opened to disastrous reviews in 1922. But the play, in spite of bad press, was doing excellent business. She was convinced that her show could be a big hit if she could borrow enough money to keep it running just long enough to outlast the effect of the reviews.

"How much?" Rothstein asked.

Miss Nicholas said she needed twenty-five thousand dollars and offered him half of the show's profits, but Rothstein told her he wasn't in show business. He would give her the money at ten percent interest plus the customary insurance policy. Miss Nicholas agreed. *Abie's Irish Rose* ran over five years and half the box would have netted A.R. over a million dollars instead of the three thousand he earned on a straight business deal. From then on he laundered some of his money in the high-risk investment in Broadway shows.

Mobsters have long had a vested interest in Broadway. Frank Costello, the mob boss of New York, was a patron of the theatre, and at least one big-name singer's involvement with Lucky Luciano has been documented in many places. I remember, as a child, a tall, thin man often came to our home, trying to convince Dad to play at his night spot, the Hotsy Totsy Club. I remember the man well because he always gave my brother and me a crisp, new twenty-dollar bill. He was Jack "Legs" Diamond, a friend and colleague of Arnold Rothstein. In the fall of 1927 Dad didn't care where Rothstein's money came from, just as long as it kept paying off Waller debts.

James P. and his lyricists, Henry Creamer and Clarence Todd, along with Dad and Andy, wrote twenty-two numbers, out of which two were hits. James P. and his team were responsible for "Sippi," and "Willow Tree" was contributed by Pop and Andy. Curiously, the showstopper "Give Me The Sunshine," was written by the director, Con Conrad.

Just before rehearsals began, the black community was saddened by the death of Florence Mills. Her death produced one of Harlem's most fantastic funerals with parades, concerts, eulogies, and an outpouring of public grief unusual even by Harlem's standards. Ralph Peer convinced Victor that a memorial record honoring Mills should be issued. Ralph asked Dad to write a song about this legendary vocalist and also asked singers Bert Howell and Juanita Stinette to record it. Pop thought it would be a treat for wife and infant son to take the long trip to Camden. Just as the session was about to start, Ralph asked Mom if she'd like to stay and watch—*if* she could keep the baby quiet. Juanita sang "Florence" with Dad softly accompanying her on the pipe organ. He also cut an organ solo, "Memories of Florence" and backed up Bert Howell on "Bye Bye Florence," but neither were ever issued. (My mother told me that I listened attentively throughout the session and didn't cry once.)

On December 1, 1927, Dad was back in Camden, teamed again with Thomas Morris' Hot Babies. They cut "He's Gone Away," "I Ain't Got Nobody," "Geechee," as well as "Red Hot Dan" and "The

Digah's Stomp". The last two records featured Thomas Morris and (for the first time on a recording) Fats Waller singing.

With the Miller-Lyles show deep into rehearsals, there was time to make only one more recording, this time for Columbia. On January 17 he did an organ accompaniment to Johnny Thompson singing "Nobody Knows How Much I Love You." Columbia suggested more work, but Dad had to take a rain check.

Keep Shufflin' opened on February 27, 1928, in Daly's Sixty-third Street Theatre. Featured along with the show's Miller and Lyles was Blanche Calloway, Cab's younger sister. The show was an immediate hit and everyone connected with it was walking on air.

Dad and James P. were hired to play duo pianos in the orchestra, Jimmy doubling as conductor. (My yellowed copy of the program reads: "on the white keys, Fats Waller—on the black keys, James P. Johnson.")

Miller noted the popularity of the two men and thought it would be a fine idea to have them play at intermission. They enjoyed the opportunity, but would race back to their dressing room each night for some refreshment. Years later Miller recalled how he had to push James P. and Dad out into the theatre pit every night to make sure they would play.

"Sippi" was chosen to demonstrate their collective talents. They would begin their miniconcert by playing the theme once through without any development or departure from the melody. Then, employing all that they had learned from Godowsky, they would perform a range of exciting variations, both melodic and harmonic, continually extending the germinal motif, sometimes even beyond their own expectations. Jazz improvisations between two pianists were (and are) very rare, but these men knew each other so well from their teacher–pupil relationship and appearing at rent parties together, that each was able to anticipate what the other would do and augment it. Their performances were tremendously popular and the audience rarely left the theatre at intermission.

"Sippi" and "Willow Tree" were very popular with the theatre audience and (when they were free) a year later Ralph Peer was astute enough to record them for Victor. He collected Jabbo Smith and Garvin Bushell from the pit of *Keep Shufflin'* and had them cut both numbers and the current Rodgers and Hart smash, "Thou Swell." They were recorded under the name of the Louisiana Sugar Babes featuring the Waller–Johnson piano duo and Jabbo Smith on trumpet and Bushell playing reeds. The original intention was to record "Sippi" in the same style as the song was played during those intermission performances. But, as is so often the case, the improvisation never really took off on the record. The disc's time restrictions (three minutes) stilted any creative development of the theme and the playing sounds rushed and stiff.

During the run of *Keep Shufflin'* Fats Waller was a contented man. He had plenty of money, his wife was carrying his second child, and he was cutting up at the theatre like crazy. There was a constant parade of his cronies from Harlem and downtown coming backstage to wish him well, among the Irving Berlin, Paul Whiteman, and George Gershwin, but Dad did most of his cutting up with Andy Razaf and Arnold Rothstein. According to Andy, Dad quickly learned that Rothstein was one of Broadway's softest touches, if approached at the right moment. Andy said that one day they found him in a particularly good mood.

"How 'bout some trash for a cab?" Dad asked.

"Sure, boys," Rothstein answered. "How about five hundred apiece?"

From then on, according to Andy, Dad always referred to him as "the goose who laid the golden eggs." But Rothsetin's generosity left him about the same time his wife Carolyn did. He was late in his royalty payments on the show, owing Dad more than a thousand dollars.

While conducting and playing in *Keep Shufflin'*, James P. undertook the ambitious project of composing a rhapsody based on the notorious Yamecraw section of Savannah, Georgia. Like Charleston, South Carolina's Catfish Row in Gershwin's *Porgy and Bess*, Yamecraw was filled with colorful characters and was perfect inspiration for James P.'s musical gifts. *Yamekraw,* as he called his rhapsody, was enthusiastically received by the critics, and the people at Vitaphone asked him to expand its themes into a folk opera to be filmed with an all-black cast, starring James P. *Yamekraw* so impressed W. C. Handy that he intended to use it as the highlight of a concert celebrating the twenty-fifth anniversary of the publication of his jazz classic, "Memphis Blues." The concert, to be held on April 27, 1928, at Carnegie Hall, was a full program of Handy's works, black spirituals, blues, and jazz pieces. James P. was to play solo piano for *Yamekraw* with a forty-piece orchestra backing him up. He was understandably thrilled that his work was to be performed at the most prestigious concert hall in America.

Unfortunately Miller and Lyles wouldn't let him out of his conducting responsibilities for even one night. Jimmy suggested Dad conduct the show, but that too was unacceptable to the actors, although they were willing to allow Dad to take Jimmy's place at Carnegie Hall. Handy, who considered Fats Waller a friend and a colleague, was amenable to the substitution, but the concert's promoters had never heard Dad play the organ. An audition was arranged, and after some consultation, the promoters not only agreed to use the new musician but suggested that besides playing *Yamekraw,* he be featured on Carnegie Hall's enormous pipe organ.

My mother remembered that concert at Carnegie Hall and spoke of it frequently because she regarded it as the turning point in Dad's life: "It was a Friday night, and the city was hit with a wild, spring storm. It rained all day and the streets were so windy you couldn't walk around. With all that bad weather you'd think no one would go out and I was surprised to see that hall filled to capacity. Your father had recorded "Beale Street Blues" the year before with Alberta Hunter, and W. C. Handy thought it would be the right selection for your father to play at Carnegie Hall." Dad played "Beale Street Blues" as a solo and then again with Katharine Handy, W.C.'s daughter, doing the vocal.

After his night at Carnegie Hall, Dad returned to *Keep Shufflin'* and the duets with Jimmy. People were buying tickets, Dad and Jimmy were cutting up on and off stage, and the money was coming in. Things were going so well that Fats and Anita Waller were saving money to buy a house, and, even more incredibly, Edith was getting her alimony on time. But then Rothstein started to fall behind on his royalty payments. (It was rumored that he was financing an illicit drug operation and had overextended himself, but this was not the sort of thing that one discussed with A.R.) So, when the offer came from the Grand Theatre in Philadelphia to play organ and piano, Dad quickly accepted. Springtime in Philly.

On the road again, Dad suffered from a relapse of his amnesia and totally forgot about Edith's alimony. We were in Philadelphia from June to October 1928, and in those five months Edith never received a cent. Mom assumed the whole while that Dad was maintaining the payments, just as he had been during the time he was working in New York. When we returned to Manhattan Edith was waiting with an arrest warrant. Mom was livid: the arrears were staggering; Dad had been irresponsible; and it was very unlikely that he would get off with another lecture.

Looking over the history of Dad's nonpayment, the family-court judge decided stricter measures were called for. Immediate payment would have to be made and a bond posted to guarantee future payment. Dad hadn't nearly enough money to cover the arrears, let alone the bond, so it was off to jail. But the judge had another surprise in store for him. It wasn't going to be a cozy thirty days in Brooklyn's Raymond Street, but the prison facility on Welfare Island. Mom would have to appeal to her mother one more time to bail Dad out. But this time Mother Shepherd hadn't the cash. Dad sat in prison, dejected and humiliated that his pregnant wife and mother-in-law had to run around the city, trying to scrape up enough money to pull him out of jail, all because he had been so irresponsible.

Naomi came to the prison with the news. Edward had suffered a heart attack and had died after two days in the hospital. The two men had never been as close as a father and son could have been, but a reconciliation had been made, and they had come to mutually respect each other. Dad felt grief and shame. Although the prison officials would have allowed him to attend the services, he decided not to go to the funeral, reasoning that Edward would have been embarrassed to see his son in chains.

Mom continued seeking out Dad's friends, hoping to raise the necessary funds, but they were all either out of town or tapped out themselves. She was able to raise some cash but it fell far short of the necessary amount. On visiting day Dad hit on the idea that if Arnold Rothstein paid the back royalties they would have more than enough to cover the arrears and bond. That was on election day, November 4, 1928. Mom promised to go to Rothstein Realty the next morning and collect the debt. But fate played another dirty trick on them.

Rothstein was sitting at his favorite table in Manhattan's Lindy's Restaurant when an old friend invited him to join a poker game with George McManus, an "associate" of the New York political boss, Jimmy Hines. A. R., who loved a good card game, played for a few hours before quitting to listen to the election returns. He had bet heavily that Hoover would beat Al Smith and he wanted to know the results. A little after midnight the desk clerk heard what he thought was an explosion on the third floor and raced up the stairs. Rothstein was clinging to the bannister, holding his side. "Call me a taxi," he said, "I've just been shot." A. R. was rushed to Polyclinic Hospital, where he died two days later.

Mom had gone through the list of all of Dad's friends and still hadn't succeeded in raising enough cash. But those buddies who hadn't the loot themselves passed the word around that Fats Waller was in jail and he needed bread to get out. Eventually Gene Austin heard about Dad's situation and contacted Mom. He would post the bail to spring Fats.

Back in family court the judge who had originally sentenced Dad wanted more than bail before freeing the prisoner.

"Is there a good reason I should let him go this time?"

Dad looked at Mom. Neither had even considered any alternative to a suspended sentence. But Gene quickly came to the rescue.

"I need this man to play piano for a record session this afternoon. . . ."

The judge snapped back, "So what?"

"If he doesn't play, it'll put several other men out of work, and these are hard times, your Honor."

It worked! The judge accepted bail after he gave Dad a scathing tongue-lashing and stipulated that all future alimony and child support be made directly to the court. This guaranteed that the court would know the moment dad fell behind.

Pop was jubilant. Released from jail and reunited with his expectant wife, he even had a job to repay Austin for his kindness. Dad rushed out of court, put Mom in a cab, and headed off to the recording session. But the day's hardships weren't over. When he arrived at the studio, he found out, as did the orchestra, that he was the only black hired to play. As soon as they saw him, the white musicians announced that they were not going to play with "Austin's nigger."

Gene wanted Fats Waller to do the recording, and Dad was in no position to huff out of the studio after his friend had just posted bail for him. Eventually Gene was able to effect a settlement. The orchestra was placed at one end of the studio, grouped around a microphone, and the black pianist at the other end of the room with his own mike.

Afterwards, Dad rarely spoke about the incident, and I've never found out what the name of the record was. The company didn't think it was necessary to credit a black musician if he wasn't working on race music.

Load of Coal helped bring fame to Fats, here shown with Paul Douglas before a Saturday Night Swing Club radio broadcast. *Courtesy of Frank Driggs.*

Chapter 9

1928-1929

Fats Writes *Load of Coal*

My brother Ronald was born on October 26, 1928, and Dad was happy to be at Mom's bedside rather than on Welfare Island. But as relieved as he was, he was still low on funds. Once again the word went out that Fats Waller was looking for some trash and needed work.

The Immerman brothers had an offer. Impressed with the money brought in by the black revues, the Immermans decided to take advantage of the phenomenon while it was still hot. Would the Waller−Razaf team be interested in writing material for a show at Connie's Inn?

"Would we consider it? Speaking for my partner and myself, I can say that we *insist* on it!"

An advance was agreed upon, and, after leaving Connie's, Dad figured that he better let the other half of the team know that they were employed again. Andy was not indisposed to the gig, so the next day they sat down with their new employers to plan out the show, which was to open in March.

Marriage had made Fats Waller a more responsible man but he was still prone to go off on a binge, and, with a deadline in front of them, Andy feared the worst. He suggested that they go down to Asbury Park and hole up in his mother's house to write the music. Pop argued that he couldn't just up and leave for southern Jersey a couple weeks after his wife had given birth. Andy went to see Mom and she agreed that Harlem's nightlife was not conducive to making deadlines. Dad reluctantly bought a train ticket. Meanwhile, Andy arranged to rent an upright piano and have it delivered to his mother's house.

Andy was not a man to waste time. The moment they arrived he asked to hear some themes and snatches of melodies that Dad had written. Andy liked the phrases and Pop began to expand them into complete songs. (Usually a song contains four eight-bar sections. The first eight bars, or the A section, are repeated and then a B section of eight bars is developed. The B section is commonly known as the release, or bridge. The first eight bars are repeated again, completing the song.) Dad had written down the first eight bars for a couple of numbers and played them for Andy.

"My Fate Is in Your Hands," a ballad, was worked out in less than an hour. Pop played a catchy tune for Andy, which he liked, but felt needed a stronger rhythmic background. After a few minutes of improvisation, the melody was enriched. Andy approved and produced the lyrics for "Zonky," a solid uptune for the show. Barely two hours had passed and they already had come up with two good songs for their musical. Having completed a day's work, Dad's concentration began to wane and he soon began plotting a return to New York.

Andy pushed on and asked Dad to work on a soft-shoe number, a vital part of any show. Halfheartedly, he drifted over to the piano and started tinkering with a tune while his mind floated off to Harlem. Andy stirred him back to reality when he became very excited about a particular passage. In a short while they were satisfied that they had the melody for their third number. Andy started working on the lyric, but he kept stumbling on one particular phrase: "Ev'ry honey bee fills with jealousy when they see you out with me." Seeing that he was having trouble with the lyric, he suggested that Dad polish the first two tunes while he worked on the words. Dad labored at the tedious chore for over an hour, all the while trying to keep his mind from wandering off to Harlem.

"Look, I gotta go to New York," he told Andy. Andy protested, but Dad was firm. "You work on the lyric and I'll meet you at Connie's tomorrow afternoon." Andy tried pleading. He reminded his partner about the rental fees on the piano. Finally he appealed to the renowned Waller appetite. "How about my momma's fried chicken?" Nothing worked. Dad grabbed a chicken leg, walked out the door, and caught the first train to New York.

Andy wasn't nearly as upset as he had let on to be. They were expected to write four tunes for *Load of Coal:* a ballad; an uptune (or rhythm song); a soft-shoe routine; and *one more piece,* probably another ballad. Three out of four wasn't bad for one day's work, and Andy knew it. He spent the rest of the afternoon trying to fashion an acceptable lyric for the soft-shoe routine, his effort carrying into the early evening. Andy finally felt he had the right lyric for the lilting melody, but the melody was still incomplete. He decided to call Pop to have him finish the tune.

When Mom answered the phone she was surprised to learn that Dad wasn't in Asbury Park. Andy began methodically calling all the places where Dad hung out, but he had no luck. Then he remembered a little bar next to the Lafayette. The bartender on the other end of the line told Andy that there was no Fats Waller in the house. Andy persisted, repeating over and over that no, he wasn't a process server, he was Fats' partner, Razaf. Andy Razaf.

Dad finally, grudgingly, came to the phone and spoke with his collaborator.

"I finished the song, Fats."

"That's good."

"The lyric for the soft shoe. I want to run over it with you."

"I don't remember the melody," Dad sadly told him.

Andy volunteered to hum it over the phone. The first phrase was sufficient to bring back the whole melodic structure to Dad's mind. Andy now sang his lyrics and Pop was pleased, especially with the last words: "honeysuckle rose." Everything was fine but Andy couldn't recall the eight bars that made the bridge, and neither could Dad.

"It's okay, Andy. Read me the lyric and I'll come up with a bridge."

After some thought, Dad hummed a melody into the phone. He had to repeat it a few times before Andy knew it well enough to sing the lyrics to it. It sounded fine over the telephone but Andy wanted to check it on the piano to make sure that it really did work.

Andy took a while but he soon found all the right notes. The lyrics and melody worked fine together. He returned to the phone with the good news.

But up in Harlem it was three gins later. "You better write down the notes, man. I forgot 'em."

"Don't worry, Fats. I already did."

As agreed, the songwriters met the next afternoon in Connie's and performed their work for the much surprised Immermans. With the music completed, the show could now be more definitely blocked out. As is often the case with music written for revues, a song's placing in the show determines its future success as a recording. "Zonky" and "My Fate Is in Your Hands" were feature numbers and were consequently recorded by several groups. Both received quite a bit of air time and the latter became quite a successful hit. But "Honeysuckle Rose" was relegated to the chorus as a forgettable tap number. It wasn't until much later, when the film short of the same name highlighted it,[1] that it gained popularity. Over the years it has proved

---

[1] When Andy saw the film he was incensed by its depiction of the song's creation. The screen version claimed that two white men wrote "Honeysuckle Rose" while they were in jail. Dad felt that the film treatment was inconsequential and refused to join Andy in a lawsuit. Andy then wrote a letter to Louis B. Mayer, the president of MGM,

to be one of Pop's most popular pieces, second only to "Ain't Misbehavin'."

Ralph Peer learned that Dad was free to do some studio work, now that the songwriting was completed for *Load of Coal*. Captain Maines knew that Peer wanted to capitalize on Dad's growing popularity, following the success of *Keep Shufflin'*. Maines argued that Fats Waller would be an even more valuable property as soon as *Load of Coal* opened at Connie's Inn, but Victor still wasn't ready to offer an exclusive contract. Even without the contract Dad was quite happy to do his first session after nearly a year of orchestra pits and composing. But he also had some very serious celebrating to catch up on. After all, he had just met a deadline for the Immermans. Peer was very aware of what could happen to the recording date if the celebrations reached their potential, so when he hired a guitarist for the session he assigned him the added task of making sure Fats Waller was in Liederkranz Hall, behind a keyboard, March 1, 1929.

Eddie Condon hadn't met my father, but he knew that Connie's Inn would be a good place to look for him. And sure enough, there was Fats Waller, holding court. All Eddie had to do was come up with a convenient introduction. He walked over to the table and gave it a try.

"Earl Hines told me to look you up."

"Oh, Earl, that's fine. Sit down and let me get a little gin for you. We'll have to talk about Earl."

In Eddie's book, *We Called It Music*, he said that Dad was "so agreeable, so good natured, that I felt almost ashamed of my mission, but I performed it."

For the next three days Eddie tried to get Dad to talk about the session, hoping he could get him to plan it out. "After we got the band together, what'll we play?"

"Why, we'll play music," Dad replied.

The night before the session Eddie stuck to Dad like glue and when he began to drink gin heavily, Eddie joined in. The next morning they were both sleeping it off at Connie's Inn. Eddie woke up, checked the time and was horrified.

"It's half past ten. We're due at the studio at noon."

"That's fine! That's wonderful! That's perfect!" Dad answered, waking up with a smile. "Now, let's see about a band. Look around for

---

expressing his resentment and remarking that the film was both an affront to Dad and himself, as well as to all their race.

Mayer did not reply directly to Andy, but wrote in *Variety* that the songwriters "were poor sports," and should be "proud to have had their song featured so prominently in a big Hollywood musical." Andy's reply was short and to the point: "I wonder how they would've placated Irving Berlin if they had presented a scene showing 'Alexander's Ragtime Band' as being written by a colored boy behind bars."

some nickles so I can make the telephone go." After a few calls he had gathered three musicians for the session.

They hailed a taxi and Pop began to hum a melody, explaining to each musician what he was supposed to do. At exactly ten minutes to twelve they walked into the hall and Peer thanked Eddie for getting everyone there on time.

Eddie played banjo, and Dad's friend from *Keep Shufflin'*, Charlie Gains, was on trumpet. For lack of a better title, Victor named the group Fats Waller and His Buddies. Dad considered that afternoon to have been one of the finest impromptu sessions of his career. The group recorded "Harlem Fuss," "The Minor Drag," and two piano solos, "Numb Fumbling," and one of Dad's favorite pieces, "Handful of Keys." "Keys" became a most popular solo, performed by many of Dad's followers. Many jazz connoisseurs, myself included, feel that the best rendition of the classic was recorded that afternoon.

After it was all over, a Victor executive pulled Eddie aside to congratulate him for getting a fully rehearsed band to the studio on time. "An excellent example of the wisdom of planning and preparation."

Despite his hangover, Eddie smiled a thank you.

The Immermans were just as pleased with *Load of Coal* as Dad was with his Victor session. Captain Maines was soon called in to negotiate a contract for a new show. Connie Immerman wanted the downtown white trade to understand that the revue was an all black, very upbeat production, so he decided on the title *Hot Chocolates*. With a free hand on the music, the Waller-Razaf team turned out a fine score, and Leonard Harper, the director, was given enough money to hire a cast to match the music. As soon as he heard that Louis Armstrong's group had arrived in New York from Chicago, Harper contacted Satchmo and the band to do the show. (LeRoy Smith's band alternated with Louis' during the run of the revue.) Cab Calloway was hired, and subsequently skyrocketed to fame. *Hot Chocolates* also helped establish two other members of the cast. James Baskette later portrayed Uncle Remus in the Disney classic *Song of the South,* and Eddie Green came into prominence as a regular on the radio show "Duffy's Tavern."

Connie's Inn was packed for ten weeks, and the Immermans started discussing the possibility of taking *Hot Chocolates* downtown to one of the Broadway theatres. Captain Maines thought that the show would need another number or two to make it a critical success. The Immermans took his advice and asked Andy and Dad for a couple more songs. The two additional pieces were probably the finest they ever produced: "What Did I Do to Be So Black and Blue?" and "Ain't Misbehavin'."

Everyone seems to have his own "true version" of how "Ain't Misbehavin'" came into being. One story has it that my father would always put on an innocent smile and exclaim, "Ain't misbehavin'!" whenever he was caught in the middle of scheme or mischief. Andy supposedly got the idea for the song after hearing the phrase. Then there's Walter Winchell's version that Fats Waller wrote the song *and* lyric while serving time for failure to pay Edith's alimony. A variation on that erroneous theme is that Dad wrote the music in jail and then gave the lyric idea to Andy to write. There's also the story that one of those honky tonk ladies of the Daisy Chain gave Dad the idea while he was playing piano in that institution.

Actually, the true story is a bit more mundane. The two songwriters had a job to do for *Hot Chocolates'* transition to Broadway, so they went over to Andy's Harlem apartment to write some music. Dad sat at the piano waiting to become "pregnant with an idea," as he used to put it. Andy sat silently with a pad and pencil, methodically ticking ideas off. He came up with the first two lines and asked Dad his opinion. Pop thought for a moment and then tried to match music with lyric. Dad's melodic line triggered the key phrase ("ain't misbehavin')" in the lyric and Andy's lyric launched more music. In less than half an hour the two men fed each other ideas so successfully that the song was almost an effortless lark. When Pop finished the melody he got up and told Andy he had an important date downtown. But Andy had no intention of repeating the "Honeysuckle Rose" episode and wouldn't let his partner leave the apartment until he put the notes on paper.

Hot Chocolates was scheduled to open on June 20, 1929. A show that opened after Memorial Day had to be a blockbuster to survive in July and August in those days before air conditioning. The Immermans wanted the show to have every chance to succeed, so they augmented the Connie's Inn cast with the best black talent available. Because of the rhythmic score, the emphasis was to be placed on dancing. Extra tap routines were written for the Eight Bon Bon Buddies and Jazzlips Richardson. Baby Cox (a woman whose voice probably kept her career from maturing) led the female chorus line, the Hot Chocolate Drops.

Early in the rehearsals Harper realized that "Ain't Misbehavin'" was destined to be a big hit, so encored and reprised the piece as often as possible. Harper also determined that a song should be written for the talented Edith Wilson about the woes of being black. The result was, in my opinion, the best Waller–Razaf song ever written. The last line of each verse, a simple repetition of the song's title, is particularly haunting: "What did I do, to be so black and blue?"

The show opened at the Hudson Theatre on the evening of June 20, 1929. Dad and his close friends, Captain Maines and Nils T.

Garland among them, stayed up through the early morning hours, waiting for the city edition of the *New York Times* and the *World Telegram and Sun*. The party turned into a celebration, champagne for all, when the reviews were read. The enthusiastic praise in Harlem's *Amsterdam News* was more than enough encouragement to convince the Immermans that they should keep the show running simultaneously at Connie's and the Hudson Theatre.

The energetic cast worked every night at the Hudson from eight to ten-thirty and then would head up to Harlem to do the show at Connie's Inn after hours. The Immermans were packing them in uptown and downtown and when "Ain't Misbehavin'" became a hit, *Hot Chocolates* was the hottest ticket in town. Louis Armstrong, who sang the song in his raspy style, was partially responsible for the popularity of the show and did a bit extra to promote it uptown. Edith Wilson, Dad, and Satchmo did their own specialty, not included in the Broadway production, at Connie's Inn. "Thousand Pounds of Rhythm" was a special favorite with the late-night crowd.

Dad's name was frequently mentioned in the New York papers and Edith was reading how much money he was making as a musician. She successfully petitioned the family court for an increase in alimony and child-support payments. Edith was correct that Dad was earning quite a bit of money, but he was spending it at about the same rate he was receiving it. When he was informed that he would have to write out larger checks he panicked. Visions of Welfare Island probably pushed Fats Waller into making the worst financial decision of his career.

On July 7, 1929 Dad sold all his rights to *Hot Chocolates* to Irving Mills. For the incredibly low sum of five hundred dollars, Mills bought the package of "Ain't Misbehavin'," "Can't We Get Together?" "Say It with Your Feet," "Sweet Savannah Sue," "What Did I Do to Be So Black and Blue?" and fifteen other songs. Mills Music would collect royalties on the music for the twenty-eight years of the copyright.

Captain Maines had been constantly telling Dad that his earning potential was increasing daily, and Victor's decision to record the music from *Hot Chocolates* bore out Maines' predictions. But Dad had already made his offer and sold his rights to Mills. Had he listened to his agent, he would have had more than enough money to pay Edith.

The August 2 session for Victor kicked off a four-month round of thirteen recording dates. Dad frequently cut his own material, his piano or organ work helping establish the record as a hit. But now he was only entitled to the musician's share of royalties. The string of songs recorded in the last four months of 1929 made more money for Irving Mills than for Fats Waller.

On August 24 he was back in Camden playing the pipe organ and although several songs were recorded, only "That's All" was issued. Five days later he was off to a New Brunswick studio for Victor to record "Baby, Oh Where Can You Be?" (unissued) and "Waiting at the End of the Road" (issued several years later by Blue Bird, a Victor subsidiary). Immediately after Labor Day he was back at the Victor studios, recording "Going About" (originally unissued as a single) and "My Feelings Are Hurt." Okeh Records also wanted to cash in on the popularity of *Hot Chocolates* and its composer, so they formed a session for a group they called the Little Chocolate Dandies, including Dad, Don Redman, Benny Carter, and Coleman Hawkins. They recorded "That's How I Feel Today" and "Six or Seven Times." There were two more recordings on the Victor label in September. "Smashing Thirds" was recorded as a solo. "Looking Good but Feeling Bad" and "I Need Someone Like You" were done by Fats Waller and His Buddies. The buddies included Jack Teagarden, Gene Krupa, Otto Hardwick, and Charlie Gains.

It was a fantastic six weeks for Dad that opened doors to even more jobs, one of which was to become an annual event for him. Pop's friend, Jesse Crawford, was the regular organist at the Paramount Theatre. When he was unable to appear for several weeks, he recommended Dad as his replacement. It was financially rewarding, at seven hundred fifty dollars a week, and the people at Paramount were so impressed they asked Dad to return on a regular basis.

The Paramount job wasn't the only engagement Pop received as a result of his recordings. The Regal Theatre in Chicago contacted Captain Maines, wanting to book Dad for several weeks as a piano soloist. Contracts were signed, an advance paid, tickets bought, bags packed, and Dad kissed us goodbye. But he never made it to the Regal. Long before the train got to Chicago Dad decided that he missed his family—and Harlem. He was back in New York before nightfall.

Ronald and I were noisy babies and that was all the encouragement Dad needed to make Connie's Inn his second study. During the summer of 1929 he would spend most of his afternoons in Connie's revising material for *Hot Chocolates* and writing new songs. A lot of stories came out of Connie's Inn, and probably half of them were true. Mary Lou Williams often told me about her first visit to the club.

"I remember meeting your father one summer afternoon at Connie's Inn. Leonard Harper had brought me there to watch a rehearsal and there was Fats sitting at the piano and sipping some bourbon. It was a rehearsal for the girls of the chorus and Fats was telling them some funny, off-color stories. There was more laughing than dancing and Leonard was getting pretty angry.

" 'Hey, Fats, did you write any new songs, yet?' Leonard shouted. Your father sat at that piano and quick as a flash he dashed off five or six good songs. He was actually making up the music as he watched the girls dance. After the rehearsal Leonard bet Fats I could play all of those songs from memory and Fats took the bet. I played the songs and your father was astounded. He picked me up and gave me a big kiss."

Most people in Dad's circle knew that he could be found in Connie's, so it hardly came as a surprise that one day Loren Watson, a Victor executive, phoned him there. Could Fats get a couple musicians together to do a session tomorrow morning? There was "this man" who wanted to record with him. Dad said okay and picked up Zutty Singleton, a drummer from New Orleans, and Bubber Miley, one of Ellington's trumpeters, for the gig. When the musicians showed up at the studio the next morning, they almost turned right around and walked out. The man who wanted to play was already there—dressed in a kilt, with a bagpipe under his arms.

Dad looked at Watson. The executive reassured the trio that they were not the butt of some elaborate joke. "This gentleman wishes to make some jazz records with you. The records will be for his private use only. They will not be released."

Dad smiled. He didn't mind as long as they were paid for the session. Quickly they decided what would be played and then got right to it. Remarkably the bagpipes blended well with the trio and they were all pleased with the result. The takes never were released, but somewhere in Scotland a Highland piper has some fantastic recordings.

After the disastrous sale of the *Hot Chocolates* material to Mills, the Waller–Razaf team picked up Joe Davis as their new publisher. Andy and Dad gave him some good numbers to push across, including "Keep a Song in Your Soul," and "Blue Turning Grey over You," which has, in my opinion, Andy's best lyrics. Davis, a hard-nosed businessman, offered Dad a job, a contract for management, and asked for right of first refusal (a guarantee that he would be the first publisher to hear Dad's music). Davis also wanted Dad on hand to play piano for any songwriters or vocalists who visited the office. He agreed to pay Dad a weekly salary, royalties, and two bottles of booze a day. It was a new and very unpleasant experience for Fats Waller: from ten to five, writing songs in a small room. But Joe Davis worked closely with my father and several of his best piano solos were written or developed under Joe's supervision. He helped refashion "Charleston Stomp" and renamed it "Alligator Crawl." Davis was also the overseer on "African Ripples" and "Clothesline Ballet."

Joe was extremely pleased with his new client, and helped keep him in almost constant demand for recordings. On November 5 he joined Don Redman's group, McKinney's Cotton Pickers, which included Coleman Hawkins and featured Don both on the alto sax and vocals. The session lasted several days and resulted in "Plain Dirt," "Gee, Ain't I Good to You," "I'd Love It," "The Way I Feel Today," "Miss Hannah," "Peggy," and "Wherever There's a Will."

Gene Austin was recording Dad's "My Fate Is in Your Hands" for Victor, and he demanded that Fats Waller play piano for the November 25 session. Three days later it was back to Liederkranz Hall for another Victor recording. Dad and James P. were teamed up with the Jimmy Johnson Orchestra and King Oliver on trumpet. Eva Taylor and the Keep Shufflin' Trio handled the vocals. The records, "You Don't Understand," and "You've Got to Be Modernistic," offer a dazzling display of duo piano playing.

On December 4, Victor had Dad record two piano solos, "My Fate Is in Your Hands" and "Turn on the Heat." Later that month Victor got Fats Waller and His Buddies together again, but this afternoon was apparently more of a jam than a straight recording session. There was a crowd of buddies in the studio on December 18, 1929, including Jack Teagarden and J. C. Higginbotham on trombone and Otto Hardwick on trumpet. They cut "When I'm Alone," "Ridin' but Walkin'," "Won't You Get Off It Please," and "Lookin' for Another Sweetie."

In 1929 Jack Teagarden, Gene Krupa, and Eddie Condon were all happy to play with Fats Waller, as his buddies, and they constituted the first black-and-white band to do so. For musicians of such caliber to appear with a black artist was quite a blow to Jim Crow-ism. My father appreciated it, and I believe that he was just as proud to work with these men as he was for having composed Hot Chocolates.

Fats the recording artist as a Thirties car fancier. *Courtesy of Frank Driggs.*

Chapter 10

1930-1931

Fats Becomes a Recording Regular for RCA

Hot Chocolates has always been associated with "Ain't Misbehavin'," and that song has always been associated with Louis Armstrong. In fact, Satchmo credited a great deal of his success to that number: "From the first time I heard that song . . . it used to send me. I believe that great song, and the chance I got to play it, did a lot to make me better known all over the country."[1]

Satchmo's rendition of "Ain't Misbehavin'" was one of the highlights of *Hot Chocolates* and the Immermans were very disappointed when Louis told them he would not do the road tour after the show closed on Broadway early in 1930. George and Connie Immerman decided that Dad would be the best replacement. He discussed it with my mother and she agreed it would be wise for him to go since they needed the money. Dad packed his bags and his favorite Nick Carter novels and departed for Pittsburgh.

Usually Dad wrote home frequently when he was out of town, but after the show opened we didn't hear from him for quite some time. Mom decided to call the theatre, and became suspicious when a cast member told her Dad wasn't available. Mom knew her husband well enough to assume that if he wasn't available to answer the phone, he must have been making himself available to someone else. She took the first train to Pittsburgh and stayed there until she was certain there was no more misbehaving.

When Dad returned to New York he had to start scrambling for work again. He was able to come up with a Victor recording session.

---

[1] Armstrong made the comment in the program for the Fats Waller Memorial Concert of April 2, 1944.

The two piano duets, "St. Louis Blues" and "After You've Gone," were recorded March 21 with Bennie Paine, but Victor had originally intended something very different. Bennie recalled the story in a May 1952 *Jazz Journal* article:

> The record was made quite by chance. Someone at Victor had the idea of turning out a double sided piano record with one side played by a real old time jazz pianist and the reverse featuring swing piano. But the other guy didn't show up. I was hanging around so Fats grabbed me for the date, 'just a little rent money,' as he put it. But our styles of playing were so similar [that] they teamed us up on two pianos. It was a pity, in a way, that the other fellow didn't show up, as I think the Victor people had an interesting idea in that contrasting style stunt. The other player, by the way, was to have been a New Orleans pianist by the name of Jelly Roll Morton.

The piano duo was the only recording session that Dad could pick up, and by the end of the month he was beginning to worry about making rent and alimony payments. Things were a bit tense until word came from the Regal Theatre that they were willing to forgive and forget last year's no-show. They still believed that Fats Waller would be a big attraction, but the theatre management wanted some sort of promise that their attraction would actually make his curtain call this time. Anita Waller supplied the guarantee. She sent Ronald and me off to her mother's house, and got on the train with Dad for Chicago.

In 1930 Chicago was a battleground for gangsters shooting it out with each other to control the rackets. Even New York Mafia boss, Lucky Luciano, after a couple weeks in Chicago, remarked, "That city's a crazy place. People aren't safe on the streets." Mom had other reasons for disliking the Windy City. She always associated it with Dad being arrested and carted off for nonsupport. One evening she had an experience that forever cemented her attitude.

Dad was finishing his performance and was taking his bows when Mom decided to leave the theatre and wait for him outside. The stage door led to a dimly lit alley and, as soon as she was a short distance from the stage entrance, several thugs grabbed her. They began to force her toward a waiting car, mistaking her for a showgirl some mob boss had taken a liking to. The stage doorman heard Mom's screams and rushed to see what was going on. Sizing up the situation, he shouted to the kidnappers, "Hey... don't you know who that is?" The leader of the gunmen pointed his pistol at the doorman and told him to mind his own business, but the doorman shouted again, "That's Fats Waller's wife."

This time the gunmen stopped and stared at Mom's face. She was terrified, mumbling a prayer.

"She ain't the one," said the leader.

"Look, sister, if you wanna keep outta trouble, you'd better forget this ever happened," he threatened.

Mom watched as they got into their sedan and sped out of the alley. As soon as they were gone she ran to the stage door and embraced the doorman while she sobbed.

By the time Dad reached the exit, Mom had composed herself well enough to tell him what had happened. Remembering his own experience with Al Capone, he calmly told her, "Never mind honey, they'd never hurt you." Unconvinced, she clung to Dad until the end of the Regal engagement and their departure from Chicago.

Back in New York there were no recording sessions to be had. Deeply concerned, Pop went off to see his publisher. Joe Davis began discussing "marketability," and tried to explain that being a fine pianist wasn't necessarily sufficient to guarantee recording contracts. Joe reminded Pop of the days when he used to go around with Andy trying to sell their material to publishers. Why not sing the material on records? Pop protested that his voice wasn't good enough to warrant recording. Joe then suggested introducing some nightclub patter onto records and again Pop declined, arguing that most of his wisecracks bordered on the blue. Joe refused to give up and he told his client to think about it. But radio, rather than managerial advice turned Fats Waller into a singer.

Early in November the programming people at CBS were planning a show with the heads of Paramount. "Paramount on Parade" would feature good music and a commentary on the latest fashions—a strange, but, as it proved, very workable combination. The show was scheduled to air three times a week for fifteen minutes at the noon hour. The original intention was to run "Paramount on Parade" on a trial basis for thirteen weeks. Some executives remembered the organist who had filled in for Jesse Crawford and they asked Dad to play the show. He readily accepted and the series began on December 8, 1930. Unable to mug to a radio audience, Pop began to sing, and it proved to be the beginning of a new phase of his career. By the fourth week the show was so popular that it was expanded to a half hour and was renewed for another thirteen weeks.

Joe Davis now had the lever to push his client as a vocalist as well as pianist. He approached Victor for a recording date, but they weren't interested in a singing Fats Waller. Davis persuaded Frank Walker, the popular-music director of Columbia Records, to tune in "Paramount on Parade" to listen to the new Fats. Walker liked what he heard and looked around for a session. The next group scheduled to cut a Columbia disc was Ted Lewis' group. Walker sat Lewis down and convinced him that no one but Fats Waller should play and sing that date.

The Ted Lewis Band featured Ted and Benny Goodman on

clarinet, Bud Freeman on tenor sax, and Muggsy Spanier on trumpet. On March 5 and 6, 1931, the group cut "Egyptian Ella," a new Waller–Alex Hill song, "I'm Crazy about My Baby," "Dallas Blues," and "Royal Garden Blues" (with Dad doing vocals on all but the first cut). An annoyed Lewis was aware of the very strong possibility that the real star of the recording was Fats Waller. Never one to be upstaged, Lewis walked over to the microphone, and right in the middle of Dad's "Royal Garden Blues" piano solo, the bandleader shouted "Is everybody happy?"

If Lewis was unhappy with the new singing Fats Waller, Columbia certainly was not. A recording date was immediately set up for Dad to play and sing solo. On March 31, under the name Thomas "Fats" Waller, he cut "I'm Crazy about My Baby" and "Draggin' My Heart Around." When "Paramount on Parade" finally went off the air, Dad was signed to do "Radio Roundup." Joe Davis was satisfied that Fats Waller was marketable as a pianist and vocalist.

Otto Hardwick, who had played many dates with my father, had quit Duke Ellington's group and formed a band of his own. He asked Dad to play piano. Several jazz greats, at one time or another, played with the Hardwick group: Tiny Walters, Garvin Bushell, and Doctor Rhythm, with Albert Prime, Alberta Hunter, and Drusilla Drew doing the vocals. Hardwick got his group booked into the popular Hotfeet Club, owned by Paul Walsh. Located on West Houston Street, right in the center of the Village, the club was popular for its hot jazz groups. Many of the city's night crowd, including Mayor Jimmy Walker, came down for the still illegal booze, the jazz, the risque show and the funny pianist who told off-color stories. It was here that Dad first began to tell those stories that later became his trademark: the cocked eye brow, the finger punctuating the air for emphasis, and eyes rolling heavenward whenever he said something blue. He capped his little act with Andy Razaf's double entendre "My Handy Man," which was a hit for Ethel Waters. Dad frequently made twenty-five dollars a night in tips and it was an ideal situation until Walsh journeyed to Chicago, planning to open a Midwest version of his Hotfeet Club. The Chicago element tried to persuade him to buy his liquor, napkins, silverware, and everything else from them. A few days after he refused, Walsh was found dead. The Hotfeet Club was closed shortly after that.

During Pop's last days at the Hotfeet Club a rumor was spreading that a young accompanist for singer Adelaide Hall was the new king of the heap. When Pop knew the Hotfeet Club was closing, he made it a point to look up the young pianist, Art Tatum.

Art was born and raised in Toledo, and he picked up most of his early experience playing in and around northern Ohio and learning from James P.'s and Dad's piano rolls. Tatum developed his own style from stride, a giant step in the evolution of jazz and its techniques. He used new and unusual harmonies, augmented with unbelievable arpeggios and multitime patterns played by both hands. While on tour, Reuben Harris heard Tatum play in an Ohio nightspot and urged him to go to New York. Art did so and soon landed his first job as Adelaide Hall's accompanist. The people who heard his new style soon spread the word around that a new king of the keyboard had appeared on the scene.

Dad walked backstage at the Lafayette unannounced, and introduced himself to the eighteen-year-old Tatum. He arranged to show Art the town the next night and then sat backstage to listen to the new challenger. He only heard Art play background chords for Adelaide and was totally unimpressed with the newcomer. Confidently, he looked forward to the next night's meeting.

The next day Dad showed up at the backstage entrance with Willie The Lion, James P. Johnson, and Lippy Boyette. Before leaving the theatre, Art wanted to pick up Reuben Harris, with whom he was staying while in New York. Dad didn't mind—the more the merrier.

They roused Reuben out of bed and hit the town, stopping at a few speaks to quench their thirst. James P. and Dad were eager to do battle with Tatum at the piano, so they searched for a club with a suitable instrument, eventually choosing Morgan's, a small Harlem bar. One of the entourage sat down at the piano and began warming up in anticipation of the main event. The crowd at Morgan's must have felt the excitement in the air because the place took on the atmosphere of a rent-party competition.

Pop urged Art to take the stool and show off his stuff. Art played the main theme of Vincent Youmans' big hit, "Tea for Two," and introduced his inventive harmonies, slightly altering the melodic line. Good, but not very impressive. Then *it* happened. Tatum's left hand worked a strong, regular beat while his right hand played dazzling arpeggios in chords loaded with flatted fifths and ninths. Both his hands then raced toward each other in skips and runs that seemed impossible to master. Then they crossed each other. Tatum played the main theme again and soared to an exciting climax.

Reuben Harris looked around at the opened-mouthed faces of Harlem's Waller, Willie The Lion, and James P. Jimmy took the stool and played "Carolina Shout" as if his hands were possessed by a demon. But it wasn't good enough. Next Dad took over and played his own specialty, "A Handful of Keys." The crowd cheered when their hometown boy finished, but it appeared as if Tatum still had a slight lead. Tatum followed Dad and had the place jumping with "Tiger

Rag." James P. had one last trick up his sleeve, his brilliant version of Chopin's "Revolutionary Etude." Dad told me he never heard Jimmy play so remarkably, but the performance fell short. Tatum was the undisputed king. In comradeship, the four men threw their arms affectionately around each other and Tatum was duly toasted.

James P. remembered the occasion and commented, "When Tatum played "Tea for Two" that night I guess that was the first time I ever heard it really *played.*" Dad never forgot the event and always regarded Art Tatum with reverence. Years later Dad was playing at the Yacht Club, and one night Art stopped in to hear him. Pop stopped and introduced Tatum to the audience. "I just play the piano," he said, "but God is in the house tonight." Just before his death Dad granted an impromptu interview to the *New York Times,* and commented about Art and James P. Johnson. Remembering that night at Morgan's, Dad said:

> That Tatum, he was just too good and it looked like they were running him out of the city. He had too much technique. When that man turns on the powerhouse don't no one play him down. He sounds like a brass band.

Dad interrupted the interview to play "Tea for Two" and Murray Schumach of the *Times* commented:

> There was an unreal quality to the music, like something in an opium den. It was soft, liquid and lingering, the rhythm slow and subtle. Intricate runs fluttered around the melody. Fats was hunched slightly, cigarette almost touching his chin and the smoke drifting lazily past half-closed eyes. He seemed to have forgotten the handful of listeners.
>
> "That's music," he said after he had finished. "Subdued and not blatant. None of this boogie woogie stuff that's just monotonous. Boogie woogie is all right if you want to beat your brains out for five minutes. But for more than that you got to have melody. Jimmy Johnson taught me that. You got to hang onto the melody and never let it get boresome."

In 1931 Tatum's style, especially his harmonic progressions, was revolutionary. My father, James P., and Willie The Lion had led a revolution that changed the rhythms and patterns of piano playing, but Tatum was changing the way *music itself* was structured.

That summer, Spencer Williams had returned from Paris and was making the rounds of the Harlem haunts. Naturally he found Dad and soon they were writing a few songs together. Spencer kept talking about all the good times, great women, and jazz lovers that could be found in postwar Paris, a city where he claimed to have suffered no racial discrimination. Spencer longed to return to Paris and he suggested to Dad that a lot of money could be made in France for two smart black musicians. Fats Waller had to go to Paris to be part of the action. He began to fill Mom's head with tales of Paris and she accepted the inevitable, that he would want to go. When he believed the right moment had come, Dad finally took the leap.

"'Nita, honey," he started. She knew what was up because he always called her 'Nita when he wanted something. "I'm going to Europe with Spencer."

"For a little vacation?" she asked.

"No, to pick up a little of that French gold."

'Nita didn't argue. She figured that if her husband had been planning on this trip for the last couple months, sooner or later he was going to pop the question, and it would have been fruitless to say no.

Spencer and Dad now had to find a way to pay their passage. Naturally enough, they figured the most sensible approach would be to write a few songs and sell them. The two men locked themselves up in Spencer's place and set down to their task. Dad's different friends have different estimates as to how many tunes were knocked off in those two days; some claimed that they actually wrote over one hundred songs. They did write at least twenty-seven, because that's how many they were able to sell. Of that grand total, only one, "Down on the Delta," was ever published. As far as Dad and Spencer were concerned, they had achieved their goal: money for two tickets on the Ile de France.

When the luxury liner left the pier that August morning a lot of hungover friends straggled off the ramp. It didn't take long for Dad to get his sea legs and soon he discovered that all of the ship's bars had pianos. He was giving concerts every night, accepting drinks as tips. Spencer said, "We sure saved a lot of money that way. If we had to pay for everything Fats drank on the trip, we never would've made it to France."

Spencer wasted no time finding them an inexpensive hotel on the Right Bank's rue Pigalle. In the heart of the artists' quarter (along the Left Bank) there were dozens of small cafes and intimate bars. Their first night there, Spencer showed his friend around the town and it was very much to his liking. Here, at last, was a city where the drink poured unhindered by the laws of Prohibition. Blacks and whites mingled freely everywhere, even intermarried. Best of all, the French loved their jazz hot! Dad made the rounds night after night, stopping most frequently at L'Enfer, Boudon's Cafe, La Rumba, which was Dad's favorite, and, of course, Bricktop's, where Josephine Baker and Ada Smith had established a bit of Harlem in Paris.

In Paris Dad met the critic, Hugues Panassie, one of the first to make a scholarly study of jazz and to recognize its artistic value. Monsieur Panassie became a Waller enthusiast and devoted a tribute to Dad in his book, *The Real Jazz*. In 1946 Panassie described his encounter with my father at La Rumba in the *Yearbook of Jazz*. More than anyone else, I think, he captured the spirit of Fats Waller, the man and the musician:

> I found almost as much pleasure in watching him as in listening to him. His appearance when he played was a complete reflection of his style. The body leaned slightly backwards, a half smile on his lips which seemed to say, "I'm really enjoying myself; wait a bit, now listen to that, not bad, eh?" He rested his hands on the piano and hardly moved them at all, his fingers alone seeking out the necessary notes.
>
> He only raised his hands a very little from the keyboard. Thus the incredible power of his playing proceeds not so much from the rapidity of his attack as from its heaviness. Its force is not nervous at all, but muscular. Instead of bringing his impetus from a height to strike the keys brutally, rather Fats attacks them very closely, and seems to want to bury them in the piano. This is surely why his playing, in spite of its terrific force, appears so much more placid than that of other pianists.
>
> . . . He lived music constantly but thought on it never, and it was only by questioning him that one had the opportunity to hear him make some exceedingly intelligent observations.
>
> In reality, he loved life in all its aspects, he loved to laugh, he loved to drink . . . and couldn't he drink! I have never known a man able to imbibe so much at one time.
>
> . . . In everything he did can be recognized an indomitable vitality, an easy force sure of itself, a joy in living which really does you good. That is why all the jazz musicians liked so much to play with him, to feel behind him the solid rock-like support, voluminous, unchanging. As in addition to all this Fats was a grand creator, an admirable piano technician and had the greatest possible swing, it is no exaggeration to say that he was one of the four or five great personalities in jazz music.

By mid-September Dad realized the funds he and Spencer had raised would soon be depleted and, not knowing where or whom to sell songs to in Paris, he began worrying about collecting some trash. He and Spencer didn't have the forethought to buy return tickets to New York and if he didn't come up with an idea soon, he'd be stranded. Dad wired some of his cronies but no one had the funds necessary for the passage. Then he remembered Saul Bornstein of the Irving Berlin office, a man who had lent him money many times in the past. Bornstein cabled the money off to Paris and Dad bought his return ticket. None of this was mentioned to Spencer, who was quite unaware of his friend's intentions.

That evening the two sat in a cafe, eating dinner, and Spencer noticed that his companion was becoming increasingly interested in a mademoiselle. When the pianist and Frenchwoman left the cafe together Spencer just smiled. Fats Waller was up to his old tricks. But when the mademoiselle returned sans Fats, Spencer suspected something.

Spencer ran through the dark narrow streets to the hotel, but he arrived too late. Fats and his bags were gone. Lying on the bed was a train schedule for Le Havre.

Mom, Ronald, and I escorted Dad back from the pier to the apartment in Harlem. James P., The Lion, Eddie Condon, and dozens of other friends were waiting there with cases of booze. Stories of Parisian adventures—and drink—began to flow. Jimmy played a rag, and drink was poured. Eddie strummed his guitar, and more drink was poured. After five days at sea, and five nights in the ship's lounges, Fats Waller was at something of a disadvantage. He walked into the bedroom and collapsed, out cold. Mom, James P., and Buddy Allen tried to revive him.

"Fats, you got company. Wake up."

"C'mon man, it's your party. You're the host."

Dad rolled over and saw James P. kneeling over him. "I just quit the job. I make you the assistant host." He rolled over and conked out for the rest of the night.

With the trip to Paris concluded and the partying over and done with, Dad got into the regular routine of things . . . looking for work. Jack Teagarden offered him a Columbia recording date with one of the most fantastic bands ever assembled. Jack sang and played trombone, with Tommy Dorsey, Artie Shaw, Bud Freeman, and Pee Wee Russell as some of the other members of the combo. On October 13, 1931 and a subsequent November date, they cut "You Rascal You," "That's What I Like About You," and "Chances Are" (issued by Okeh).

Joe Davis gave Dad his old job back and he even found him a manager, a young man named Marty Bloom. Steady work and royalties kept Dad's spirits buoyed for the rest of the year.

As was customary, a big party was thrown at the end of the year. Honored as the Musician of the Year was Duke Ellington. Dad, James P., and Willie The Lion found a convenient basement speakeasy for the celebration. "It was one helluva party," The Lion related. "All those musicians were making a racket that could be heard all the way over to East Harlem. There was a whistle and somebody yelled 'The cops!' Naturally, I ran. I didn't want to spend time in the can. I found me this back door that led out into an alley filled with garbage and one scrawny tree. I didn't see no one else. I figured I was the only one who made it to safety. Nobody could've run faster than me outta that basement.

"I could hear the cops roundin' everybody up. It was still Prohibition, you know. The only thing to do was climb the tree and pray hard that nobody saw me. I made it up to the first branch and tried to cover myself with the leaves. All of a sudden I heard a voice coming from the branches over me. 'What's up, Lion? Cops after you?' Damn, I nearly fell outta the tree. It was Fats. Can't figure how he ever got outta that place before I did!"

Fats during an early network broadcast in 1932.

Chapter 11

1932-1933

Fats Goes to Work for WLW

Besides spending most of his free afternoons in Connie's Inn, working with Leonard Harper on stage shows, Dad was a regular performer there, both on piano and on a special piano-shaped Estey organ that the Immermans had installed especially for Fats Waller. And a great deal of Fats Waller's popularity (and income) came from Connie's—directly or indirectly. Prohibition had made the club one of the hottest spots in the city for good shows, hot jazz, and a place to drink without being hassled by the police.

But if the police were more relaxed about the Eighteenth Amendment by 1932, New York's gangsters were not. Organized crime had many factions, and each wanted to control the profitable sale of alcohol to the Harlem clubs. For several years Vincent "Mad Dog" Coll and Arthur "Dutch" Schultz had competed with each other to sell their beer to Connie's. At one time or another the Immermans had purchased their booze from either Coll's or Schultz' operation. Coll decided that the Immermans needed only one beer distributor, and he planned to persuade them that Schultz was not the correct choice.

One night, during a break in his performance, Don Redman was standing in the doorway, trying to catch a breeze of fresh air, when the thugs came in. Redman stood with his back to them and he never saw who asked, "Is Connie here?"

Without turning, Redman answered, "I don't know, but George is, if you want him."

Coll wanted any Immerman he could get his hands on and George would do well enough. They held him for three days before beginning negotiations for his ransom, probably weakening George's already frail heart. The payment was arranged, but when Coll brought George back to the Inn, the police were waiting. There was a shoot-out and Coll got away without a penny. Very shortly after the kidnapping, the

Immermans sold Connie's. There would be no more floor shows featuring Dad's music, and no more Estey upon which he could entertain New York's most influential music crowd.

The Inn had always been something of a second agent for Fats Waller. The club's demise coupled with the "exuberant" Waller character convinced Marty Bloom that he wasn't the man to manage this particular career. He decided to take the comparatively calm job of producing floor shows at the Sherman Hotel in Chicago (easier managing thirty leg-kicking starlets than managing one gin-drinking piano player). Luckily for Dad, Marty's friend, Phil Ponce, agreed to take on the job Marty was so eager to leave.

Captain Maines had been a sort of guiding light for Dad, but Maines had fallen too ill to offer his assistance any longer. Phil Ponce filled his place admirably. His experience in show business spanned many years, and he had even fathered a singing group, the Ponce Sisters. Phil was the kind of man who sat back and analyzed a situation, found a solution, and then put a plan into action. He saw that he had a client who was a good entertainer, who had written a Broadway show and hit records, had established himself on records for Victor, Columbia, and Okeh—yet who was still on a treadmill. He felt Pop needed recognition, a chance to develop his name on a national level. Dad's records were good, but not quite strong enough. Phil knew the answer was radio, and there was one station that was received in almost every city in the United States: WWL of Cincinnati. He arranged a one-shot appearance for Dad on the station and prayed they would give him a return engagement. The station expressed some interest, but not enough to inflate anyone's hopes for the future.

Mom knew Dad was feeling a little low because of the closing of Connie's and his uncertain career so she decided to throw a surprise birthday party to raise his spirits. That party on May 21, 1932 had a guest list that read like a *Who's Who of Jazz*. Naturally, James P. and Willie The Lion were there, but so were the Dorsey Brothers, Eddie Condon, Zutty Singleton, and Ralph Peer. Some others, like George Gershwin and Paul Whiteman, sent wires of congratulation. It wasn't too long before all the boys were jamming and having a high time in our small apartment. About five in the morning the music was interrupted by the loud rappings of someone at the door. Standing in the hallway was a big, tough-looking cop, who said that if they didn't break up the party he'd be forced to bring them all down to the station house. Pop smiled and extended an invitation. "Have a drink. Take your coat off. Enjoy yourself." The policeman was handed a drink and soon he was tapping his feet to the music. The party lasted for several more hours and I still wonder how that cop explained his alcohol-induced smile to the desk sergeant.

A few weeks after the party, Eddie Condon was approached by Banner Records, a Columbia subsidiary, to put together a group for a session. The Rhythmakers included Eddie, Dad, Pee Wee Russell, Pops Foster, Billy Banks, and Zutty Singleton. On July 26, 1932 they cut "I Would Do Anything for You" and "Yes Suh!" on the Banner label, and "Mean Old Bed Bug Blues" and "Yellow Dog Blues," which was released by Columbia. The second recording proved to be extremely popular with European jazz buffs, and it was subsequently released by Brunswick, Parlophone, and other companies in England, Ireland, France, Italy, Switzerland, Germany, Czechoslovakia, and Australia. As successful as these records were, they turned out to be Fats Waller's last 1932 sessions. Phil Ponce had made a connection.

Phil's tireless efforts had landed not one more appearance on WLW, but a two-year contract. The Wallers moved to a new home. I remember living in that little white house near the Cincinnati airport. I *knew* we were a long way from Harlem when I first saw those trolley cars equipped with cowcatchers. But Cincinnati, not Harlem, offered Dad the radio gig that would finally secure him the national prominence he had so long failed to achieve.

The *WLW* staff began to fashion a show around Pop and his piano. A black singing group called the Southern Suns, four brothers and their sister, was retained for the show and the all-white house band was renamed Fats Waller's Rhythm Club. The show opened with "Underneath a Harlem Moon" and then segued into Gershwin's "I Got Rhythm." A sinner, played by one of the Southern Suns, came on to confess to a deacon that he loved jazz, the devil's music. As the deacon sermonized on the evils of jazz Dad began to swing in the background. Soon the deacon was finger snapping and toe tapping with total abandon. The show always ended with Pop and the house band breaking up the place with a wild jam session.

Ever since Dad had started singing on "Paramount on Parade," he had grown constantly more comfortable with his singing. During the WLW stint he began to augment his vocals by satirizing the often inane lyrics of popular songs. Playing with the moon—June rhymes, inserting his own brand of comic deflation, and playing on the keyboard to develop what was originally a simple tune soon established Fats Waller's show as something of a good-time hour.

But one night, after receiving his quarterly ASCAP royalty statement,[1] he deviated significantly from good times. He never mentioned

---

[1] Most songwriters belong to either Broadcast Music Incorporated (BMI) or the American Society of Composers, Authors, and Publishers (ASCAP). These two societies function as monitoring, licensing, and royalty-collecting agencies for composers. They see that songs are cleared by radio and television stations and set minimum royalty payments for broadcast as well as jukebox play. "Listeners" are hired to

Mills Music specifically, but continually told his audience how music publishers were stealing the earnings of the poor artists who created the music. The insinuation was that *all* music publishers were dishonest. At the end of the program Paul Stewart, the announcer, said, "Now it's time to say goodbye to Fats Waller and his music, and even if it weren't time, it would be a good idea."

Another of Dad's chores at WLW was playing the organ for "Moon River," a popular program which was broadcast throughout the Midwest. At one in the morning he played a half hour of uninterrupted romantic organ music, carefully chosen by the station manager. Dad had a raucous and comedic reputation from "Fats Waller's Rhythm Club," and as the management of WLW didn't want him identified with "Moon River" he was never billed or given credit for that show.

In Dad's last recording session before coming out to Cincinnati, Una Mae Carlisle had done the vocals on "Mean Old Bed Bug Blues." Una Mae, an exceptionally gifted pianist, was in New York during her summer vacation from high school when she cut that record. I don't know why she was picked to sing if she was a pianist, but she must have left a lasting impression on my father, in one way or another, because he remembered her in December.

Una Mae lived with her family in Xenia, Ohio. Dad knew that she was still attending school, so he waited until Christmas vacation to invite her out to Cincinnati, to appear on his holiday-week shows. Her parents were reluctant to let her go, but eventually they gave in. She came to Cincinnati, accompanied by her older sister, and went straight to the station where Dad was rehearsing the show. One look at the trim and attractive Una Mae and rehearsals were nearly forgotten. Dad phoned home to say that he was going to be late that night, very late. He saw to it that Una Mae went on the air that evening and stayed himself to make sure she had proper accompaniment on the organ.

In short order Una Mae became Dad's shadow. Everywhere he was, she was close behind. Pop taught her to drink and to stay up late and party. Their relationship soon went far beyond the protégé—master level. Una Mae moved into a boarding house just across the street from where we were living, and when Christmas vacation ended, she refused to return to Xenia or school. Her mother came to town to fetch her but, after Una Mae carried on, vehemently, Mrs. Carlisle returned home without her. The only concession Una Mae would agree to was to move across town to live with friends. If Mrs. Carlisle was unhappy, my mother was no more pleased with the turn of events. And when Una Mae became a regular on the show, Mom started

monitor broadcasts and check that stations correctly report performances, hence, regulating royalty payments.

talking about how she'd prefer to go back to New York to place me in a Harlem school.

With or without Una Mae the program was a tremendous hit, and the Keith promoters approached WLW to arrange a summer tour. Phil Ponce agreed to the tour and negotiated Dad's contract. WLW had a very good radio show but it had to be fashioned into a vaudeville attraction, and that was not an easy task. Paul Stewart, who later went to Hollywood as a writer-producer, wrote blackouts and sketches as well as scripted the entire format of the show. It was booked onto the RKO circuit and scheduled to premiere at the Cincinnati Palace.

Spending the summer with my father and Una Mae was too much for Mom to stand. She announced that she was returning to Harlem, "to take care of Maurice's education." Mom, Ronald, and I got on the train for New York, and Dad remained in Cincinnati.

The show opened as scheduled. Dad was unsure of his reception, but once he cracked his first joke, started to mug and cut up through his opening number, the audience was all his. The crowd knew Fats Waller from his radio show and was ready and waiting for his off-the-cuff remarks. Dad's confidence grew and his mugging and funny lines came at a faster pace as the show traveled along.

That summer tour proved to Dad what Joe Davis had insisted the year before, that the singing and patter would help his act. And Phil Ponce was justified in his suggestion that the extra dimension would make Fats Waller a star.

The tour was doing very well but the relationship with Una Mae wasn't. The young woman was something of a firebrand, every bit as insistent as my father on having her own way. Their verbal battles grew increasingly more frequent and developed into ugly scenes, embarrassing cast members. By the time the show hit Indianapolis their screaming matches were reaching Herculean proportions, often ending in mutual threats of desertion. Una Mae decided to prove that her companion could get along without neither her personal nor musical presence; so she drank a small quantity of oil of wintergreen, and soon became violently ill. This effort failed to win any substantial increase of affection, and had it not been for someone else's quick departure, Dad might have let Una Mae leave, as she was constantly threatening to.

When the tour opened in Youngstown the road manager left town with all the cash the show had received from its previous bookings, plus the Youngstown advance. They were stranded without a dime or an opportunity to make money. Una Mae contacted a relative who lived in Youngstown, and was able to get everyone safely back to Cincinnati. Una Mae's action probably postponed the inevitable breakup with Dad.

WLW bailed everyone out financially by immediately rescheduling the radio show, and booking the tour in a country club in nearby Louisville. They had three weeks off, so Dad and Una Mae jointly purchased a car to make the short trip to Louisville. He promised to pick her up at six-thirty the next morning for the drive down to Kentucky, across the river. However, Dad had another plan. He intended to leave her behind, hoping her wounded pride would prevent her from joining the show in Louisville.

Una Mae should have known better than to expect Fats Waller that early in the morning for *anything,* but she was up, dressed, and ready to go. It wasn't unusual for Pop to be late for an appointment, but five hours *was* unusual, even for him. She hailed a cab and went over to Dad's house at the other end of town, and discovered that he was gone and the garage was empty. Una Mae bought a railroad ticket for Louisville, and upon arriving there she called the best hotel in town and learned, that, yes indeed, a Tom Waller was registered there. Furious, she headed for the hotel and on her way she spotted Dad, one of the Southern Suns and a pair of local beauties driving along in the car that she had purchased with Dad.

Una Mae stepped into the middle of the street, raised her arms, and stopped the car. She began to scream at my father at the top of her lungs. The beauties and their new friend took off. Reconciled to his fate, Dad shrugged. "I was coming for you honey . . . but it was getting late. I knew you'd make it here all right, so I took off."

His engagement at WLW lasted until the end of 1933 and when it wasn't renewed Dad immediately packed his bags and headed for Harlem, where he knew Una Mae wouldn't follow him. I don't remember any pots or pans flying through the air when Dad returned home, but Ronald and I knew enough to stay out of mischief for a few weeks.

Phil Ponce started planning once again, hoping to capitalize on the radio gig. He booked Dad into a Harlem club known as Pod and Jerry's, and continued to look for other work. Once again, help came from an unexpected source. This time it was from George Gershwin.

Mrs. Harrison Williams was giving a party for the great composer and hired Paul Whiteman to provide the music. Whiteman was an admirer of Fats Waller and knew of his friendship with Gershwin so he asked Pop and Willie The Lion to entertain that evening. It was quite an affair, with some of the biggest names on Broadway gathering to pay tribute to Gershwin. Dad played piano most of the night and was at the keyboard when William Paley, the president of the Columbia Broadcasting System, walked in with his young daughter. She was impressed with Dad's playing and antics and she dragged her father over to hear him play. Paley was also impressed and asked Gershwin who the funny man at the keyboard was. Good old George did a real selling job. Years later (on June 25, 1943) Dad told a *New York Times* interviewer about the meeting:

> Gershwin told Paley to get hold of me. So Paley comes over to me at the piano and says, "Drop over to the office and see me." Man, I'm stiff... but stiff, and I don't know what he's talking about. But the next day I realized what happened. Bull Am! [One of my father's favorite exclamations, along with "Wheemp!"] I didn't waste no time. And that's how I got my start in radio.

Dad showed up at WABC (a CBS station in 1934) and Paley told him he was planning a radio show with Dad as the star. Paley and Ponce were to work out the details and financial arrangements. According to Phil, as soon as Dad left the office, Paley picked up his phone to talk with the WABC program director.

"Where can we fit Fats Waller in?"

"We haven't room for him just now, Mr. Paley."

"Then make room," Paley ordered.

Paley was true to his word and Dad made a whirlwind series of appearances on WABC until a program of his own was established. In March, 1934, Pop was featured on the "Saturday Revue." In April he was a guest several times on Morton Downey's "House Party," as well as on the "Columbia Revue." Ponce knew this was the break Dad needed and began to hammer Victor for a regular recording contract. Dad wasn't aware of Ponce's negotiations with the record company and, probably out of habit, he still scrambled to make a dollar wherever he could. Two old friends, Willie The Lion and Adrian Rollini gave Pop an opportunity to pick up a little extra trash.

Rollini, a bass saxophonist, xylophonist, and author of "Goofus," had been the proprietor of a small popular club known as the Whitby Grill, located in the Whitby Hotel on West Forty-fifth Street, in the heart of the theatre district. The Whitby Grill became an unofficial hangout for every unemployed musician in New York because Rollini was always good for a handout. When his lease expired, the Whitby was pressured by a local Catholic girls' school not to renew the lease and Adrian began to search for a new home. He found a vacant basement in the President Hotel just one block down the street from his former club. Rollini dubbed it Adrian's Tap Room and hired Willie The Lion to play. Willie ran into Dad one day and invited him to come to the club's opening. It was a date Dad was certain to keep, wanting to wish his friend Rollini well—and take advantage of the partying and liquor.

Adrian opened the club early, and by half past nine the place was filled with all of New York's jazz world except Willie The Lion Smith. A little after eleven Dad strode in and grasped Adrian's hand. Rollini was depressed and explained why, pointing to the empty piano stool.

"The Lion's most likely cutting up at another gig. I'll play for you," Dad offered.

Willie never showed up and Dad played at Adrian's Tap Room for nearly six months for sixty dollars a week plus tips. His presence helped to make the club a success. Tommy Dorsey, Ella Logan, and Martha Raye all appeared at the Tap Room, contributing substantially to its fame. Ella Logan, who later starred on Broadway in "Finian's Rainbow," and Martha Raye, who later starred in everything, engaged nightly in a scat duel that delighted the customers. It was the kind of atmosphere my father thrived on, but he had to leave when his commitments to Columbia became too demanding. The station was unhappy over Dad's appearance at the Tap Room and they ordered Ponce to have Dad leave. Ponce knew that CBS could mean more to my father than playing a gig for some friends and he finally convinced Dad to leave before any difficulties developed.

Columbia had Dad working regularly, appearing on many programs, particularly the "Harlem Serenade." He was a name now, recognized all over the country, and Victor was ready to deal. Pop was offered a Victor recording contract which guaranteed him three percent on all records, plus a one hundred dollar advance for each selection, whether it was issued or not. Ponce and Dad carefully selected the sidemen for the Waller Band, settling on Herman Autrey on trumpet, Ben Whittet (later replaced by Eugene Sedric), Billy Taylor on bass, and Harry Dial on drums. They looked around for a good guitarist for the group and found him in DeWitt Clinton High School.

The Southern Suns learned about the new band and called Dad to tell him about their talented nephew in New York, Al Casey. Dad contacted him and was very impressed with the young man's ability. He asked Al to join the group on their first record and Al was ready to quit high school to pursue a musical career.

"Fats had a long talk with me and convinced me to remain in school. He made me see how important an education was. He promised I could play with the band on all their record dates in New York and that during the summer vacation I could tour with them. He did me a big favor . . . got me to stay in school and got me started in my career. It was fantastic. Here I was, a kid in high school, and I was playing guitar with a great group."

Victor arranged the first session for May 16, 1934. The group cut "I Wish I Were Twins," "Armful of Sweetness," "Do Me a Favor," and "A Porter's Love Song to a Chambermaid." The phrase "Fats Waller and His Rhythm" appeared on the first of many Victor labels. Victor was so pleased with the session and the potential of the cuts that they arranged another date for late summer (as I mentioned previously, New York used to shut down from June 1 to September 1).

Paley's program director was finally able to push someone out of a time slot, and in June, 1934, Dad got his own radio show. "The Rhythm Club" was aired on Monday and Thursday nights. Radio personality Fats Waller also did a program of organ music on Saturdays, appeared every other Sunday as a guest artist on Ukelele Ike's show, and was a regular on the "Columbia Variety Hour." It was a demanding schedule but my father had turned the corner and was well on his way to becoming the man he wanted to be. His records were selling very well and Victor pushed up his next session from September to August.

On August 17, 1934, Fats Waller and His Rhythm cut "Georgia May," "Have a Little Dream On Me," "Then I'll Be Tired of You," and a tune from the Fred Astaire—Ginger Rogers film, *The Gay Divorcee,* entitled "Don't Let It Bother You." That song begins with a bit of dialogue between Fats and his drummer, Harry Dial:

Fats: Boy, what's the matter with you?
Harry: Oh man, everything's wrong. The iceman done run off with
          my old lady.
Fats: What?
Harry: And my daughter ran off with the undertaker, and I'm about
          to die, and ain't nobody to bury me.
Fats: Son, don't let it bother you.

By the end of September, the group was back in Liederkranz Hall, recording "How Can You Face Me?" "Sweetie Pie," and one of Fats' best sellers, "You're Not the Only Oyster in the Stew." At the beginning of "Serenade for a Wealthy Widow," Fats comments, "Woman, they tell me you're flooded with currency." On "Mandy," originally from an Eddie Cantor film, Pop demonstrates both his ability to sing scat and some more of his omnipresent humor. As he begins a very fast-paced solo, he half giggles, "This tickling is so terrific. Oh, stop it baby." That September 28 session is all the more memorable because it marks the first appearance of Eugene Sedric, the great clarinettist and tenor saxophonist with the group.

Phil Ponce remembered the popular tour Dad had after his appearance on WLW and he tried to duplicate it in New York. He booked Dad to play a live show in Manhattan's Academy of Music on East Fourteenth Street. The Academy offered top line entertainment, and when Dad's band appeared, it shared billing with the Charlie Turner Band, featuring Hank Duncan on piano.

The people at Victor knew the sales value of a New York appearance, and they wanted to cash in on it. They set up two sessions in Liederkranz Hall to record and market as many songs as possible before the mid-November concert. On the first session the group cut "Honeysuckle Rose" from *Load of Coal,* "Breaking the Ice," "Believe It, Beloved," "If It Isn't Love," "Dream Man," and "I'm Growing Fonder of you." Pop so detested the lyrics from "If It Isn't Love" (from the RKO picture of the same name) that he decided to let the song self-destruct. He adopted a mock operatic voice and turned the tune into a brilliant exercise in comic deflation. To make sure that no air was left in the balloon, he added a pin-prick tag line to "If It Isn't Love," when he quipped, "It's mud to me."

Nine days later Dad was back to record four piano solos, all of which are now considered Waller classics. Each of those solos was written in the cramped room assigned to Dad when he was working for Joe Davis. The flip side of "Alligator Crawl" is backed by the incredibly rhythmic "African Ripples." Dad's humor breaks through on the musically inventive "Clothesline Ballet" and "Viper's Drag," that make up the two sides of the other disc. "Viper's Drag," an ode to marijuana smoking, is an example of how rhythmic patterns and melodic variations can conjure up scenes without the aid of accompanying lyrics.

The executives at Victor were amazed by the popularity of Fats Waller records, which, because of his bawdy sense of humor, froggy voice, and distinctive style, were leading all sales for the record company. Dad was on his way to becoming one of Victor's best-selling artists. The company had assumed his records would sell well in the black community, but the discs were bought by everyone. Victor's discussions with Phil Ponce convinced him that Dad was ready for a national tour. Phil began to plan it out.

A band on tour requires a monumental piece of planning, very much like that of an army on maneuvers. Arrangements have to be made for the material to be played. A format for the show must be developed. A road manager and advance men have to be hired and briefed. Then there is the almost impossible task of working out a schedule, arranging for transportation and accommodations, and praying that everything goes smoothly.

Phil was impressed with the Charlie Turner Band from the Academy of Music and they were retained to work as Dad's band on tour. That group was an impressive one, including Rudy Powell and Don Redman (who also did some of the arrangements) on alto, Gene Sedric and Bob Carroll on tenor, Herman Autrey as one of the trumpeters, Charlie Turner on bass, and Hank Duncan on piano. The group had to be rehearsed thoroughly and my father had a unique system to reward inventiveness in improvisation.

Pop kept two bottles of gin on a table during the rehearsals. One bottle was for himself or anyone who happened to be visiting. The other bottle was the "encourager," as he called it. When one of the band excelled in an improvisational section, Dad would stop the rehearsal, pour him a healthy shot of gin, and the two of them would toast each other. If you wanted to drink at rehearsal, you had to shine. It might have been an unorthodox method, but that band had some fine solo work.

By the end of 1934 everything was ready and the band was ready to go, but the Victor people wanted Dad for one more recording session before he left New York. On January 5, 1935, the band journeyed to Camden to cut "I'm a Hundred Per Cent for You" (with and without a vocal), "Baby Brown" (with and without a vocal) and "Because of Once upon a Time" backed by "You Fit into the Picture." The nonvocal sides were used for juke boxes. Dad played piano on these three selections and organ on "Night Wind" and "I Believe in Miracles." Once the session was completed Victor said goodbye and the band hit for the road.

The tour began with an appearance at the Meadowbrook Theatre across the Hudson River, in Pompton Lakes, New Jersey, and then moved on to Boston, Providence, and the Grand Theatre in Philadelphia. Dad and the other pianist, Hank Duncan, had a bit of funny business which brought the house down everywhere. It was a piano duel reminiscent of Dad's contests with James P. in *Keep Shufflin'*. Hank would burst into a rousing chorus of "I Got Rhythm" (Dad loved those Gershwin songs). From across the stage would flash a patented Waller look, eyebrows raised in feigned disbelief. Duncan then topped the first chorus with some dazzling musicianship. Dad would turn to the audience and comment, "Say, this guy can really play!" Then he would take over, besting Duncan, and the duel was on. The two of them would end the song with a fantastic duel that socked the audience.

The tour concluded with an appearance in Harlem at a new music mecca that was taking New York by storm. Earlier that year Frank Schiffman had purchased a rundown burlesque house known as Hurtig's and Seaman's, that had had a whites-only policy. After his experiences at the Lafayette and Lincoln Schiffman decided to turn the burlesque house into a black theatre, which he dubbed the Apollo. To guarantee the success of his new hall he booked the legendary Bessie Smith. The Apollo was a new phenomenon on the New York scene by the time Dad was booked and reunited with his old boss.

Just because the tour finished in Harlem, it didn't necessarily mean that Dad was going to spend much time at home. RKO had contacted Phil Ponce while Dad was on the road and had offered five hundred dollars for one day's work on *Hooray for Love*. The company was in the midst of a box-office battle with MGM, and making every effort to produce gala musicals as "spectacular" as the older company. Jule Styne, the composer, had been hired to oversee the production. The cast starred Anne Sothern and Gene Raymond. Bojangles Robinson, who was featured in the movie, suggested to Styne that Fats Waller might be available to sing a couple numbers. Styne and RKO saw the advantages of capitalizing on the successful tour, and Ponce saw the advantages for his client. So Dad and Mom got on the Twentieth Century Limited and set off for Hollywood. Ronald and I were getting very used to Grandma Shepherd's house.

There wasn't much time for family life after the return trip from the West Coast. Victor was glad to see their top recording artist, and immediately scheduled two sessions, each lasting a full day. Considering that forty-four songs were cut (and all subsequently released), they must have been *very* full days. The public's demand for Fats Waller records seemed insatiable, and Victor was going to waste no time in making every effort to take advantage of that appetite. On March 6, 1935, a few of the records the band cut were "Dust Off That Old Piana," "Cinders," "Louisiana Fairytales," and "I Ain't Got Nobody." On that last number Dad urges Rudy Powell to achieve a wild clarinet solo, shouting, "Make that thing sweat, boy! Make it sweat!" Rudy managed some of his best improvisational licks on that cut.

Five days later Dad and Rudy were at the Associated Program Service (later to become Muzak) studios. The two men cut thirty songs that day, some of which were "Dinah," "Zonky," "Handful of Keys," "Tea for Two," "Somebody Stole My Gal," "Ain't Misbehavin'," "Honeysuckle Rose," "California, Here I Come," and "You're the Top" (all issued on an LP). With this session completed, Dad was able to return to the road.

The merry-go-round began during the spring of 1935 and continually spun faster and faster. We now had a part-time father, a visitor we saw only when commitments and schedules allowed. The Fats Waller Band went on a tour of the Midwest and we were resigned to one more extended absence. Playing at the Forest Grove in Detroit, Pop set an attendance record that stood for nearly thirty years. The band played in the main ballroom and music was piped into two other halls. In all, nine thousand people danced to Fats Waller and His Rhythm. The tour stopped off at every major Midwestern city before heading South, where they were greeted by more crowds of record-breaking proportions. But the strain of the tour was something that no one had considered.

Dad's behavior was becoming somewhat erratic. The constant

travel was taking its toll on his stamina and he was definitely losing some of his enthusiasm. If something about a city or a hall disturbed him, he would take advantage of this annoyance and skip the date. Tour promoters do not consider this sort of conduct in their best interest, and Phil Ponce suffered countless days of frustration trying to reestablish his client's good reputation. When the band hit Atlanta a summons was waiting. At first Dad suspected it was for once again neglecting Edith, but the court order turned out to be from Durham, North Carolina, where the band had failed to show for a concert. Phil had had enough. He canceled the rest of the trip and pulled the band back to New York.

Phil booked Charlie Turner back into the Arcadia Ballroom and arranged more sessions for Dad. On May 8 the band recorded Billy Rose's "Lulu's back in Town" backed by "Sweet and Slow" and "You're the Cutest One" with "Hate to Talk about Myself" on the flip side. Another song was needed to back "You've Been Taking Lessons in Love." One of the Victor people suggested a song that had been published already but that no one had thought enough of to record. A piano copy was brought to the studio and a desperate Victor executive insisted Dad and the band do it. They had no arrangement for the song and Dad wanted to cut it another day, but it had been an extraordinary session so far and the Victor personnel wanted to take advantage of the momentum to record the tune then. Dad played it on the piano several times and began to assign parts to the musicians who had to learn them by rote. The band rehearsed the number until each member felt comfortable. "I'm Gonna Sit Right down and Write Myself a Letter" became the most popular number the band ever recorded, and the song became forever associated with Fats Waller.

The money earned from all those records and concerts enabled us to move from our small apartment to something quite grand on Morningside Avenue bordering on Columbia University and City College. Fats Waller now had enough money to provide himself with something he always wanted: a Hammond organ. We were nearly evicted the day they installed it because Dad spent the greater part of that night breaking it in, much to the chagrin of the neighbors. Once he had his family and new organ safely tucked in their new home, it was time to pack again.

On June 24, 1935, Pop and his band traveled down to Camden for a long session before hitting the road. Again the Victor people tried to squeeze in as many songs as possible. Some of the highlights that day included: "Dinah," "There'll Be Some Changes Made," and one of his funniest and best rendered songs, "Somebody Stole My Gal."

By now Waller fans were buying the records just to see what the funny man would add to the song. The records were beginning to take on the characteristics of live stage performances. On "Somebody Stole My Gal" there's a monologue never intended by the lyricist: "Sherlock Holmes, go find that woman. . . . She's gonna come back in *June?* . . . Well, go get her. . . . Oh, Sherlock, bring her right back." On recordings from that afternoon the record buyers really did get something more akin to a stage than a studio gig. On "Dinah" Dad calls out to his friend and trumpeter, Herman Autrey, "Move that thing, Herman." Fats introduces "Blue Because of You," just the way he would at the Apollo, with "Aw, don't make a fat man blue." And trying to ply more than just his piano playing, the fat man makes an offer to his imaginary female listener at the end of "Twelfth Street Rag": "Aw, look what you can get for nothing, baby."

The band boarded a train and set off for its tour, but six weeks later they were back in Victor's studios. Records were selling so fast that the company had pulled them off the road to do a day's recording. On the list of material that Victor handed the band was "I'm on a See Saw," a song detested by my father. He objected to doing the number, but the company's decision prevailed. Forced to do material he so disliked, Dad resorted to one of his WLW tricks, satirizing the lyrics as he sang them. Ironically, on this and other material that Victor coerced him to record, the comic interpretations made the discs best sellers. And when, due to the popularity of the songs, he had to perform the distasteful numbers on stage, Dad added the extra dimension of his mugging.

The band hit the road again and one of their first stops was the bustling resort, Atlantic City. Myra Johnson was also playing a date in the Jersey resort. Myra had previously worked with the Charlie Turner Band, but when Dad took over the group she felt there was no place for her, and joined the Lew Leslie Band for a European tour. "Fat Man" Turner, Dad's bass player, constantly sang her praises, and upon learning she was in Atlantic City Dad made sure he got to hear her. He was very impressed with her voice and dynamic stage presence. When Dad first asked her to join the band she refused, not wanting to compete as vocalist with the group's leader. But Dad was persistent, and when the band set off again on a fall tour Myra was with them.

Pop and Myra worked out several great duets together (which they later recorded). When it was time for her to make her appearance, Dad would bellow out, "Come on out here, you fine Arabian thing, you!" As soon as she was on stage he'd check out her figure, which was ample and well proportioned, and raise his eyebrows approvingly. Whenever they sang "Shortnin' Bread" he always made reference to her body by improvising his own lyrics:

> Oh, momma, momma, don't run so fas'
> You're gonna show your big fat ass.

His favorite duet was "Two Sleepy People," which he insisted on calling "Two Sloppy People." In it is probably the most notorious example of how Pop would kill a sugary line. Myra would sing the lyric:

> Do you remember the reason why
> we married in the fall?

to which he would reply:

> It was a shotgun wedding as I recall.

No matter how many times they pulled that routine, the audience was always devastated—especially when Myra threw her arms around a grinning Fats Waller, who very obviously was *not* looking for a hiding place. She was an important addition to the band and soon became a virtual member of our family. Ronald and I were in love with her. She wore an infectious smile and always carried some sort of treat in her bottomless pocketbook. That purse also served the band with many a button and aspirin.

Despite her ability with a needle and thread, no one treated her "like a woman." She was just one of the boys. To the guys in the band she was always known as Johnson. Once a member of the press was interviewing her and the conversation got around to her relationship with the group. Did she have a sweetheart? "The whole band's my sweetheart," she answered. That night they were all sitting around in a Pittsburgh-bound Pullman, swapping lies and passing the bottle. The boys were unusually quiet and polite and Myra suspected something was up. She began to feel drowsy, said goodnight, and slipped into her berth. A moment later the whole band threw back the curtain and shouted in unison, "So Johnson's the sweetheart of the band?" The ensuing brawl almost had them thrown off the train.

Myra, a prankster herself, plotted revenge. In those days a forerunner of the knock-knock joke was sweeping the country. It was based on altering song lyrics in response to a challenge, working something like: "Jimmy?" "Jimmy a little kiss, will ya, huh?" The band was playing Chicago at the State Theatre. Shortly before showtime everyone but Myra was sitting around backstage. The boys heard her moaning, "Oh, oh, oh!" in a faint voice. They rushed to her dressing room where she greeted them with the chorus, "Oh, you beautiful doll!"

The tour moved through the Midwest and into the South, playing both all-white and black theatres. And this time no shows were canceled. (This was partly due to the presence of Bobby Driver, Fats' "companion," hired by Phil Ponce). When they started their swing back home, RKO took advantage of the band's Philadelphia booking. For the price of a balcony ticket, audiences were able to see Fats Waller perform "I've Got My Fingers Crossed" and "Livin' in a Great Big Way" in *Hooray for Love.* And when the film ended, the band would come onstage and do the numbers live.

Twentieth Century—Fox had expressed some interest in Dad when he was working on *Hooray for Love,* but had offered nothing definite. When they saw the fantastic drawing appeal his Philadelphia appearances demonstrated, Phil Ponce started receiving phone calls. A lucrative offer was made and Fats Waller was signed for *The King of Burlesque.* He was to play the small role of an elevator operator and sing "Too Good to Be True," "Spreading Rhythm Around," and "I've Got My Fingers Crossed." Starring Warner Baxter, Alice Faye, and Jack Oakie, the film's plot was a spin-off of the down-and-out producer saved by the talented newcomer who puts on a show with his pals. In this case the elevator operator saves the day. The picture was something of an event for Pop, not because of what he did in front of the cameras, but because of something he did behind them, something he was always proud to talk about.

Dad had been embarrassed about not standing behind Andy when he protested over the treatment given the creation of "Honeysuckle Rose." The original script of *The King of Burlesque* called for Dad to play a Stepen Fetchit part. He objected vehemently to his part and the way blacks in general were treated by the film. After long and vehement arguments, the producer gave in. Instead of being the butt of all the jokes, the elevator operator would be able to make fun of the other characters, and do so in an ironic fashion. In one scene for instance, Jack Oakie is riding in the elevator and talking to himself: "If I hadn't have been such a dope our sign would now read 'Bolton and Cooney, Partners.' I guess I'm just a big ignorant sap." As Dad opens the elevator door, he says "Yes sir. Yes sir!" A black man getting the last laugh was something of a minor victory in 1935.

Back from Hollywood, Dad found two recording sessions already scheduled for him and the band. Three records were cut on November 29, 1935: "Sweet Thing" backed by "A Little Bit Independent;" "When Somebody Thinks You're Wonderful," with "You Stayed Away Too Long;" and "Spreading Rhythm Around" with "I've Got My Fingers Crossed" on the flip side. There was a December 4 session, but none of the records were released in the states.

Shortly after the December session Dad learned that Eddie Condon was seriously ill. Ever since Ralph Peer had hired Eddie to bring Dad to the studio the two musicians had been constant companions and the closest of friends. Dad was fearful for his friend's life when he learned that Eddie had been taken to Polyclinic Hospital, infamous for its high mortality rate. He was suffering from acute pancreatitis and it was necessary that he receive a blood transfusion. Somehow Eddie was given tainted plasma and his condition soon deteriorated. He knew that he was critically ill but he maintained his sense of humor and quipped, "This must be Fats Waller's blood. I'm getting high." Luckily, Eddie recovered to make more jokes.

Fats at about thirty-one, already well-known as a composer
and recording artist. *Courtesy of Frank Driggs.*

Chapter 12

1934-1936

Fats Makes It to the Top as a Composer and Recording Artist

By the end of 1935 my father certainly had everything he wanted—except a private life with his family. Dad spent almost the entire year on the road in 1936, playing extended engagements or doing one-night stands. After a while the buses and trains and living out of a suitcase began to bore him. To compensate for the discomforts of being on the road, Pop would buy all the comforts he could when he was at home.

The first comfort he purchased was a brand new Lincoln. In the early twenties, his friend Clarence Williams was doing extraordinarily well as a composer and publisher and had rewarded himself with a shiny new Lincoln. Dad was awestruck by that car and vowed he would buy himself one some day. The car made a lasting impression because once he had the money Dad only owned Lincolns and every time he'd buy a new one he'd tell me about the one Clarence Williams owned.

There were other ways he compensated for his early years of poverty. The Lion used to call him "Filthy Waller" and that always deeply troubled Dad. Just as he was determined to have a Lincoln, he was equally determined to have a flawless, expensive wardrobe. My father had his suits custom made. It was a matter of pride and necessity for him. He just couldn't walk into Robert Hall's and pull his size off the rack. He was an enormous man and stores didn't carry his size. Dad saw to it that our whole family was well dressed and that Ronnie and I always wore long pants. He used to tell us how he wore short knickers until he was given his first pair of long pants by James P. and his wife. He always remembered when one of the neighborhood girls had invited him to a party and he felt embarrassed because he didn't have a pair of long pants. He took a pair of Uncle Larry's trousers and cut them down to size. Properly dressed, he left for the party. To his shock, Uncle Larry walked in. My uncle spotted Dad wearing his mutilated pants and it was, according to my father, one of the most humiliating experiences of his life.

Dad spent money on us lavishly but neglected some other financial matters. He fell behind in his alimony payments (but not as seriously as before) and he owed Phil Ponce some money on commissions. The IRS felt they were due more money on his last year's return and Dad's reputation for walking out of engagements was beginning to catch up with him. To make matters worse, several large fines were levied against him by Local 802 of the musicians' union, and many concert promoters were suing him for backing out of appearances. So to clear up this financial disaster, most of 1936 was seen from concert halls.

One of his many stops during his tours was the Apollo Theatre, where he and Bessie Smith were always top box office attractions. In the early years Dad and Bessie helped keep that house solvent, playing five shows a day, starting at ten in the morning—an ungodly hour for my father. He needed a little bourbon now and then to help him through the day but Frank Schiffman strongly objected to his drinking on stage. "Mr. Schiffman," he told the owner one day, "if the booze is out then I'm out. And if I'm out, then you're out. But if the booze is in, then I'm in. And if I'm in. . ." The bottle and Fats remained onstage.

Many theatres in those days promoted a band with a live appearance on a local radio show. When Dad played the RKO Theatre in Boston, he was slated to appear on the "Fox Fur Trappers' Show," sponsored by the I.J. Fox Fur Company. The sponsors knew Dad's weakness and they gave one of their young employees, Irving Siders, ten dollars to buy some bourbon and pick Dad up for the show. Siders purchased the enticement and headed backstage.

Naturally, Dad enjoyed the inducement and offered to let his new friend see the show free. Siders was so pleased with his visit with my father that he convinced the owners of I.J. Fox to give Pop an expensive fur wrap as a gift for Mom. But when Dad showed up for the radio broadcast with the band he was so drunk from Siders' bourbon that he was unable to stand. He wobbled like a bowlfull of black Jell-O. Bobby Driver and Siders wrapped the house curtain around Dad's legs and "danced" him onstage to the nearby piano. The audience knew Fats Waller was a clown and thought his awkward movements were part of the act, but the Fox people knew better.

When Pop heard that Siders was fired because of the bourbon episode, he offered him the job of advance man. (Irving loved the job so much that eventually he became a band booker in New York.) He traveled with the group through New England and then onto Chicago where they spent Christmas. Al Casey, who was on winter vacation from school, joined the band as guitarist and it turned out to be a Christmas he would never forget.

Holidays on the road are always a little depressing, spent miles away from family and friends. On Christmas Eve Dad had a Wurlitzer organ delivered to his hotel suite. Pop then arranged for room service to stock the rooms with plenty of good food and liquor. After that night's show he invited the band to his suite for a little Christmas cheer, and the party was on. Dad played every Christmas carol he knew on the organ and the boys joined in. It wasn't long before the hotel guests, the working staff, and passersby were up in the suite celebrating. Always his own best promoter, Dad kept on playing "Swing Them Jingle Bells," which he had recorded the previous month.

When *The King of Burlesque* opened in New York, Victor dragged Dad back to the city for a few more sessions and some publicity appearances. Twentieth Century Fox held a press conference at the Hotel Warwick and Dad held court like visiting royalty (or the King of Swing, as Walter Winchell had dubbed him). He played several numbers from the picture and then his own version of "Tea for Two" and "Russian Fantasy." Some reporters asked him to define "swing" and Dad replied, "It's two thirds rhythm and one third soul." He put his hands over his heart and continued, "It's got to be here first and then come out here." His hands then moved to the piano and played a few riffs to demonstrate his point.

"Isn't it just another name for jazz?" a reporter asked.

"In some respects," Dad answered, "you might call it educated jazz."

Cornered by a *Metronome* writer, Pop gave him his theories on jazz and music in general:

> The big difference between the modern pianist and the one not so modern is to be found in the left mitt. Formerly the right hand was given all the work and the other left to shift for itself, thumping out a plain-octave or common-chord foundation. There was no attempt at figuration. But that is all past. Now it's more evenly divided and the left has to know its stuff, its chords and its figuration, just as well as the right. I consider the thorough bass foundation I got in the study of Bach the best part of my training [Godowsky had him play Bach inventions as part of his training]. Whenever you get stuck for a two-bar harmonic device, you can always go back to Liszt or Chopin. Even so, it's all in knowing what to put on the right beat.

Later in the same interview, he instructed how to play with the Waller touch:

First get a thorough bass. Make it more rhythmic than flashy, a pulsating bass. Know how to play first without pedals and then always use the pedals sparingly. Study harmony so you will know the chords. Play clean both in the right and left hand. This is one of the marks of the modern pianist, he plays much cleaner than the old school. There is also much more expression to modern playing and it is necessary to know how to build climaxes, how to raise up and let down, to show sudden contrasts. Keep the right hand always subservient to the melody. Trying to do too much always detracts from the tune.

This very uncustomary discourse on style was really something of a veiled attack on boogie woogie, a sound Fats Waller considered "cheap" and "unmusical" because of its repetitiousness and very limited harmonics. In fact, he disliked the new style so intensely that he insisted it be stipulated in all his concert contracts that he not be required to play it.

Even without recording any boogie woogie, Dad cut over fifty songs in 1936. Some of the more notable were "Christopher Columbus," "Cabin in the Sky," featuring Dad playing a haunting celeste solo, "Black Raspberry Jam," "S'posin'," and "There Goes My Attraction," on which Dad urges Herman Autrey on to a fantastic trumpet solo. In June of that year he recorded one of his classics, "Big Chief de Sota," and, at the same date, angered Andy Razaf by hamming up his sentimental lyrics to "It's a Sin to Tell a Lie."

One of Dad's most discussed recordings is the band's June 8, 1936, version of "Black Raspberry Jam." The six musicians demonstrate such an incredible understanding of harmonics that they sound like a fifteen-piece group. There are probably as many good riffs and improvisations on this side as on any Fats Waller recording. And once again the record takes on the feeling of a live performance as Fats announces: "Boys, we're assembled here to give a little jam this afternoon. I think you better get yourself in line because I got mine. Look out! Here it is. I'm throwin' it at you. Here it comes." And from there he soars into a wild stomping rendition of the number. At the end of the disc he can't resist saying, "Take your finger out of my jam."

Perhaps Dad's greatest coup of 1936 was winning over Walter Winchell, the nationally syndicated columnist. It is difficult to imagine today the awesome power that Winchell held in show business in the thirties and forties, but a word in his column could mean virtual life or death to a performer. Winchell took a shine to my father and often referred to him as his favorite songwriter.

126

Shortly after hailing in the new year, the band was struck with a tragedy. Arnold Bolden, the group's drummer, was stricken and died from a heart attack. The band, much like a family by now, was deeply shocked, canceled their road engagements, and mourned for several days. Arnold's sudden death and memories of Eddie Condon's horrific experience only a few months earlier stirred my father's own fears of death. He contacted Phil Ponce to have a lawyer draw up a will. But the band was on the road, and shows had to be played. The musicians pulled themselves out of their collective grief and finished the tour, returning to New York in March to play the Apollo.

Victor's recording director, Eli Oberstein, noted that besides Fats Waller, Tommy Dorsey, Bunny Berigan, George Wettling, and Dick McDonough were in New York. Oberstein decided that he should take advantage of this coincidence, and put together an authentic jam session—and put a Victor label on it. More than a few phone calls were necessary to get the group together. According to drummer George Wettling, Berigan and Dorsey were on less than speaking terms, their mutual animosity so intense that the other musicians had doubts about either of the two men showing for the date. But Oberstein was a diplomat in his own right, and convinced everyone involved that the session would be worth their while musically and financially.

When the men gathered on March 24, 1937,for their jam, they learned that the session was going to be much more impromptu than either they or Oberstein had first imagined. The recording director had expended so much time making the necessary phone calls from one musician to the other that he had neglected to choose any music for them to play. Only after the group was assembled was it decided that they would play "Honeysuckle Rose" and "Blues." That agreed upon, the "pickup" band set down to business. Despite the ill will between Dorsey and Berrigan, there are some amazing musical exchanges between them on *Jam Session at Victor*. Wettling said that the interplay between all the men was so good that nobody wanted to stop. But, "when it was all over, we all took off on our separate ways. Just like that."

Upon reflection, and with the benefit of hindsight, it is interesting to note that no one at Victor or any other studio ever again took advantage of the opportunity to gather such jazz greats together for another jam. In 1937 the big bands were shuffling in and out of New York every day, and a trip to the Jazz Mecca on West Fifty-second Street was often rewarded by the appearance of the Dorsey brothers, Louis Armstrong, Jack Teagarden, Glenn Miller, Benny Goodman, Art Tatum, and, of course, Fats Waller.

Phil Ponce was beginning to suffer from failing health, and felt that he could no longer handle all of his responsibilities. His search for a partner settled on an AR man at Victor, Wallace "Ed" Kirkeby. Fats Waller was a difficult client and it would take a very experienced individual to handle him. Phil thought that Kirkeby had the right credentials. He had spent over twenty years in the music business, had discovered and managed many groups. It was his Memphis Five that recorded "I Wish I Could Shimmy Like My Sister Kate," and his management skill in the early twenties that put together the Dorseys, Adrian Rollini, and Red Nichols to form one of the first successful white swing bands. In 1935 Kirkeby first mets Fats Waller in the Victor recording studios. The AR man noticed the band's "encourager," half full of gin, sitting on a table. Kirkeby's voice came through the intercom, "Is that your last drink?"

"No, it's my first bottle."

Ponce was satisfied with Kirkeby's experience in the business, and his familiarity with my father. Even if he wasn't successful in curbing Fats Waller's drinking, Ed Kirkeby was one of the few men willing to take him on. Gradually Phil handed over management of his client to his new partner. (Phil Ponce died in 1940 of emphysema, brought on by acute asthma).

About the time that Kirkeby came in as manager, two more changes were made in the band. "Slick" Jones was hired to replace Arnold Bolden on drums, and Buster Shepherd was hired to replace Bobby Driver. Buster was one of Mom's cousins, and long familiar with Dad's antics, but on the long road trip, immediately following his employment, Buster learned that the stories he had been told were anything but exaggerations.

Buster was soon exposed to all of Fats Waller's proclivities, the partying, the booze, and female companionship. But Buster was surprised to see those aspects of the bandleader that never got into the gossip columns, like the nightly reading of the Bible to the assembled band. Adeline and Edward had left a mark on their son Thomas.

Buster recalled an incident in rural Mississippi. The band was playing a tent dance, and a young man standing near the stage kept on shouting for Dad to do his hit "Big Chief de Sota." The band was working hard that night, receiving more requests than they could possibly do, and when it came time for the break they hadn't played "de Sota." Dad got off the piano stool and headed for a well-earned, and needed drink. But the young man was standing there, barring his way.

"I saved a cent a day for half a year to come to this show, and I ain't leaving till you play that song."

Dad looked at him for a moment and then turned around and played "Big Chief de Sota" before taking a rest.

That tour was exhausting, tiring even the most road-experienced musicians in the group. To make matters worse, on a stopover in New York, Kirkeby informed Dad that after the Boston concerts the group would immediately turn around and head back to the New York Victor studios. Not surprisingly, Dad had had no time to do any composing on the road. He contacted his two friends, Andy Razaf and J.C. Johnson, asking them to join him on the six-hour haul up to Boston for a work session. The result of that train ride is "The Joint Is Jumping," my favorite Fats Waller comic song. The three writers put together a tune ("Pay Your Quarter at the Door") to be sung by Myra and Dad, as sort of celebration of a wild rent party. The gimmick would be the background party noises and a running commentary by Fats Waller.

Andy and J.C. met Dad when the band showed up at the New York studios. The two lyricists brought along some male and female friends to supply the necessary party sounds. As the partying increases, so do the ad libs:

> "No baby . . . not now, I can't come over right now."
> "Don't you hit that chick. Dat's my broad."
> "Put this cat outta here before I knock him through his knees."

With a siren wailing off in the distance, Dad reassures the group, "If we go to jail I got the bail." The cops are at the door (or so the drummer's patrolman's whistle suggests) and Dad sticks in his last words; "Remember, don't nobody give his real name."

"The Joint Is Jumping" is only one of the nearly hundred singles recorded in 1937. The writing, recording, and uncountable miles of road and more road were taking their toll. Fats Waller was beginning to reestablish a bad name with promoters again. The drinking increased and there were repeat performances of the "Fur Trappers" fiasco. Dad was making nearly as much money as President Roosevelt but his behavior was preventing him from seeing the rewards of his earnings. Promoters were constantly complaining to Ed Kirkeby about Fats Waller either stumbling onto the stage in a near stupor, or not getting to the stage at all. His sense of responsibility was sadly lacking. One of his favorite stunts was to walk out of a hotel, hand Buster his bags and say, "Holland Tunnel." The car would head off to New York, leaving the hotel manager holding the unpaid bill.

Local promoters began to shy away from signing the Waller Band after a disastrous Southern tour. When the group hit South Carolina and northern Florida they were confronted by group of red-necks, who, for some unstated reason, had decided to boycott the band's performances. All the musicians were long familiar with racial prejudice, but they were unprepared to cope with it economically, even if they could handle it emotionally. Attendance fell sharply. In the few cities where the boycott proved ineffectual, the bigots employed another tack. After playing to a full house in Panama City, Florida, the band came out of the hall to find all the tires on their bus slashed. At another stop sand was poured into the bus crankcase.

Kirkeby finally had to cancel the tour when he learned that the individual in charge of bookings had been bleeding the backers for a large portion of the gate. Money was lost on the trip, and to make matters worse, when the group got to Philadelphia for the premature conclusion of the tour, a summons arrived from Durham (where a date had been skipped), and the box office was attached for nearly a thousand dollars.

Kirkeby knew that something had to be done immediately to make the act appear more attractive to promoters. As big bands were sweeping the nation, Kirkeby suggested taking on that sound. So Don Donaldson was hired as a second pianist and arranger. Kirkeby, Donaldson, and my father traveled around Harlem clubs, searching for more musicians. In Small's Paradise they heard a quintet, featuring Cedric Wallace on bass and Jimmy Haughton on trombone. My father was so impressed that he asked Kirkeby to hire the whole group. The Fats Waller Band was now substantially expanded. To check out the viability of the big-band sound, Kirkeby booked an engagement in Scranton, Pennsylvania. Exhausted, but satisfied with the gig, everyone piled into Old Methuselah, the company bus, and arrived back in New York, Sunday morning, December 12.

Sunday was a special day for jazz enthusiasts because WNEW's disk jockey Martin Block held a weekly jam session at the Criterion Theatre. Someone told Dad that Louis Armstrong, Cozy Cole, and Jack Teagarden were all at the Criterion doing the show. Dad grabbed Myra Johnson, Al Casey, and Zutty Singeleton and hustled over to the theatre to join the proceedings. It was the first time my father had seen Satchmo in nine years and it was a grand reunion as they all cut up with "Honeysuckle Rose," "Jeepers Creepers," "On the Sunny Side of the Street" and "In the Crack." Louis and Jack, in Louis' All Stars, would always improvise the lyrics to that last song, so it was only natural for Dad to get into the act.

After the show Pop was introduced to Martin Block, a man who greatly admired my father and his music. Martin became a friend of the family and frequently spent his Sunday afternoons in our diningroom, enjoying Mom's feasts, and in the livingroom, enjoying Dad's concerts.

The big band hit the road in 1938, but it was not a very happy tour for the group. Donaldson had spent many hours writing new arrangements to feature the different musicians, and the crowds were always ecstatic; but promoters were still reluctant to deal with Fats Waller. Perhaps the incident that most indelibly marked the tour was that suffered by Jimmy Haughton. Jimmy's trombone solo in Donaldson's arrangement of "In the Gloaming" had become one of the show's highlights. Buster Shepherd told me:

> One night we were all waiting backstage to go on when the stage manager hands Jimmy a telegram. His mother had died that afternoon. Jimmy was shocked. Fats asked if Jimmy was all right and he said he was. Jimmy wanted to go on, just to get his mind off his tragedy. The band came up to the "In the Gloaming" set and Jimmy stood up for his solo. Tears flowed freely down his cheeks and I've never heard anyone play with such emotion. Everybody in the band had to fight off tears. It was the saddest thing I ever saw.

The band returned to New York ready for a long rest. Kirkeby was desperately trying to hit on some tactic to revitalize promoters' faith and interest in Fats Waller. If the Waller reputation couldn't be changed, there might be some way to pick up enough publicity to overshadow fears of a no-show. Jazz was beginning to become very popular in Europe, and Americans who performed there were getting quite a bit of good press. Kirkeby arranged for a ten-week tour of Britain and Scandinavia. His client quickly agreed to the idea.

My mother was eager to go along with my father to Europe, remembering his glowing accounts of his previous visit to France. I was ten years old at the time and I longed to take the trip, too. I had heard Dad and his friends talk about Paris so much that I had all kinds of fantasies, but Mom and Dad wouldn't consider it. It would be summer with Grandma Shepherd for Ronnie and me. Before they left for the tour Dad wanted to see his sister. Naomi had recently married and was about to move to Florida. They hadn't seen each other for nearly ten years, so their brief meeting served as a reunion and, unknowingly, a farewell. They would never meet again.

Ed Kirkeby had elaborate preparations to make before the trip began. Wanting all the stateside publicity he could get, Kirkeby quickly arranged a recording session with Victor so they could have Fats Waller singles for the fall months. He set up a nationwide appearance on NBC, that was a combination concert and public relations event. All of America was told that night that Fats Waller was leaving to conquer Europe. It was a good ploy because every wire service carried a story about Dad and his impending trip. Biographies, press blurbs, and photos were sent to England and Scotland to ready the press for his first appearance. It was all very orchestrated indeed.

Dad had been whisked into the recording studios as soon as he returned from his road trip. Kirkeby hadn't allowed for a moment's rest, reasoning that the pre-European publicity was as important as the tour itself. So by the time my folks boarded the SS Transylvania in mid-July, the Atlantic crossing was regarded as something of a much needed rest. Of course, for Fats Waller a rest certainly did not preclude jamming every night with the ship's orchestra. When the boat reached Scottish shores at Greenock, the press corps boarded and began a round of interviews and heavy drinking. At the pier in Glasgow the Bill Mason Band struck up "Honeysuckle Rose" the moment Dad appeared on the gangplank.

Pop was absolutely overwhelmed by the reception the Scots were giving him. He couldn't believe that they not only knew his music, but could play it so well. My parents arrived on a Sunday morning, and as Dad's first performance was on Monday night they had time to travel to Loch Ness with Billy Mason. While they were standing there enjoying the scenery, Dad was touched and surprised that a passing bicyclist stopped to ask for an autograph.

My father had left New York a little unconfident about the trip, unsure of the European reaction to his music, and to him personally. He also was keenly aware of the difficulties Ed Kirkeby was having booking him in the United States and he knew this tour had to be "gloriously triumphant" if he was to recapture his American bookings. It was a huge responsibility and he wanted to give the tour his best. He and Kirkeby carefully planned the act to appeal to the packed house at the Empire Theatre in Glasgow.

An introduction was made to the enthusiastic audience and then out stepped Fats Waller, dressed in a traditional tartan kilt. This was a calculated gamble, as no one was sure how the Scots would react. Dad, with his hulking frame wrapped in plaid, looked outrageous— and the audience loved it. He sat at the piano doing his usual routine, looking down at his large bottom and the small piano stool. "Fatsy Watsy, are you all there?" he asked himself. The crowd roared. Then he played the first sixteen bars of the popular Scots tune, "Loch Lomond," and he had the crowd eating right out of his hand. In the next eight bars Dad began to lightly swing, not heavily, but with just a hint of the Waller touch. He then followed with his repertory of "Handful of Keys," "Honeysuckle Rose," "St. Louis Blues," "Ain't Misbehavin'," and "I'm Gonna Sit Right Down and Write Myself a Letter." The Glaswegians "accepted" the kilted pianist, demanding no less than ten curtain calls.

The reception in Glasgow did a lot to restore Dad's confidence and he was now looking forward to the rest of the tour. The next stop was Edinburgh, where Pop repeated his act with the same degree of success. The Glasgow and Edinburgh appearances were nothing short of triumphant, but London was next and Dad knew he had to be extraordinary there. He and Mom boarded the train for London and she reassured him, trying to keep his confidence buoyed.

Arriving in London the next morning on a typically rainy day, they were met at Victoria Station by Dad's good buddy, Spencer Williams (whom Dad had wired before leaving New York). Pop's first performance at the Palladium wasn't until the following night so they were able to spend a pleasant day with Spencer in his home at Sunbury-on-Thames. When they arrived, Spencer rolled up his sleeves and cooked a tremendous lunch of Southern-fried chicken. It was a comfortable afternoon with good food, good liquor, and good friends, and soon Dad was doodling at the piano. He caught the rhythm of the steady pitter patter of the rain and started to improvise. Ed Kirkeby and Spencer liked what he was doing and the three of them were soon at the piano working on the song. Kirkeby suggested the title, "A Cottage in the Rain" and the work was begun in earnest. It turned out to be a relaxing day and a profitable one, too.

The next morning Spencer helped Mom and Dad find an apartment. They were going to be spending time in England and Mom preferred a flat to a hotel suite. Once a suitable one was found, Dad, Spencer, and Kirkeby headed for rehearsal at the theatre. Pop was to share the bill at the Palladium with British stage stars Max Miller and Florence Desmond, and he was thrilled when he saw his name over theirs on the marquee. He stayed at the theatre all day, rehearsing and resting. That night, dressed in a dinner jacket, he grabbed the house curtain and hulaed out to the piano. London loved it. In fact, after the performance the audience demanded several encores and asked him to make a speech before leaving the stage.

The press notices were excellent and business was brisk. Dad settled in for a solid run in London; and Spencer acquainted him with the town's night life. My parents spent their after-concert hours visiting many of London's fine clubs, frequently going out on the town with Spencer and Adelaide Hall, the star of *Keep Shufflin'*. Their favorite nightspot was the Nest, where Edmundo Ros was the featured drummer. Dad and the boys jammed every night, giving Ed Kirkeby the idea for a Fats Waller commemorative album, celebrating his first trip to Europe.

Kirkeby began to discuss the possibility of such a record with the executives at His Master's Voice (a Victor affiliate), who said that they would be interested if enough jazz sidemen could be found. Kirkeby corraled all the capable musicians he could find, plus Ross' band.

Two sessions were set up, one with Dad and the band, "Fats Waller and His Continental Rhythm," and a session with Dad alone on the Hammond. Dad and the group cut a few current English favorites, "A Tisket, a Tasket," "Flat Foot Floogie," "Pent Up in a Penthouse," which was written by Spencer Williams, and "Don't Try Your Jive on Me," as well as Dad's "Ain't Misbehavin'." (Originally only released in the United Kingdom, the records were big sellers.)

The second session was memorable in many ways. Going back to his roots, Dad chose a program of spirituals particularly adaptable to the big Hammond organ. They included "All God's Chillun Got Wings," "Go Down, Moses," and "Deep River." He played like a man possessed, filling the hall with rich rolling chords, expanding rhythms, and a sense of deep inspiration. The last selection to be recorded was "Sometimes I Feel Like a Motherless Child" and Dad rose to the occasion with a fantastic, sensitive effort. But just before the end of the piece, he stopped and began to weep uncontrollably. Adelaide Hall, who had come to the session with my father, rushed to the organ to find out what the trouble was. The song had reminded him of his mother Adeline, whom he had been thinking about ever since he had seen Naomi. Later he told Mom that the music made him remember how much his mother liked that particular spiritual and how proud she would have been of him, in Europe, a star.

When Dad settled down the engineer wanted him to try another take but he refused. Instead, he suggested that he back up Adelaide in a pair of tunes, "for old times' sake." Once the HMV officials and Kirkeby realized that Dad would not continue with the spirituals they agreed to the duo. Adelaide recorded "That Old Feeling" and "I Can't Give You Anything but Love," a tune, incidentally, that my father always insisted he had written.

The remainder of the London stay was spent in a storm of activity. Pop was the guest artist on the popular BBC jazz show, "Melody out of the Sky" and then again on BBC with Adelaide on the "Broadcast to America" show. Pop was asked to sign autographs at the Gramophone shop to help promote his switch from the Palladium to a new site. During his last two weeks in London he played at the Holborn Empire and the Finsbury Park Empire. It was now time to move on to the continent and Dad was eager for new ground to conquer.

Mom and Pop took a small boat across the Channel to stop over in France before continuing the tour. Dad proudly escorted my mother to all the places that he and Spencer had haunted a few years before. One of his friends had heard about Dad's sensitive recordings of the spirituals and spread the word through the French jazz community. Consequently, my father was invited to play those same spirituals on the massive organ at Notre Dame before a limited audience. To this day, Dad is the only jazz musician to have ever played at that ancient cathedral, an honor that he cherished more than anything else in his life.

Their short stay in France ended and it was time to move onto Copenhagen. Dad was excited about appearing there until he learned that it was necessary for them to travel through Nazi Germany. Hitler was still smarting from the thrashing his supermen had received from Jesse Owens and he had been making all kinds of derogatory remarks about jazz. It wasn't the ideal place for a black jazz musician to be, and as Ed Kirkeby described the incident in his Fats Waller biography, *Ain't Misbehavin'*:

> . . . when he heard the journey would take him through Hitler territory, he wanted no part of that. "No man . . . ugh, that rascal Hitler don't like my kinda music," Fats said, and it was not until arrangements were made for him to lock his stateroom door and be undisturbed until he changed on to the Danish train in Hamburg, that he agreed to go at all.

During the trip they ran into a group of German soldiers at the station in Vlissingen, Holland. In Kirkeby's words:

> We made our way up the platform towards the restaurant to get some breakfast but had just turned the corner when we ran slap bang into some of Hitler's legions as they goose stepped through the station to be loaded aboard the troop train. Fats turned pale. "Man!" he said, "I may have to be gettin' outta here fast, and outta here is the best place I know of!" However, I grabbed his arm and we boarded the Copenhagen train without further incident.

They arrived safely in Copenhagen for a series of concert appearances with the popular Danish musician Sven Asmussen. For two weeks they crisscrossed Denmark, Norway, and Sweden, well received wherever they went. However, Hitler was rattling sabres in Holland, threatening to invade Norway and Denmark. Fearful that they would be caught right in the middle of an international crisis, Kirkeby canceled the balance of the tour. He wired Britain to arrange transportation back to the States and upon learning that the earliest ship leaving was the Ile de France, he booked passage.

There was enough time before their departure for Dad to give three more concerts in England and to appear on a BBC program called "Alexandra Palace." Fats Waller, to his own surprise, was appearing on a new media called television. He was fascinated to see himself live on the monitor and hoped to see commercial television arrive in America.

The Ile de France was bothered more by heavy seas than by

German U-boats on the return voyage. When not clinging to the rails, Pop spent most of his time in consultation with Kirkeby, the two of them planning how to handle the press in New York. The trip to Europe had been a great success, but its real effect was meant to put Fats Waller back in American concert halls.

Pop was ready to ham it up as soon as the cameras started clicking. Did the European crowds like his music as much as the Americans? "When Fats Waller sets down to a piano he just storms up a mess of jazz. He makes people dance, stomp, and cut up." But when a reporter asked him about the difference between American boogie and the music preferred in Europe, the hamming ceased: "For years I've been trying to sell the idea of softer stuff over here. I used to tell 'em down at Victor I ought to tone down, but they'd just say, 'No, go ahead and give 'em that hot primitive stuff.'"

Dad wasn't just attacking boogie woogie this time. Fats Waller was going through something of a transition. He was becoming more introspective, considering his achievements and potential as a composer. He constantly talked about his admiration for Gershwin's *Rhapsody in Blue* and *Concerto in F*. He was introducing more and more classical themes into his music. Fats Waller began to study the violin, something he would have never considered only a few years earlier.

Ed Kirkeby went to work, trying to capitalize on the success of the tour. Dad wanted to spend some time with his family so he asked his manager to find something close to home. Kirkeby found the perfect gig, a long-term engagement at the Yacht Club, one of the most coveted "rooms" of all the jazz clubs along West Fifty-second Street between Sixth and Seventh Avenues. It had flourished during Prohibition, featuring stars like Helen Morgan and Texas Guinan, who made popular the expression, "Hello sucker." Dad gathered the faithful— Autrey, Casey, and Sedric—plus a couple of newcomers, and began rehearsals. For the first time in nearly seven years, my father had something of a permanent base, allowing him to travel around the city, checking out the action and the new musicians on the scene. Part of his investigation took him every Sunday to another club just down the street, known as Jimmy Ryan's, the home of weekly jam sessions that every musician on the block was sure to attend. Dad never missed one of those Sundays while he was playing at the Yacht Club. Another of my father's regular stops along Fifty-second Street was the Onyx Club, where the house band featured a young pianist named Billy Kyle. Dad listened to him several times and was very impressed with his style and technique, especially the difficult modulations he would do from one key to another. Pop asked Billy where he learned that particular trick, and Billy sheepishly confessed, "Took it off a record of yours." He also admitted he used to buy Fats Waller piano rolls, teaching himself to finger the keys from playing them. Amused, Pop told Kyle how he used to buy James P.'s piano rolls for the same purpose.

There was one ugly incident that marred the engagement at the Yacht Club—so ugly, in fact, that nobody in the family would talk about it. (My sources are Buster Shepherd and Harry Beardslee.) Uncle Larry had come to the club to see Dad, and during a break between sets the two of them were outside the club enjoying a cigarette and some family gossip. Two white couples came out of the club and the women approached Dad for his autograph. Their dates didn't approve and began cursing the women and Dad with equal fervor. My father didn't want to create a scene so ignored their comments, but when the men began to slap the two women around, Uncle Larry intervened. One of the men drew a .22 pistol and fired at Uncle Larry, wounding him in the leg. Infuriated, Dad charged the man with the pistol and proceeded to beat him unconscious. Somebody from the Yacht Club whisked Dad inside before the police or an ambulance could arrive. The incident was kept out of the newspapers because the people involved wanted neither a court appearance nor the attendant publicity.

Dad finished out 1938 at the Yacht Club and Ed Kirkeby booked him into the Apollo Theatre. My father wanted to include the spirituals he recorded in London in his act at the Apollo but the theatre didn't have an organ. So Buster was duly sent off to the family's house, now in St. Alban's, to fetch the Hammond. "It wasn't that much of a trip from St. Albans to Harlem, but I ran into a lotta problems. It took me more time than I thought it would to load the thing into the car and I was late. I got on the road headin' for the Triborough Bridge when a cop pulled me over for a moving violation. That cop read me the riot act and I was already late. Fats and the band didn't know what happened to me. They kept calling Anita, but she told them I was long gone. When I finally got to the theatre it was ten minutes before the curtain. Fats was in a fit of rage until he saw me. That organ was set up in record time and the audience loved it and Fats."

A guest spot was set up for the Howard Theatre in Washington. Kirkeby's logic was that the Howard performance would serve as very good advance publicity for a Southern tour he was trying to set up for the Waller Band. But word came from London that promoters were eager to have Fats Waller back for a return engagement—at a very attractive price. The original European tour had been set up to reestablish Dad in the States, and now, ironically, it was "preventing" him from working there.

There followed the usual press releases, transportation arrangements, and, of course, the rushed recording sessions. Some of those cuts included "A Good Man Is Hard to Find," "'Tain't Whatcha Do," and "Undecided." He also recorded a single with Gene Austin, "Sweet Sue," and "I Can't Give You Anything but Love" (both of which were unissued).

This time Mom decided to remain home, making sure that Ronnie and I kept up our schoolwork. The March crossing was spent mostly in the ship's bars and at the piano, but Dad was continually thinking about his composing. One evening he told Kirkeby about his admiration for Gershwin, and how much he, Fats Waller, aspired to write some "serious" music. Kirkeby suggested offhandedly that Dad might write his musical impressions of the different sections of London. Both men thought the idea had some potential, but there seemed little sense in further discussing the project until they settled into the city.

Upon his arrival in London, Dad learned that he was booked into the Holborn Empire Theatre with the Mills Brothers and the British comic Ted Ray. Plans were made for the shows, and little time was further devoted to discussing "serious" music.

One of the Mills mentioned that there was to be a benefit concert for sick and destitute musicians at the Beaumont State Theatre. Ever a soft touch, especially when it came to musicians down on their luck, Dad immediately bought twenty-five tickets. He then got on the phone and arranged to have two dozen of his London-based friends meet him at the stage door before the concert. He would then pass out the tickets and they'd all go in together. The Jazz Jamboree of 1939 promised to be a good bit of entertainment.

On the afternoon of the concert he ran into Una Mae Carlisle, who was living and working in England. She told him that she had been feeling very poorly and they began to talk. . . . Meanwhile, Ed Kirkeby was waiting at the stage door with twenty-four of Fats' cronies, all clamoring to get into the concert. Without tickets it took quite a bit of fast talking, but Kirkeby successfully got the boys in. The next day Dad meekly explained he had been visiting a sick friend.

After one week in London the show moved on the road, playing one- and two-night stands in the English provinces. The tour was well promoted and Dad and the Mills Brothers were packing them in. On the road, be it in England or the States, Fats Waller was very much a night person. After concerts he enjoyed playing some of his best music in jams with friends, either in clubs, where he would just walk in, or perhaps in apartments or hotel rooms. So it was nothing unusual for him to be wandering the streets of Sheffield at six in the morning. Ideas were floating through his head and he wanted to work them out with someone. As Ed Kirkeby later told the story to the *New York Times:*

> . . . about six in the morning the phone rings and it's Tom. "Are you up, Ed?" he asks. "I am now," I tell him. "Can't you hear me eating my breakfast in bed?"

138

"Look, Ed," he says, "I was walking through the park just now and I heard the birds singing a song. How about me coming over and getting it down?" That's all there was to that.

Dad showed up at Kirkeby's room and played his melodic idea. Kirkeby worked on the lyric, and "Honey Hush" was born. After the session, the manager reminded Dad of his desire to write a meaningful score based on his impressions of London. Pop shrugged it off, promising that he would get to work on the project when he had more time.

What Kirkeby didn't know was that his client was very serious about that London impressionist piece. Kirkeby thought it was just one more idea kicked around and forgotten because nothing more was said about it. But Fats Waller couldn't get the idea off his mind. He spent many nights with Gordon's Gin and packs of cigarettes, working out his ideas about the various sections of London. Picadilly, Chelsea, Soho, Bond Street, Limehouse, and Whitechapel all suggested different melodies; all had their own rhythms. Notebooks were filled with musical phrases and a few words about this street or that entrance to the underground.

Early one morning, fatigued from the night's work, he played his ideas for Kirkeby. He explained to his manager that he envisioned a piano suite, accompanied only by drums accenting the rhythms. Kirkeby was enthusiastic and spent several hours listening, encouraging the musician's various bits of expansion. After their session, Dad set the music to manuscript. *London Suite* was his most ambitious work.

Wanting the material recorded as quickly as possible, Kirkeby wasted no time in setting up two days in the HMV London studios. The April recordings, with John Marks on drums, intended to be a test session, were cut on acetate. Kirkeby had hoped to extend the English tour to the Continent, but Hitler had just annexed Czechoslovakia; and with war imminent, a European trip seemed too risky. A second recording session was hastily arranged for June, just days before the Ile de France would leave for New York. *London Suite* was recorded again, this time accompanied by Max Lewin on percussion. Duplicates of the session were cut and the masters stored.[1] My father and Ed Kirkeby, satisfied with the recording, set off for the States.

---

[1] After the war Kirkeby and Victor decided to release *London Suite,* but they learned that during the London blitz the acetate masters had been destroyed. Kirkeby remembered the duplicates and requested that HMV and Gramophone search for them. In 1950 HMV discovered a copy of the duplicates in a publisher's office, and had the wax copies transferred to acetate. In 1951 the record was finally restored. (In the interim Ted Heath had expanded the piece to a full orchestral score, and recorded in that form with the Ted Heath Organization for London Records.)

On the set for the film *Stormy Weather*, 1943.
Courtesy of Michael Lipskin.

Chapter 13

1937-1943

Buster Shepherd Remembers the Good and the Bad Times

A good deal of my father's professional life was spent on the road, and the man who probably spent the most time on tour with Fats Waller was my cousin, Herman "Buster" Shepherd. Buster was Dad's chauffeur, bodyguard, and companion. He covered well over one hundred thousand miles of road with the Fats Waller Band, always at my father's side. I thought it would be appropriate for Buster to give his own story about life on the road with Fats Waller.

"I was seventeen years old when I went to work for Fats. I started because his other chauffeur, Bobby Driver, just didn't know how to handle Fats and he was too much for him. I made a hundred and fifty dollars a week, driving Fats' 1937 maroon Lincoln convertible. My real job was to be his companion . . . to stay up with him all night. Fats always stayed up all night, either writing music or partying or, when we were in New York, playing all night on Martin Block's show on WNEW.

"Fats was always a lot of fun to be with. He was the greatest human being I have ever known. He had a big heart. People all loved that guy wherever we went and he had a reputation of being the softest touch around. People he never met would come up and give him a hard-luck story and Fats was laying twenty dollars on them. Once in Virginia he found a bunch of poor families and took them out to buy groceries. He gave them money, too. In Detroit he did the same thing with a bunch of musicians who were down on their luck. It was the same all over. Fats was the man who was always ready to help you out."

Buster was hired during that period that Phil Ponce was turning over the management of the Fats Waller group to Ed Kirkeby. Buster knew both men and, when asked, compared the two: "They were different men." Phil Ponce was down to earth and accepted you for what you were. He never interferred with the band. He made a suggestion now and then, but that was it. Ed Kirkeby was the opposite kind of person—very proper, always telling people how to behave or how to do something. He always had things to tell Fats about his music or the band. He was a kind of snob. Kirkeby came with us on the road, arranging our sleeping quarters or meals. He'd stay around a while and then go.

". . . I drove Fats in the Lincoln, with the top down and the Hammond organ sticking out of the back seat. We never put a flag on it, like you're supposed to, and we were always getting tickets for a moving violation.

"We played in hotels, theatres, and clubs when we played big tours but when we played in little places it could be anywhere: cotton barns, cotton factories, tents, fields. We once cut a figure eight across the United States. One time, in Fayetteville, North Carolina we played in a peanut factory. It had no walls, only a roof, and it was the dead of winter. It was so cold that Don Donaldson, Fats' sub pianist, was playing with gloves on."

In some Southern cities the band couldn't find a black hotel, so improvised arrangements had to be made. "Usually, Kirkeby set us up in people's houses and Fats would stay with a local minister. We paid these people for the room and when they saw us in the morning they'd ask us if we wanted something to eat. We'd go out and buy groceries and use their stove and dishes, and the next thing you know they give us a bill. They charged us for meals just like a restaurant.

"One time, near Baltimore, the driveshaft broke on the bus and we had to get it fixed. Ed Kirkeby and Herman Autrey saw a restaurant down the road and they went there to try to get some food for the band. We had to go to the back door to get some eats and then they'd only serve us a few sandwiches. Kirkeby told them who we were and the manager was very apologetic. 'It's against policy,' the manager explained, 'but I could set you up in the kitchen.' It was like that in some places, especially in the South.

"On a series of one-nighters we played on Lake Manitowoc in Wisconsin. We were right off the water and it was *cooold!* You never saw it so cold. Fats must have had two-feet thick of covers on him. The whole band went to the bar and emptied every bottle in the place just to keep warm.

"My partner that night was Gene Sedric. We shared a cabin and a double bed. I got into bed and fell asleep without moving one way or another. Sedric came in later on. "Man, why didn't you warm up the bed?' Sedric asked. 'Who me? Not me.' I wasn't warming up no bed. I was staying right where I was. Where I was it was nice and warm. All night I could hear Fats hollering, 'Buster, I'm cold!' He's two cabins down the road and I can hear him calling me. I finally got up and brought him a bottle.

"Nobody could outdrink him. He could hold his whiskey better than any man I've ever known. Fats was told to stop drinking and for a while he drank nothing but soda pop or Pocahontas sauterne wine. When we got to Florida, Fats didn't have his usual glass up on top of the piano and nobody believed it was really him.

"We'd get up in the morning and call room service, and before the bellhop got there with breakfast, Fats would usually finish half a bottle of Scotch. He stopped drinking Scotch, though, after he had some Cutty Sark and it made him sick. He was down on all fours on the floor, groaning and holding his stomach. It almost killed him. After that he wouldn't look at a sailing ship. Just the memory made him sick. But he always had his bottle.

"Even on stage, Fats had his bottle. I'd have it in the wings ready for him. When he felt the urge he'd work it into the song . . . 'Buster, I need one . . .' and the boys in the band knew the cue. They'd vamp something insane and rhythmic. Fats would do a funny dance over to the wings where I was waiting for him. As soon as he got there, I'd pour him a good, stiff belt. He'd wiggle around a little more and down the booze. The audience never knew. He'd dance back to the piano and resume the act.

"Fats danced a lot on stage and it was the funniest sight you ever saw. He'd take his three hundred pounds and start to do the lindy. He was a big man but he was agile on his feet. He'd always finish up the routine by shaking his behind at the audience. It used to bring down the house.

"At that time there was a group known as the Big Apple. The leader of the group was a man named Big Tiny. He used to dance onstage with a girl named Little Wilbur. When Big Tiny was finished with Little Wilbur, Fats would come onto the stage and dance with Big Tiny. Fats was big, but Big Tiny was enormous. They were something to see. The two of them would Lindy and cut up until the audience just split its side laughing.

"He had a bit he'd do whenever he played the 'E Flat Blues.' Fats recited a little poem:

She was the daughter of a butterfly,
He was the son of a bee.

Then he'd get up and do his crazy dance.

"Fats' favorite place to play was the Panther Room at the Sherman Hotel in Chicago. They treated him royally. Fats would sit for hours with the owner of the club, talking music. When Fats Waller played the Panther Room, it never closed until dawn. They knew Fats was partial to Salisbury steak and the chef fixed it especially for him—once every three hours. One night Fats rented an organ and he was playing in his room—at three-thirty in the morning. The bellhop knocked on the door and I thought he was going to tell Fats to cut it out. Instead he had a list of requests that other guests wanted to hear. We played the Panther Room for six weeks every December. All the time I was on the road with Fats, I can't remember being home for Christmas.

"Fats was always playing music all night and having people up to his room. That was the only thing he and Anita ever fought about. Sometimes she'd come on the road with us, and sooner or later they'd get into a fight. Anita was a real live wire, with a very strong personality. Wherever we were, Fats would call up people to jam with him. He'd call Earl 'Fatha' Hines or Coleman Hawkins—whoever was in the same town with him. Anita didn't like that because she was afraid he wasn't getting enough rest. Eventually they'd get into a fight over it and she'd pack her bags. He'd yell at me, 'Buster, pack your bags. You're going, too!' Anita would always leave by herself. He'd see me following her with my bags and then he'd say, 'What are you doing? Go to your room. I'll tell you when to go.'

"There were always women around. Fats didn't have what you would call a steady. Girls always hung around the band and the guys usually picked out who they wanted. You made your own arrangements over a drink or dinner or something. It was that way with Fats, and the same with the other musicians. When he made his arrangements, I had to find some other place to spend the night.

". . . I got married in Baltimore where Fats was playing a gig in a theatre. After the theatre emptied out the boys in the band cleared the stage. I was married right there on the stage, with Fats as my best man. After the ceremony there was a reception on that same stage. Fats called some caterers and they brought in food and champagne. I never saw so much food and drinks in my life and Fats paid for the whole tab. Fats was like that—very generous with the people he loved."

When they weren't on the road, Buster would "travel" through New York with Dad. He reminisced about their frequent visits to the offices of George and Ira Gershwin in the Brill Building. "Fats and George Gershwin were great friends and they deeply respected one another. They'd sit for hours, playing tunes for each other and making suggestions to one another. Ira sat there as a kind of judge. When he heard something he liked, he'd just smile and tell them, 'I like that tune.'

"We'd go up to WNEW and wait for Martin Block or Fred Coots [who left radio to become a songwriter] to let us into the studio. Fats played all night long on the radio, and during the commercial breaks they'd tie on the feed bag. Martin Block, Fred Coots, and Fats had healthy appetites and along about three in the morning Fats would send me down to the Rialto Delicatessen for pastrami sandwiches.

"Fats had a reputation for being a big eater but no one could outdo Fred Coots. He'd love to be invited out to Fats' house. Fred and Martin Block would come out there on a Sunday to talk about jazz, listen to Fats play the organ, and sample some of Grandma Shepherd's good cooking. They loved the way that woman cooked.

"Grandma Shepherd didn't go to the supermarket and buy one or two chickens like you or I would. She bought a case. When Block and Coots were over to the house, she'd get out her skillet to whip us a mess of fried chicken, and as soon as they finished the first batch she'd be at work on another. Coots loved to eat. She'd set down a pan filled with forty baked biscuits and Coots would finish them off all by himself. Grandma Shepherd would bake pies for them too. One for Anita and the kids, one for the company, Block and Coots, and one for Fats; but he never ate his pie in one sitting. Fats would eat one piece an hour.

"He was always a very generous man and he loved to see his friends and family enjoy his hospitality.

For a long while his sister Edith lived with him and Anita. And my cousin, Carolyn, lived with them for a while too.

"If there was a church social and they were serving food, Fats would be there. One time down South, Fats heard this church was having an outdoor supper to raise some money. He came down with the band and livened up the proceedings. Afterward he bought an enormous baked ham, a jar of mustard, and a knife. He called over the band to eat a little. We feasted.

"Everybody in the band liked to eat. We called Charlie Turner, the bass player, 'Fat Man.' Gene Sedric's nickname was 'Honeybear' because he looked like one, big and fat. These men were always eating up a storm and holding little contests, with side bets, to see who could eat the most. I've seen them sit down and eat a dozen hot dogs apiece. Somehow their appetites always increased as they got further South.

"Another time down South the band was supposed to play a dance for a black church. This was in Mississippi in the middle of the summer and it was hotter 'n hell. We got to the place and found the dance was held in a clearing in the middle of the woods. The church built a raised platform for the band, but there was no piano. The man who arranged the whole thing didn't think it was necessary to have a piano because a band was playing. One of the members of the church had a piano and we got up a group of men to go and fetch it. They had to drive that thing down the highway and then drag it through the woods.

"Mississippi is mosquito country, and those devils were everywhere. Between the bugs and the heat, it was *oppressive*. They brought in a bunch of fans and placed them around the bandstand for Fats and the boys. They turned them on and sheets of music were flying all over the place like those paper airplanes kids make. That didn't bother Fats and the band. They didn't need charts to make music.

"On one of these tours, Kitty Murray was booked to play with us. She did her own act and the band accompanied her. Now Kitty was a big woman with a big behind and one night onstage Fats looks at her big tail and says, 'All that meat and no potatoes.' I heard Fats say that a thousand different times about a thousand different girls, but it was the first time Ed Kirkeby ever heard it. Kirkeby sat down with Fats and together they wrote a song called 'All that Meat and No Potatoes.' The song became a big hit and Kitty asked her manager to book her all the time with Fats and the band.

"I was with Fats when he wrote all of his stuff . . . 'Jitterbug Waltz,' 'Anita,' the song he and J.C. Johnson wrote about his wife . . . all his stuff. I saw a lot of his tunes ripped off by other people. I remember one particular incident because Fats took the offender to court. It was Frankie Carle who stole one of Fats' songs and then used it as his theme song. You're allowed to 'borrow' eight bars of a tune without getting into trouble, but this was a whole song note for note. As I said, Fats took him to court, but I don't know what the result was. I'll tell you this: Fats used to curse everytime he heard the name Frankie Carle.

"That never changed Fats' attitude about people. You know he never went to the track. He'd rather bet on people. If he felt you had something to offer, he'd take a chance on you. Look how he encouraged Al Casey to finish school and then used him in the band. He did that in a lot of other ways, always lending broke musicians money . . . trying to help the church out.

". . . I got my notice from the draft board early in 1942. Fats notified them that I was on the road and couldn't report for induction. We were doing one-night stands and we usually left town just as my new induction letter arrived. This went on for a year but when I got back to New York, the letter was waiting: 'Greetings from the President of the United States.'

"Fats called them and said he needed me on the road and it worked for a while. But when we hit Philadelphia there was no escape. Fats threw me a party that night and the band dedicated the performance to me. Fats told the audience how valuable I was and how much he was going to miss me. That night we partied with the girls from the chorus and everybody got drunk. Some of us were still drunk the next day when the show started. One of the girls fell off the stage right into the lap of the band. Fats just looked up and said, 'Man overboard.'

"I went in the service but I wanted to be with Fats. Joe Louis and Sugar Ray Robinson were giving an exhibition at the camp where I was stationed, and Fats sent them a message to give me: he was planning to throw me one hell of a party for my birthday, which was in January. [He died in December.]

"When Fats died it was Captain Maines who called me and said he had arranged emergency leave for me. I was picked up by an air-corps bomber and that plane waited fifteen days in New York to take me back. Fats Waller was the greatest man I ever knew. When I got out of the army, Bill Basie offered me a job working as his chauffeur. I didn't take it. Somehow it wouldn't be the same as working for Fats."

The Fats Waller band with the Deep River Boys in their final recording session at RCA, 1942. *Courtesy of Frank Driggs.*

Chapter 14

1940-1943

Fats at His Peak as a Recording Artist and Songwriter

The English tour had successfully reinvigorated promoters' interest in Fats Waller. Official Films, a Columbia subsidiary, asked Kirkeby to arrange for Dad to appear in four shorts, singing and playing his own material. More publicity was always welcomed by the manager; and soon Fats Waller was performing two of his classics, "Ain't Misbehavin'" and "Honeysuckle Rose," plus two comedy numbers, "The Joint Is Jumpin'" and "Your Feet's Too Big" in front of the cameras. (To the best of my knowledge, there are no surviving prints.)

While in New York to film the shorts, Dad was approached by Lee Wiley to back her up on the organ. Lee performed with the Max Kaminsky Orchestra on Liberty Records, and had to ask Victor for permission to use Dad on the recordings. Victor refused to release their artist from his exclusive contract. But Lee wanted Fats Waller to play the organ on "Someone to Watch over Me" and "How Long Has This Been Going On?" So Dad did what he often had to do in these circumstances (or more precisely, what he *chose* to do). He recorded the material under the name of Maurice Waller. According to Buster, who accompanied Dad to almost all his sessions, Maurice Waller did a lot of piano and organ work in those days. There may still be some jazz buffs who think they've got records with some incredible organ work by the then twelve-year-old Maurice Waller, but I'm afraid I can't take credit for those gigs.

In 1940 Victor was billing Fats Waller as their outstanding comic performer, and thus his recordings reflected the company's promotional emphasis. His biggest hits of the year were "You Run Your Mouth, I'll Run My Business," "I'll Never Smile Again," and "'Tain't Nobody's Bizness if I Do." Despite the stress on comedy, Dad was still very intent on continuing what he considered his "serious" composing. When he was home from the road he would incessantly talk about Gershwin's *Porgy and Bess* or *An American in Paris.*

On the road, Dad would never use the telephone, always prefering to write. And now he considered me old enough to discuss what was on his mind in our correspondence. Letters would arrive from all over the country, Chicago; Salt Lake City; Millsboro, Delaware; Detroit; and Milwaukee. He wrote how he wished to raise the level of American music, as he considered his friend George Gershwin had. And when Dad wrote about *Porgy and Bess* he lamented that a black man had yet to write such a moving work of art about the black experience. And I think that my father knew from my letters, that I wanted him to be a George Gershwin.

Buster and Dad arrived in New York at three in the morning. Dad raced up the stairs while Buster warmed up the organ.

"Leave the boy alone. Let him sleep," I could hear my mother say.

"No, no. He's gotta hear this. It's a killer-diller!" Dad grabbed my robe, hustled me out of bed, and brought me downstairs. He sat at the organ and played "Jitterbug Waltz" with great gusto. A tremendous smile of self-satisfaction wrapped around his happy face.

"What do you think of that, Maurice?" he asked. But there wasn't even a chance to reply before he answered himself. "Good as anything Gershwin's ever written." I thought so too, but I never had the chance to tell him.

All night I listened to him talk about his stay in Chicago and the short trip to Detroit that followed it. Dad was especially impressed with his gig in Motor City. Michigan had been hit with a blizzard and Dad couldn't believe that long lines of people were standing in a blinding snowstorm to get into a theatre to see him.

Ten days of family life and it was back on tour once again. The letters came in from new places, but they were different in tone. The strain of one nighters was getting to him and my impression was that he wanted badly to quit the road. There were many times when the band traveled six hundred miles from one city to another to play a short date. Dad was no longer irresponsible and he was disgusted with people who were, especially promoters. Several times promoters failed to pay guarantees or bookings were canceled at the eleventh hour. He began to complain about his health. The years of hard drinking were beginning to kill his appetite and he frequently caught colds.

Dad came to New York for one of his regular appearances at the Apollo Theatre, and while he was home, Mom urged him to see a doctor. At first he resisted but Buster told her how he frequently coughed so hard that he nearly choked. (Buster told me years later that my father would often cough violently in his sleep. "I'd pick him up around the shoulders and just hold him until his chest was less congested and he'd stop coughing. Fats never woke up. The spell would pass and he'd be all right.") Mom insisted, and he went for a physical. No one was surprised with the prognosis. Liquor and late hours were slowly killing him. For over a year Fats Waller stayed away from alcohol, drinking only soda. Of course, he was still Fats Waller, so, not surprisingly, he'd go through a case of pop a day. Later he switched to sauterne, rationalizing that it was only eleven percent alcohol as compared to eighty-six in Old Grand Dad. He had his favorite brand, Pocahontas, and he bought that by the case, too, so he'd have it wherever he went.

The next road trip began with a swing through the South and then moved West. Dad was booked for a two-week engagement at the Paramount Theatre in Los Angeles with Eddie "Rochester" Anderson, Jack Benny's very funny sidekick. They continued to swing across the land, returning East through the Midwest. In Milwaukee, where the band played at the Palm Garden, in the Blatz Hotel, Pop introduced a new gimmick to his act—he played the violin. Louis Chapman, a reporter for the *Milwaukee Post,* reported the incident this way:

> At the piano, the colored star plays jazz or classical music with equal dexterity. He makes the pipes at the organ "give out" with torrid rhythms or murmur gently with solemn toned spirituals. When tired of these instruments, "Fats" turns to his violin, of which he is also a master.

Chapman gave some interesting comments about life on the road with my father:

> Attendants at Milwaukee hotels where "Fats" has stayed testify to his equal lavishness on tips and appetite. Folding money tips to bell boys and maids are a common occurrence in the musical star's life, while legends have been circulated about his immense penchant for food. Double orders are frequent on the menu for "Fats."
> "Fats" wasn't feeling so well one day. When asked by the waiter for his order, "Fats" replied that he wasn't hungry so he would have "only a dozen pork chops."
> "Fats" has a peculiar aversion to answering telephone calls. The musician who has appeared before hundreds of thousands almost always refuses to answer the phone, regardless of the distance of the source of the calls. He has received numerous calls from New York and St. Louis and other cross-country points. "Let 'em go, I'll call later," is his usual reply.

Chapman might have been exaggerating about the dozen pork chops, but, as I previously mentioned, Dad really did have an aversion to the telephone. He preferred speaking face to face with someone, and regarded letters as more personal than phone conversations.

In one of his letters from Milwaukee he told of going to a concert with Ed Kirkeby. Across the street from the Blatz Hotel the great conductor-composer Dimitri Mitropoulos was appearing with the Minneapolis Symphony Orchestra. Dad was impressed that this brilliant man was able to play and conduct simultaneously. Dad started thinking again about *his* contribution to music. Why shouldn't jazz be taken as seriously as classical music? Why shouldn't an all-jazz concert be performed in Carnegie Hall?

Dad discussed the idea with his manager, and Kirkeby agreed that they should give it a try. Elaborate preparations were made all through November and December of 1941. Public appearances, press conferences, and guest shots on radio shows were made. Victor's efforts to use the forthcoming concert to sell Fats Waller records both increased their sales and served as further publicity. It had been a good year in the studios, and Victor pushed "Pantin' in the Panther Room," "All That Meat and No Potatoes," Pop's version of "Carolina Shout," and "Cash for Your Trash."

The concert was the only topic of conversation in the Waller house during December 1941. *My father* was going to appear in *Carnegie Hall,* and he was going to wear *black tails!* Let us say I was not unimpressed. I knew that I was going to attend the concert, but I worked on Dad for days to make sure I wouldn't have to sit in the audience. He agreed to let me stay in the wings if I kept away from rehearsals. Dad felt that it would be an added surprise, if I waited for the big night to see the band. The group had been expanded to sixteen pieces for the performance, and Dad was spending every minute he had with Don Donaldson and Don Redman going over charts.

The night of January 14, 1942 finally arrived. I stood behind the curtains of a sold-out Carnegie Hall and proudly watched Buster wheel out the Hammond onto center stage, fill all the cups with oil, and then warm it up. I was totally surprised at what followed. The band didn't strike up the hula. Dad didn't wrap the curtain around his rump and dance on stage. He came out from the wings, stepped into the spotlight, bowed, and sat at the piano. He played his first number. There were no raised eyebrows. There were no jokes or comments.

Fun-making was a part of Dad's personality and you couldn't separate him from it. He was a brilliant musician and revelry wasn't necessary for him to put a song over. This departure, however, from his usual style made him uncomfortable. He played very well, but he wasn't Fats Waller.

Despite his discomfort, the music went over fairly well with the audience. Dad was applauded enthusiastically before he went backstage for intermission. When he got behind the curtains, he found a horde of his old buddies waiting to wish him well and extend their congratulations. So many toasts were offered that by the time Dad came out for the second act he was quite drunk.

The second half of the concert was supposed to begin with a tribute to Gershwin that included "Summertime." But Dad was so far gone that every number he tried to perform thereafter somehow turned into "Summertime." The concert turned into a disaster, and Dad was attacked by every music critic in the city.

He was crushed when he read the reviews. Dad had envisioned the Carnegie Hall appearance as the crowning achievement of his career, believing that it would prove to the world that he was indeed a serious musician. He had an almost messianic conviction that if jazz was performed in Carnegie Hall it would have to be accepted as legitimate, respectable music. In his own eyes he had failed himself and all the jazzmen who would have benefited from a successful concert.

Perhaps this effort to prove jazz's "respectability" affected Dad's approach to the performance and put more pressure upon him than he was able to carry. He would never discuss why he chose to cut out all the humor from his performance; in fact, he refused to discuss that night at all. I can only surmise that his sense of "mission" that night plus his departure from his usual style were too much for his nerves, and that when he went backstage during intermission, he was so agitated that he was unable to judge how much he was drinking.

I have always believed that Ed Kirkeby persuaded my father to abandon his usual style and adopt the conservative approach he used that night. Kirkeby, a conservative man by nature, probably felt it best that Dad be restrained. It was an error in judgement. No matter what my father did, some of the critics would have condemned him for appearing at Carnegie Hall, but the jazz buffs would have applauded his usual routines.

For the first time in years, Dad was happy to get back on the road. The miles between him and New York separated him from some of the trauma he had suffered. He moved out to Chicago, where he played at the Down Beat Room instead of his favorite spot, the Panther Room at the Hotel Sherman. The operators of the Panther Room were naturally very angry that Dad should be playing at a new, competitive night spot, but Kirkeby had booked him at the Down Beat because he felt that the Hotel Sherman was taking advantage of Dad's willingness to play there any time they asked.

Just as he had done at Adrian's Tap Room, Pop helped establish

153

the new club as part of the Chicago jazz scene. One night during that four-week gig, Jack Robbins, of Robbins Music, one of the more successful publishers in New York, appeared in the club. Dad spotted Jack in the house, introduced him to the audience, and then told the story of Robbins' life; how he was a poor man who had fought and worked his way up, publishing the best in popular music. He interspersed his comments with songs that the Robbins organization had published. Jack Robbins was moved to tears. That night was something he talked about for many years afterwards.

The gig at the Down Beat was notable for another reason. The club had a regular singer, who impressed Dad very much. He worked over her arrangements and insisted on accompanying her. My father's coaching, coaxing, and interest did a great deal to help Dinah Washington's career.

From Chicago the tour moved to Minneapolis and a booking at a small club called the Happy Hour. Dad enjoyed working there because of its proximity to Fort Snelling. Entertaining soldiers was one of my father's joys in life. Every year Cedric Adams, a columnist for the *Minneapolis Star Journal,* organized a benefit concert to raise money for the production of special motion pictures for the boys in uniform. The Swing Parade Concert was a big event on the Minneapolis social calendar. Dad was asked by Adams if he'd be willing to make an appearance and he readily accepted because it was for the servicemen. He was then told that Dimitri Mitropoulos was to be the guest conductor. Adams suggested that Dad and Mitropoulos meet before the concert, and it was arranged for my father to spend an afternoon at the home of the famous conductor.

The two musicians played the piano for one another, each in his own style, and they swapped notes about their techniques. Dad talked about his disappointing concert at Carnegie Hall. Mitropoulos both consoled and encouraged him. Pop remarked how much this meeting reminded him of his bull sessions with Gershwin, and Mitropoulos was flattered to be compared to the New York composer.

Dad's next letter was filled with glowing tributes to Mitropoulos, the concert at the Niccolet Theatre, and how the maestro had conducted him and the chorus in "Anchors Aweigh" and "God Bless America." The meeting and the concert having restored his confidence, Dad wrote that he was eager to make another appearance at Carnegie Hall or try another stab at writing a serious piece of music.

The band left Milwaukee and started crisscrossing the country with a vengeance, one nighters dotting the map and draining everyone's energy. On the few opportunities Dad had to take a rest, he would pass up the chance, preferring to entertain the troops at a serviceman's canteen, play for a bond drive, or do a radio spot for the war effort.[1] Finally, after the usual Christmas gig in the Panther Room, the band was sent home for the short break they so badly needed. But Dad's break was shorter than the other musicians'. Before Ronnie and I even got used to having a father in the house, Dad was back on the train, off to Los Angeles with Kirkeby to film *Stormy Weather*.

In 1942 Irving Mills was working for Twentieth Century Fox as a producer. Years ago he had backed and promoted the Duke Ellington band, and from his experience in music publishing Mills was aware of the tremendous popularity of race records. He reasoned that an all-black musical, starring popular "colored artists" dancing and singing their own material, would sell a lot of box-office tickets, no matter how inane the plot. Hence, the birth of *Stormy Weather*. Bojangles Robinson, Lena Horne, and Fats Waller were hired to make the picture a profitable venture.

Mills wanted to use "Ain't Misbehavin'," and as he already owned the copyright he was free to do with the song as he pleased. But to use any new Fats Waller material he would have to negotiate with Kirkeby and his client. An advance was paid and Dad and Kirkeby wrote "Moppin' and Boppin'" for the film.

Stormy Weather proved to be something of a working holiday for Dad. He enjoyed working on a film with people he respected and spent a good deal of his time cutting up with Bill Robinson. Dad played the leader of a band in a honky tonk, and as the group consisted of Benny Carter, Gene Porter, Alton Moore, Slam Stewart, and Zutty Singleton, a good time was had by all.

Buster Shepherd remembers that by the last day of shooting Fats Waller was beginning to behave like a movie star. Dad and Bojangles, both dressed in white satin tails, were supposed to have their final climactic confrontation with the villain. Dad was as nervous as if he were up for an Academy Award. Afraid that he might soil the tux, he had Buster constantly powdering the jacket or pants. After a toweling, Dad would peer into the mirror and ask Buster to rearrange his hair.

When he finally got to the last scene, Fats Waller the movie star reverted to Fats Waller the ad libber. The script called for Dad to open a door and react with great surprise upon seeing that Bojangles had already disposed of the bad guy. But instead of feigning shock, Dad

---

[1] My father's habit was to search out the nearest military post, and appear there on his days off, without any pay or publicity. Three days after his death, the National Council of the Army and Navy Union (the country's oldest veterans' organization) met in Philadelphia and honored Fats Waller with a posthumous citation "for his efforts to entertain the fighting men of the country he loved so well."

turns to the camera and sagely intones, "One never knows, does one?"

Prior to the filming of *Stormy Weather,* Kirkeby had been contacted by the Broadway producer, Richard Kollmar. Upon their return to New York, Dad and Kirkeby began serious negotiations with the producer about Dad playing a major part in the musical *Early to Bed.* The show was scripted by George Marion Jr., but the music had yet to be written. Dad and his manager liked both the play and the role chosen for my father. When Kirkeby learned that Kollmar had yet to decide on a composer, the manager started pushing his client. Kollmar was familiar with Fats Waller's songs, but he was unaware of Dad's writing the score for *Hot Chocolates* or his efforts in *Keep Shufflin'.* Convinced of Dad's ability, Kollmar signed him as an actor and composer. Dad went home, with a sizable advance, and began to work on the score. He was delighted with more than the money, however. He was the first black man to write the music for Broadway on something other than an all-black musical.

Marion worked on the book and lyrics in California while Dad scored the show in New York. I remember packets of neatly typed pages of lyrics arriving and Pop setting to work on new material or changing already written numbers. It became necessary for George Marion to come to New York to polish material and help prepare for rehearsals. George arrived in New York in early spring but rehearsals were held up because of his usual Waller appearance at the Apollo Theatre. After the Apollo engagement we lost our father again. He wasn't on the road, but the only evidence (after breakfast) that he was still in the house was the occasional chords of his piano working out a new tune. It soon became apparent to all concerned that Dad was going to be unable to rehearse his performance in the show, and supervise the rewrites and orchestrations, so, reluctantly, Richard Kollmar released Dad from his performer's contract.

Early to Bed went into rehearsals in March, quickly shaped up, and was scheduled to premiere at the Shubert Theatre in Boston on May 24, 1943. There was an excitement in the Waller home from the day rehearsals began. My mother was determined to be in Boston on opening night. Dad instructed Kirkeby to get hotel accommodations for him and Mom, and Kirkeby booked them into one of Boston's finest. When the desk clerk saw my folks, he refused to honor the reservations, insisting they were never made. Indignant, Kirkeby demanded to see the manager but it was to no avail. Other arrangements were made.

Mom told me that our usually cool father was a nervous wreck on opening night. He continually fidgeted in his seat, his heart stopping after each number while he waited for the audience to applaud. During intermission he paced constantly and had to get some Old Grand Dad to brace himself for the second act. Dad made it through the rest of the show as well as he could but, despite the audience's laughs and applause, he wasn't relieved until he saw the next morning's favorable reviews. As the box office was doing brisk business, it was decided to take advantage of the audience reaction and extend the Boston run by two weeks to work out minor rewrites in the script or choreography. Two weeks was too long a wait for my nervous father. To settle down a bit he took a one-week engagement at the Cove Club in Philadelphia.

Dad returned from Philadelphia and started counting the hours until the June 17 opening at the Broadhurst Theatre. He was still a bit scarred from the Carnegie Hall experience, and regarded *Early to Bed* as his vindication. Unable to do anything more for the show, he waited in a state of limbo. I watched the great confidence he exuded after the Boston opening slowly ebb away. He tried to hide his uneasiness with outbursts of joviality and we all pretended to have a good time, but we all knew how anxious he was.

I tried to wait up for Mom and Dad the night the show opened but they went to a club to wait for the reviews and I fell asleep long before they came home. The next morning I got up early and ran to buy every newspaper I could. The reviews were excellent and the show promised to be a long runner. Dad returned to his usual relaxed self, even if annoyed that *Early to Bed* had been a better show when it began rehearsals. In his opinion, some of the deletions made in Boston had cut out the very heart of the show. But business was very good and there were long lines outside of the theatre, so it didn't matter much to anyone except my father. *Early to Bed* had a very good run, but it could have been even longer. The rather risqué story shocked people in 1943 and word of mouth had marked it as "only for the daring." In fact, Mom agreed with the general consensus that the show was "for adults only." Which is why I wound up waiting at home rather than at the Broadhurst on opening night.

Usually one or two commercial singles from a show have a tremendous impact on ticket sales. But none of the singles from *Early to Bed* were cut because the musician's union, Local 802, was involved in a dispute with the recording companies. In fact, very little of anything was recorded during the summer months of 1943 because of wartime restrictions. This, too, had an effect on the longevity of the show. It wasn't until the fall of 1943 that any of the songs were cut and they were done by Dad on V discs for the servicemen.

Toward the end of June Kirkeby discussed taking advantage of *Early to Bed's* publicity and the pending opening of *Stormy Weather* to launch another tour. Dad hadn't been on the road since Christmas of 1942 but he was still physically drained from his work of the last six months. Another tour was arranged, but Kirkeby made efforts to make it a less strenuous one. Dad was scheduled to play the Tic Toc Club in Boston and he was looking forward to it. A few days before the date the East was suddenly engulfed in a horrendous heat wave. Due to the war effort, air cooling and fans were strictly forbidden. The Tic Toc Club had poor ventilation and even in cool weather was a hot box at best. Dad became ill with fatigue and heat prostration and the engagement was canceled. He returned to New York and decided to wait out the summer on Lake Ontario in Canada at the home of Murray Anderson, the producer of "Anderson's Almanac." Mom had always promised that I could go on the road with Dad some day. But as I wasn't old enough to do so, Dad's enforced holiday was the first real vacation we ever spent together. It was a summer of partying, songwriting, speedboat trips on the lake, and long talks.

Our vacation was cut short when Pop had to return to New York in late August to plug *Early to Bed* on the popular radio show, "Lower Basin Street." He talked with the interviewer and played some of the songs from the show. The next morning ticket sales increased.

It cooled off considerably in late August, but even after the extended vacation he seemed tired and listless. Kirkeby booked Dad into Palumbo's in Philadelphia. In the middle of the two-week engagement he was slotted for a guest shot on the "Million Dollar Band Show" on NBC. So after the evening performance at Palumbo's it was off for a quick run to the New York radio studios, say good night, get back on the bus, and head back down to Philly. After the second week at Palumbo's there was a Boston engagement to make up the canceled date at the Tic Toc Club. Dad came down from Boston on a one-day stopover before leaving for the West Coast. He appeared haggard, very worn from the zigzagging between New York, Philadelphia, and Boston. That afternoon in October was to be the last time I saw my father alive.

Nils T. Garlund, Dad's old friend from the early days and the man who introduced him to radio, was operating the Zanzibar Room, a chic club in the Florentine Gardens. He wanted Pop to appear in the floor show there, and Dad was more than willing to accept. He liked Hollywood and the warm, balmy weather and it was a chance to help an old friend out. Ed Kirkeby booked him into the Beachcomber, a jazz club in Omaha, so they wouldn't have to make the long trip West in one shot.

The letters started to come in again from the road from my father but they were different. His handwriting seemed changed and his letters were succinct, something that Dad never was. He was trying to cheer himself up, but there was little on this trip to be cheerful about. His first letter told of how he was denied the use of the hotel diningroom where he was staying and, even more critical for him, how he was also denied room-service privileges because he was a black man. it hurt him to think this kind of thing could happen outside the South.

Pop played the Beachcomber and it must have been a tonic for him because by the second week in Omaha he went back to his old routine of entertaining servicemen wherever he could find them. He performed concerts for air cadets, wives of officers, and most important to him, the men stationed at Fort Crook. Two weeks of playing for the troops was to pay off in an unexpected dividend.

During the war, the entire railway system was under the control of the military, due to its need to move troops across the country in vast numbers, and on schedule. The only way to travel from Omaha to Los Angeles was on the Los Angeles Streamliner, but the Streamliner didn't stop in Omaha. Kirkeby mentioned something about this during one of the performances at Fort Crook and one of the officers vaguely replied that it wasn't the sort of problem one should worry about. A few days later my father received a phone call telling him that the army command in Omaha had arranged a special stop in the city for Fats Waller to board the train.

The train pulled into Los Angeles and Dad was soon at his hotel, the Clarke, meeting old friends and partying. He opened at the Zanzibar Room, doing his usual act and plugging *Early to Bed*. Dad was always popular in Hollywood and he packed the house every night. He was also in demand for a long list of radio shows and he eagerly made every appearance, the first of which, for Garland, was on "What's New." But Dad's constitution wasn't ready for any extracurricular activities and he soon began to weaken. As his health declined, he was, unknowingly, exposing himself every night to further physical punishment. The Zanzibar Room was cooled by an early form of air conditioning that blew air across refrigerator coils. Dad's piano had been placed under one of the ventilators. As he got into his act he would perspire freely, and the cold air did him in. At the end of the second week at the Zanzibar, he came down with a severe case of the flu that infected his lungs. He was ordered to the hospital but he wouldn't go. Instead, he stayed in his hotel room for ten days, recovering. The doctor examined him and said he was able to return to work but he should take it easy. No extra activities, no drinking, no being Fats Waller.

He immediately resumed his gig at the Zanzibar Room and his

radio appearances. First there was "Colored U.S.A.," followed by a performance on CBS with Bud Abbott, Lou Costello, and Dinah Shore. The next night he was joking with Charlie McCarthy and Edgar Bergen and clowning on the piano with their bandleader, Ray Noble, on NBC. He also appeared on NBC's "News from Home" and the "Hollywood Canteen." All of this was in the space of one week after recovering from his bout with the flu.

Pop finished his engagement at the Zanzibar and had a press party scheduled before leaving for New York and the Christmas holidays. The night before his scheduled departure was spent partying with his friend Benny Carter. (Dad had gone off the bottle for about two years, but sometime before he went off to film *Stormy Weather* he started drinking again—heavily.) Dad showed up for his press conference the morning after in an advanced state of fatigue, barely able to keep his eyes open. It didn't seem to matter because in a few hours they would be on a sleeper for New York and he'd get plenty of rest.

Back home I knew my father was on his way and I waited in expectation. I hadn't seen him for months and now he was coming home for Christmas to be with us. I was disappointed that I had come down with a case of the flu, and thought it was particularly bad timing that I had caught the very same thing that my father just recovered from.

Fats with his sons, Maurice and Ronald. *Courtesy of Michael Lipskin.*

Chapter 15

Maurice Remembers His Father

I mentioned earlier that my father and I shared a mutual bond in our love for music. I was a shy child and always held my father in awe. Afraid of his reaction, I was nine years old before I worked up the courage to ask for piano lessons. I can still remember his reply.

"What the hell took you so long, Maurice?"

He went out and found the best piano teacher available, Mrs. Tallarico, who I remember as a pleasant fat woman who came to the house twice a week to beat scales into my head. I once made the mistake of complaining to my father about my teacher's predilection. I received a three-hour dissertation on the importance of scales. And I now had a second teacher. A year later when Ronnie began to study baritone sax I had a third teacher.

When Dad went off on his European tour Mrs. Tallarico entered me into a children's competition in Town Hall. I couldn't wait to show Dad my silver medal and demonstrate my proficiency with Schubert and Mozart. When Dad returned home he was very pleased with my recital, and for my reward he took me to the Apollo Theatre, where he was playing for the week. I was sitting in the wings, watching him like I usually did, when he turned to the audience and said: "Hey, I want you to meet my son, Maurice. He's a real killer-diller."

Suddenly Buster was pushing me onstage and I was bowing to the audience. I was scared to death! Even if you can't see beyond all the lights you know there's an audience out there. You can feel them. The next thing I knew Dad got up from the piano, sat me down, and told me to play. I thought to myself, "Oh, my God, what the hell am I going to do now?" The only thing I knew by heart were selections from the "Magic Flute," so I began to play. I wasn't aware that the Apollo crowd preferred hot pianos to magic flutes. Dad didn't mind. He wanted me to perform in public. He beamed at me while I played, even though the audience was wondering what they were listening to. When I was finished I got an ovation, but it was out of respect for my father. He plugged me with that audience just as if I were Art Tatum or Al Casey, or any of the other people he gave a helping hand. It was a fantastic thrill for me to know I was playing solo piano in front of the best jazz band in the United States.

Dad kept impressing on me the importance of being a professional in both performance and attitude. But he didn't want me to make the devil's music. (When I refer to jazz as the "devil's music" I'm only half joking. Dad made a great effort to make sure Ronald and I attended church regularly, and he would always make every effort to help churches in financial need. But my father never went to church services himself. I believe he really did feel he had committed some kind of a sin, not so much by playing jazz on the church organ but in failing to use his abilities to perform religious or "serious" music, as his father would have desired.) It was the classics for me and hot jazz for Dad. His parents' teachings had rubbed off on him and he was now trying to influence me the way they would have. Of course I played popular songs—on the sneak. If Dad were home and upstairs asleep, I played as softly as I could, but eventually he'd wake up and I'd hear him shouting from the top of the stairs, "Maurice, don't play that stuff. Stick with Mozart and Beethoven."

Sometimes I'd inadvertently play a song he had sold to another composer and all hell would break loose. One afternoon I was playing, "I Can't Give You Anything but Love," and he heard me. Dad came storming down the stairs in a rage.

"Maurice, I don't want you to ever play that damn song. I don't want you to even whistle it. Do you understand?"

I didn't understand, but later on he explained how he had sold that tune or other tunes just for drinking money and it bothered him terribly that they had become hits.

Many times Dad accused Fletcher Henderson, Irving Berlin, or other writers of stealing his material. The most vivid memory I have of one of those incidents dates back to the time when we lived on Morningside Avenue. Dad was listening to the radio one Sunday afternoon. Suddenly he became infuriated and smashed his fist through the livingroom's beautiful glass French doors. The song was "On the Sunny Side of the Street," a hit record credited to Jimmy McHugh. Dad had sold the song for a few bucks when he was broke back in the twenties. McHugh also "wrote" "I Can't Give You Anything but Love, Baby."

Pop was a severe taskmaster for me. He saw to it that my fingers were perfectly arched, not sloppy like his. He made certain that I sat absolutely straight in my chair, tapping rhythm out for me with the regularity of a metronome. He introduced me to George Gershwin and told me to listen to what he had to say. After I heard *Rhapsody in Blue,* I became a musical snob and Dad's music just didn't measure up any more. At that time I was ashamed to tell him what I felt about his music. Eventually I learned he wrote music for his personality, and I learned that my approval was something he really valued. He never made me feel as if he were patronizing me when he asked my opinion. If I didn't like something, he wanted to know. There were many times he changed a melodic line or a rhythmic pattern because "little Maurice didn't like it." When he wrote "It Pays to Advertise" I had him change the bridge twice. And while he worked on "Supple Couple" I urged him to change the harmony. I believe I had one of those rare fathers who was genuinely influenced by the opinions of his children.

Reciprocally, Ronnie and I were always ecstatic when our father approved of something we had accomplished. My brother and I used to play around, writing tunes together. Around the time *Early to Bed* was opening, we came up with something by varying the basic chord structure of "Sweet and Lovely." Dad was so impressed with what we had done that he took the manuscript with him to one of the promotional press conferences for *Early to Bed.* Dad added the Waller touch and played the song for all the assembled reporters. When the tune was mentioned the following day in the *New York Times* I was walking on air.

Of course there were times that Ronnie and I didn't win Dad's approval. Ronnie, a precocious six-year-old, answered his teacher's "What does your father do?" with a one liner that raised the roof at home. Ronnie just smiled and replied: "Drinks gin." I don't know if my father ever considered himself an alcoholic, but I do know that by the time the doctor ordered him off booze, Dad knew he had a serious problem, and it certainly wasn't something that he boasted about. Often he would drink his whiskey out of a coffee cup onstage. If someone asked what he was drinking, he would answer, "Tea."

Eventually, like any youngster would tend to do, I began to sneak a shot of Old Grand Dad out of the liquor cabinet when Dad was out of the house. One afternoon he caught me nipping and I thought he was going to be madder than hell. Instead he sat me down and said, "Maurice, I didn't know you were interested in drinking." I didn't answer him because I didn't know what to say. He got up and went to the bar and poured me a good stiff drink in a cocktail glass.

"Come on, Maurice, we'll have one together." He put the glass in my hand and urged me to drink it down. "Next time you want a drink, take it right out and drink it down. I don't want you sneaking drinks and I don't want you drinking stuff on the streets. If you gotta have a drink, take it from here." He never lost his temper with me. He just made me drink all afternoon. The next morning I learned my lesson. I never knew that a person's head could hurt in so many places. I didn't touch another drop of liquor until I was eighteen years old.

Dad's generosity was a strange thing. Although he was almost consistently late in paying Edith her alimony and child support for his own son, Dad willingly helped support all my uncles and aunts. He was always setting up someone with a business stake. Uncles Bob and Larry thought that Dad was out of his head to give away his earnings, but they accepted his "loans" when they were stuck for cash. Our home in St. Albans was usually filled to capacity with members of Dad's or Mom's family. Aunt Edith lived with us for many years, until she died at forty from diabetes. She was Dad's favorite sister and was more of a second mother than an aunt to Ronnie and me. The Waller home was a halfway house for any cousin or friend of the family with a problem.

The only time I think I ever suffered from Dad's extended-family attitude was when Buster Shepherd's younger sister, Caroline, was staying with us. Caroline and I were both about eleven, and one day we were doing a bit of innocent sexual investigation, playing doctor. Mom walked into the middle of the examination. Caroline was sent home to her parents and I received one of my few spankings.

Ronnie and I were the recipients of much of Dad's lavish generosity. As a nine-year-old growing up on the edge of Harlem, I received twenty-five dollars as my weekly allowance. America was just climbing out of the Depression and most men were earning less than that as a weekly salary. There was no way I could spend that much money on myself every week, so I eventually wound up taking all my school pals to the neighborhood ice cream parlor, where we all feasted until our young stomachs bulged.

Dad never came home from a road trip without bringing Ronnie and me some fantastic present. My brother loved to build model airplanes and Pop always brought him one more marvelous than the previous one. Ronnie spent his childhood locked in his room with balsa wood, paint, and glue.

Ronnie and I rode our bikes in Morningside Park almost every day. One day a group of kids came up and began to talk to us. They asked if they could have a ride and, because we were so naive, we agreed. When we realized what was going down we chased after them. They gave the two of us a beating and ran off with our bikes. After this experience Dad thought we should have a dog to protect us, so Locai, a German Shepherd, came into our lives.

166

Locai was about four or five years old when we got her. She was extremely well trained and loved Ronnie and me just as if we were her own pups. You could come into the Waller home but Locai wouldn't let you leave unless someone in the family said it was all right. Of course this sort of devotion also presented its own problems. Whenever we went to the neighborhood store on an errand we had to carry a little note with us if Locai was along. The note instructed the storekeeper to place the change on the counter and not to touch us in any way. If the man failed to read the note, his offending hand would promptly be firmly held between Locai's jaws. It was a sad day for the whole family when Buster buried her in the backyard.

When I was about to graduate from grade school, Pop asked me what I wanted most in the world, and remembering a bronze horse he had bought me some time before, I said a pony. Dad was playing at the Apollo and didn't come with me to the ceremonies. He would have never been able to get up that early. My mother and I returned in the early afternoon to see a truck parked in front of our house.

"What's the truck doing there?" I asked my mother.

"Let's go take a look," she said, already walking with me toward it.

Grandma Shepherd came out of the house when she saw us and shouted, "Maurice, look what your daddy got you."

The driver opened the gate and inside was a beautiful black and white pinto. Dad had already arranged to board the horse at the Holliswood Riding Academy in Queens.

White Sox had formerly been a show horse and could manage eight different gaits. I didn't know how to ride and she was much too much horse for me, so I made a deal with the owners of the academy. They could rent White Sox out to anyone who could ride her if I could ride any horse in the stable. They agreed and I started with an easy horse, Blue Steel, until I learned to ride properly, and then stuck with White Sox. I often rode her eight hours a day in Cunningham or Alley Pond Park. There were four other kids who rode with me and we wanted to buy ourselves smart-looking stallions to start the first all-black polo team. I kept White Sox for four years before I sold her. My intention was to buy a younger horse, but I never got around to replacing her. Dad died and I lost my interest in riding.

When your father spends most of his time away from home you learn to relish those few holidays you get to spend with him. Whenever he had the chance, Dad would scoop us up into the Lincoln and drive out to Coney Island or Rockaway Park. As soon as we'd get out of the car he's say "Let's tie on the feedbag," and we'd head over to Nathan's. We'd consume enough hot dogs, hamburgers, French fries, and cokes to assure Nat Handworker of his day's profits. Dad enjoyed riding the roller coaster for hours, even after eating a dozen franks. He loved all of the rides at Coney Island and went on them all, including the carousel. It was an amusing sight to see all three hundred pounds of Fat Waller sitting on a carousel horse.

On Sundays he'd take Ronald and me on a tour of all the clubs on West Fifty-second Street where he'd usually jam with friends of his. We'd stop at Jimmy Ryan's and he'd play for hours just accepting drinks for pay. Sometimes I think he perfected his left hand just so he could keep a glass in his right. Wherever we went, Dad would play with the least bit of encouragement, especially if he knew the boys in the band.

Dad's fondness for jamming necessitated that the rest of the family learn to sleep through anything short of an artillery barrage. As I was going to school, I had to be up early in the morning. Dad would come home nightly with an entourage which usually included Martin Block, Fred Coots, Al Casey, Willie The Lion, and anyone else who happened to be in town. Pop and cronies partied, drank, and jammed until dawn, while the rest of the family peacefully slept upstairs. On the other hand, when we came home from school at three, Dad would be, more likely than not, asleep. We also learned to be very quiet children.

Some Sundays the family would go out to South Jamaica to visit James P. and Lil Johnson. Their children, James Jr. and Oceola, were the same age as Ronnie and me, so it was a trip we always looked forward to because it gave us the opportunity to play in the "country" with kids our own age. When I was a child I never realized how brilliant a pianist James P. was. A shy, retiring man, he had long ago given up the clamor of the business. Jimmy had elected to live off of the income from his record and writing royalties. Jimmy Jr. played piano and we'd jam together just like our fathers. Oceola sang and danced and we had a good little act going there. Lil Johnson was one of my favorite women. Outspoken, with a mouth capable of making any man blush, she was also a lovable, generous woman—who more than once belted me across the jaw for talking out of turn or being wild.

Ronnie and I were always excited when Buster picked us up to go to the Johnson house. It was a special treat. Clarence Williams and Eva Taylor lived across the street from the Johnsons, so the entire day was a social event. We ran through the backyards and played up a storm. When we were called in there were the *two* pianos to play. We thought the place was paradise.

Dad knew how we all enjoyed this little journey to the country. One Sunday afternoon he got all of the family together to announce we were going to Long Island. Buster drove us over the bridge, but we didn't head for South Jamaica, which puzzled all of us. Pop took us to Sayres Avenue in St. Albans, an upper-middle-class neighborhood, not very far from South Jamaica. We stopped at a house and he ushered all of us out of the car.

"Maurice, Ronnie, and Anita . . . this is your new home," he announced as casually as he would say: "And now, for my next number. . . ."

The house was a surprise to all of us. It was like a dream for the whole family. Pop loved that house in St. Albans, and it was a source of great pride to him. He had finally gotten his family out of Harlem and away from the city.

Two or three days after we moved into our new home we became aware of an air of tension between ourselves and our white neighbors. They resented our presence and they were not trying to hide their feelings. Dad kept us all in the house, hoping the situation would not erupt into an ugly incident. One night we heard noises on our lawn and we were shocked to see a cross burning there. A group of people were milling around the cross and they seemed very menacing. Dad was furious. He searched the house for a weapon to defend us with and found my baseball bat. Mom called the police and we waited, praying the crowd would leave us alone. I was scared for myself and my father. He gripped the bat very tightly and I was worried he was going to go out and take on the mob. It was quite a while before the police arrived and dispersed the crowd, and those moments were filled with fear, anxiety, and hate. The night raiders never returned but Dad was afraid to let me go to the local school. I continued attending the Little Red School House in the Village, and every day I'd have to get up early and travel nearly two hours on the subway to go to school.

Ronnie and I had no friends because the white children in the neighborhood were forbidden to play with us. If we wanted to play we took the short bus ride to visit Jimmy Junior and Oceola. After we moved out to St. Albans in 1939, other black entertainers also emigrated to the suburbs. Count Basie lived directly across the street from us and, over the years, Lena Horne, Jackie Robinson, and James Brown all moved into that immediate area. Dad rarely socialized with these people when he was at home. He had his usual clique of Block, Coots, and The Lion over to the house all the time, but he tried to keep our home exclusive from his business and friends. Bill Basie was one of the few neighbors we saw, occasionally coming over for lessons on the Hammond organ. Dad always regarded the Count as one of his closest and dearest friends and felt badly that he didn't receive the recognition he deserved earlier in his career. I remember Dad remarking to Martin Block that Basie was a superb stylist with a unique approach, a man whose originality might have hindered him.

The Count was one of the few friends who was permitted to visit our house. Dad believed his home was a sacred place and it should be solely for his family (except for jam sessions). When he was on the road we rarely saw his regular cronies except Eddie Condon or Willie The Lion, who would come out to check on us and to take home a sampling of Grandma's good cooking. Willie used to sit with me for hours, telling stories about my Dad and "adjusting" my playing style.

One Sunday afternoon Dad violated his "nonvisitation" rule; and it was one of the most exciting experiences of my childhood. My uncle, George Shepherd, had quit his job as a sergeant on the Detroit police force to become a personal bodyguard. The man he was protecting was Joe Louis, who had just won the heavyweight championship. All of Harlem was buzzing with his exploits. Uncle George was sitting in the livingroom with Dad and the Champ. I didn't know who he was but I kept staring at his massive hands that looked as big as baseball gloves.

"Hey, Maurice, come over here. I want you to meet somebody. This is Joe Louis, Maurice," Pop said, as if he was introducing me to nobody special. I refused to believe I was meeting the Champ, saying hello to him and shaking his hand. My little hand got lost in his as we shook. The next day my friends in school would be bored with my story.

That whole afternoon I sat staring at Joe Louis and listening to him talk with my father. Like Dad, he felt an obligation to his country and frequently toured the army camps entertaining the troops. Dad ran into him several times on the road and they became very good friends, Dad rarely missing one of his fights. I remember watching the Champ at Dad's funeral, sitting in a nearby pew, tears streaming down his cheeks. It seemed so incongruous a sight: this man, a symbol of brute strength, crying like a child.

What I am trying to say about my father is that he made every effort to share his life with us. He was a man of great taste and was never ostentatious with Ronnie or me, whether he was introducing us to George Gershwin or Joe Louis. Part of my father's pleasure was involving us in his life, and he had the enviable talent of doing so gracefully, totally free of any condescension.

Mom would never allow us to join Dad on his road trips, but Ronnie and I were permitted to travel with Dad on short hauls, as far as Philly or the Howard Theatre in Washington. I loved riding in that Lincoln convertible with the top down so the Hammond could fit in the back seat, sitting and talking shop with Dad and Buster. I was thirteen and felt like a seasoned veteran as we talked about musicians, arrangements, and the people we were going to meet.

My favorite acts were the dance numbers. It didn't matter if it was a chorus line, the Step Brothers, or Peg Leg Bates. As soon as the dancers started, I was in the wings, watching attentively. At the Howard Theatre I watched Peg Leg Bates do his five shows and charm the audience. I wanted to tell him how much I loved his act, but when I got to his dressingroom door, Peg Leg was sitting in front of his makeup table crying. I looked at him, not understanding why. Dad pulled me away and led me down the hall. He explained to me that Peg Leg's wooden leg was very painful and that he frequently cried from the stinging and throbbing. Dad didn't make any speeches, but just let the message sink in. Of the millions of people who derived happiness from this man's dancing, few knew he was in constant pain.

Two years later, backstage at the Howard one night, Dad had an announcement. "Ronnie and Maurice," he said, "you're getting to be big boys now. I don't want you playing with yourselves; you'll go blind. Let me know when you think you're ready . . . and I'll get you laid." I was totally taken by surprise, and was too shy to speak up, anyway. But Ronnie, who was thirteen at the time, wasn't.

"I guess I'm ready, Pop," he said.

"How about you, Maurice?" Dad asked.

"Well, if Ronnie's ready, I'm ready."

One of the girls in the chorus line had caught my eye. I'm sure she had better things to do that evening, but, as a favor to Dad, she put up with my fumbling and generally maladroit virgin efforts.

Ronnie, as usual, couldn't keep his mouth shut, and soon he told Mom about our Howard outing. She was not amused. In fact, I can't remember seeing her *less* amused than she was about Dad "introducing you two boys to the seedy side of life."

Dad wasn't able to get Mom to allow me into a theatre or a club again until that summer in Burlington, Ontario. The place was built like a ship, the upstairs serving as a hotel, with rooms fitted out like an ocean liner's staterooms and stairways leading downstairs to the main room, which resembled a captain's quarters. I would go downstairs every morning to practice the piano for a couple hours. One morning I met some Canadian musicians and we started to jam. I began playing "My Country, 'Tis of Thee," and the musicians suddenly dropped out. I figured they dug my piano playing, so I started developing a jazz improvisation on the theme. They looked at me aghast. After a few minutes of this Dad yelled down to me. "Maurice, stop that right now!"

I stopped playing and the musicians disappeared. A moment later Dad was downstairs, bathrobe wrapped around his massive frame.

I thought the "Star-Spangled Banner" was everybody's national anthem.

"Up here it's called "God Save the Queen" and you can't swing it. It's very disrespectful."

He sent for the musicians and had me apologize to them. It was all forgotten when the bunch of us got up to the bandstand and began to jam on "Honeysuckle Rose." Dad looked on approvingly, smiling like a babe.

My father was never the kind of person who went out and played ball with us or took us camping, but he did encourage us to do all these things. He once told me, "Maurice, I believe in childhood because I never had one." He saw to it that we had baseball bats and gloves, footballs, bikes, ice skates, and anything else he could think of. One of his gifts, a sled, almost spelled disaster for us. Shortly after Christmas the city was covered by a substantial amount of snow. Ronnie and I cajoled Dad into taking us to a nearby park so we could try out our new sleds. Reluctantly he agreed and we all trekked through the snow to the park. Ronnie came careening down a hill and into a concrete park bench. He rolled off the sled, unconscious. Dad ran to him, picked him up, charged off and to the hospital. I watched helplessly as my father paced up and down the hospital emergency room, cursing the day he bought the sleds. Ronnie was all right but Dad canceled a brief engagement to be with him during his convalescence. Ronnie recovered but our sleds were left in the park.

When I was six or seven I developed a strange kind of dizziness that the doctors suspected might be spinal meningitis. Dad saw to it that I had the best doctors available and went with me everyday to their offices. He was distraught and even began to pray again. I was taken to a Dr. Styles, who never correctly diagnosed the illness but was certain it wasn't meningitis. Soon, with medication, rest, and proper diet, the dizziness was under control.

"Maurice, I'm gonna throw you a helluva party," Dad happily announced when he learned my illness wasn't the dreaded child-killer. Somehow he never got around to the party. That plague, the road, interfered once more.

When your father is a famous man, he really isn't your father. He belongs to everyone. You're allowed to steal him for a few moments from time to time, but that's all. Even though we led a very private life, our father was only in it part of the time. The rest of his life was devoted to Victor Records, the road, and his music. When your father is a famous man you reflect in his glory. You know Gershwin and spend your summers on Lake Ontario. You go to the Little Red School House and you have everything you want. You don't realize that other children aren't as socially or materially fortunate as you are. They don't know Gershwin or Joe Louis or go to a private school.

Sometimes you can reflect in your father's glory too long. You find yourself without a personality of your own and you learn that if you want to do anything like your father, people measure you by his accomplishments. Living off of his reputation becomes very frustrating and self-defeating, and you can never have a standard of your own. I reflected in my father's glory for a long while, but luckily my parents gave me the kind of education and upbringing that allowed me to eventually break out of that pattern.

Publicity photo for the announcement of Fats' Carnegie Hall appearance on January 14, 1942. *Courtesy of Frank Driggs.*

Chapter 16

1943

The Death of Fats

The Santa Fe Chief would take Dad and Kirkeby to Chicago, where they would change trains to make their New York connection. They reached their berths and Dad sighed with relief as he hit the mattress. "Oh, man, I can't take this much longer."

Kirkeby replied that, in fact, Fats Waller never would have to do any more of the grueling travel and one-nighters any more. Royalties from records and shows, concerts, and (possibly) Broadway appearances would be sufficient to guarantee a very acceptable living from now on.

Dad got his second wind and began discussing business matters with his manager. When they got back to New York there was to be a guest appearance on "Stage Door Canteen." Richard Kollmar was already negotiating with Kirkeby about Dad composing another score for a Broadway show. From my discussions with Dad I know that this second Broadway show meant quite a bit to him. He had already done Broadway work before *Early to Bed,* but he considered most of that work to be frivolous and superficial. He had no illusions about Broadway musicals, but he felt that if he could contribute to the Broadway scene he might *eventually* create something as significant as *Porgy and Bess.* Perhaps thinking of a more satisfying career, he fell asleep.

Kirkeby describes the following journey into Kansas City in his book *Ain't Misbehavin':*

> Later that day we walked along to the club car, where Fats was greeted, it seemed to me, by people from all over the world. "Hey, Fats, glad to see ya," and the party was on again! Eventually we took some people up forward to our room, but near on midnight, I started taking off my coat and I said I was going to bed. It was the only way to break things up.

At eleven o'clock the next morning, I woke and asked Fats how he felt.

" 'Man, I'm sure gonna get some more shut-eye!" he said, and turned over with his face to the wall.

"Good idea," I said. "I'll meander down to the diner and get some breakfast. If you want anything, just ring for the porter and I'll tell the diningcar steward to be on the alert."

Fats slept all that day—not really unusual, for at times he used to hibernate the same way at home. From time to time I checked the porter and the room, content that Fats was at last really getting the rest he needed so badly. Meanwhile, I passed the time with our friends of the night before, and kept them from disturbing Fats.

About two that morning I opened the door to the sleeper and was hit by a blast of cold air.

"Jesus, it's cold in here!" I said, as I saw Fats was awake.

"Yeah, Hawkins is sure blowin' out there tonight." Fats replied.

The train was roaring through the Kansas plains in a howling blizzard, which reminded Fats of the blustery sax-playing of his friend, Coleman Hawkins.

"Are you warm enough?" I asked.

"You'll be okay when you get into bed," he replied.

So I washed quickly and piled into bed.

[Kirkeby informed the reporters the next day that the discussion occurred about four-thirty in the morning. Shortly before six he heard Dad choking.]

Quickly I switched on the light and saw Fats over there in bed, trembling all over. I jumped out of bed, and shaking him by the shoulders, called him to wake up. It seemed he was having a bad dream, but I couldn't wake him. Frantically I rang for the porter."

The train had pulled into Union Station in Kansas City because of the storm, allowing a doctor to board and attend several passengers who were ill with heavy colds or influenza. Ed rang for a porter, but they were apparently all inside the station. He slipped into a robe and raced down to the club car to find a steward.

Returning with the bar steward, Kirkeby saw that the porter had already come back to the car; but my father was now lying motionless. Kirkeby demanded that the train not leave the station until medical attention was obtained. No one had a chance to tell him that the doctor who had boarded the train had been summoned. The doctor arrived in the midst of the confusion and immediately ordered everyone be silent. After a few moments, he turned around and said, "The man is dead."

Under Kansas law an autopsy had to be performed. By now the blizzard had virtually locked in the city, and it was several hours before the police could remove the body and the coroner, G. C. Leetch, was able to give the postmortem. On December 15 my father had died of bronchial pneumonia, a condition he had apparently had for some weeks, either brought on or aggravated by the Zanzibar engagement. Kirkeby, as a matter of procedure, had been held by the police until the results of the autopsy were announced. It wasn't until three hours after my father's death that Kirkeby was able to call New York with the news.

I was upstairs, in bed with the flu, when the phone rang. I could hear my mother speaking very quietly. And then she called upstairs: "Maurice, your father's dead."

I understood the words, but they didn't make any sense. There was no emotion in my mother's voice. I put on my robe and went downstairs. Mom was holding onto a counter for support, still staring at the telephone. In a monotone she told me that Dad had died on a train in Kansas and that Ed Kirkeby was taking care of arrangements. She then sharply told me to get back to bed.

Years later I learned that while Dad's train was stalled in Union Station another train, coming from the opposite direction, was also stuck in the terrible blizzard. Aboard the westbound train was Dad's old friend, Louis Armstrong. When he saw the arrival of the police and ambulance he asked a porter what was happening. The porter told him that Fats Waller had died on the other train. Louis told my mother that he cried all night long. He couldn't believe that Dad was dead at thirty-nine.

The storm in Kansas City kept raging on and soon the city was snowed in. Kirkeby had to make arrangements for the embalming, the casket, and the eventual transportation of the body to New York. He also had to find a hotel room, but because of the storm, every available room was occupied. The manager of the Muehlbach was kind enough to offer his own quarters. A funeral home was notified and the process begun. Shortly before they had left California, Dad had signed his will. As Kirkeby had witnessed it, he was aware of what Dad wanted.

Ronnie came home from school and raced up to my room before Mom could get hold of him. I told him what little I knew, and he sat there staring at me for a long time before he said anything.

Soon the phone calls started coming; what seemed like hundreds of friends expressing their condolences and offering help. Mom called the Abyssinian Baptist Church to arrange for the funeral. She thought it fitting to have Dad eulogized there because of his family's long relationship with that church. Even though Dad never attended church services, he had maintained his boyhood friendship with its minister, Reverend Adam Clayton Powell, Jr.

In Kansas City Kirkeby was flooded with calls from all the wire services and soon the radio news was telling the world that Fats Waller had died of a heart attack on a Kansas City train (despite the contradictory coroner's report). Kirkeby called again from Kansas City to tell us it was impossible to estimate when Dad's body would be returned to New York. The blizzard was still roaring through the West and Midwest and the train schedules were a myth. Late the second day the funeral home had finished the arrangements and my father's body was brought to Union Station for the trip back home to New York. But this time no one was shouting, "Buster: Holland Tunnel."

The train arrived on the night of December 19, and the body was taken to the church. The next morning Mom woke us up very early and made sure we were dressed impeccably. It was her feeling that Dad was going to be given a royal Harlem sendoff, and she thought he would have us dressed for it. When we arrived at the church I saw my father for the first time in many weeks. Adam Clayton Powell escorted us to the first row, where we were to wait for the services to begin. A stocky, well-dressed woman and a young man in a corporal's uniform came into the church and walked up to the casket. I stared at them. I had never seen them before. The Reverend Powell then escorted them to share the first row, reserved for the immediate family. I was shocked.

"Who are these strangers?" I asked my mother.

"That's your father's first wife and your half brother, Tom."

I couldn't believe it. I had no knowledge that there had been a previous marriage, and that somewhere there was another young man who shared my father. Illogically, I hated the army corporal who sat next to me, my brother and yet totally strange to me. I looked at the stocky woman. I didn't know what to feel only that I wanted to chase them out of the church.

Slowly the church began to fill with mourners and dignitaries. Aunt Naomi had come up from Miami. Andy Razaf, J. C. Johnson, Don Redman, Claude Hopkins, Andy Kirk, James P., Donald Heywood, and Clarence Williams were the honorary pallbearers. Friends and relatives came in. The entire band, and members of previous bands who had previously worked for Dad, were there. The cast of *Early to Bed* filled several pews. Before I knew it the entire church was filled to capacity and yet more people were coming. The deacons of the church were making hasty efforts to install some kind of loudspeaker system outside the church to accommodate the overflow crowd. Over twenty-five hundred people came to the services and many had to stand outside on the church steps in the freezing December weather to hear the services.

The services lasted an hour and a half. I kept staring into the open casket as the different speakers made their remarks about my father. Andy Razaf paid tribute to him on behalf of all the musicians who worked for him. Gene Buck, president of ASCAP and composer of the Ziegfeld Follies, said that Fats Waller had "brought great distinction to his family, his race, the nation, his colleagues, and friends." It meant nothing to me then. Everything only sounded like so much cacophony.

Richard Kollmar said, "I have lost a great friend and fellow worker, whereas the loss to the musical world is inestimable. Waller was a pioneer in his particular field of music, an inimitable personality, and a pleasant associate. I have never worked with anyone of any race with greater pleasure and understanding."

The last speaker was the Reverend Adam Clayton Powell, Jr. "Fats Waller always played to a packed house. We are gathered here this morning to mourn the passing of a simple soul, a soul touched with the genius of music which brought relief from our cares and woes." The Reverend then told of their relationship from childhood. When Dad first became interested in music, the only place he could go to practice was the church, where there was an organ. Adam showed Dad how to force the basement window open and sneak in. Adam always came with Dad, pushing the window open for him, and then holding it until Dad's massive frame slipped through. It was Adam who pumped the pedals for my father as he played his sweet and hot music, as he experimented, as he learned. Adam Clayton Powell never forgot that. He also told how Dad began to play portable organs on the streets around the West Forties. Dad would play and Adam Clayton Powell, Sr. would preach. "Because God gave him genius and skill, he in turn gave the world laughter and joy for its difficult and lonely hours. Thomas Waller and his songs shall live again. His sweetest songs are yet to be heard . . . in glory."

I looked around the church. People I had never seen were crying. People who had known Dad over the years were weeping uncontrollably. Only when we left the church did I begin to realize how many people were actually there. The vestibule of the church was filled with mourners. The stairs and even the streets were overflowing. People were standing on rooftops on Amsterdam Avenue, while others were milling in doorways and leaning out of windows. There must have been close to ten thousand people in all. As we moved in the cortege toward Seventh and Lenox Avenues more crowds lined the streets and rooftops. My mother slipped something to me she had removed from the casket. It was the citation posthumously awarded to Dad by the National Council of the Army and Navy Union.

We had moved only three or four blocks before the sea of mourners flooding the streets halted the funeral procession. People took roses and carnations from the floral tributes. Some of the women tossed the flowers onto the casket; others took them home to keep as remembrances. The cortege moved along Harlem, down to 125th Street, across the Triborough Bridge, and out to Maspeth, Long Island, and the Fresh Pond Crematory.

The urn of ashes was turned over to an aviator known as the Black Ace, a pilot famous for his World War I and Spanish Civil War exploits. In compliance with my father's wishes, this man went aloft and saw to it that the ashes of Fats Waller were released into the air, to fall to rest upon Fats' beloved Harlem.

After the services the cortege returned to St. Albans. Only the family and Dad's closest friends were allowed to attend the wake. Willie The Lion was there. He couldn't look at me and I couldn't look at him. Whenever our eyes locked, they flooded with tears. I tried to ask him about Dad's first wife and my half brother, but I didn't have the courage. It wasn't until years later, after my mother told me the story of that first marriage, that I no longer felt bitter. I don't think Ronnie was as sensitive about it as I was, but I know it did have an effect on him.

I began to realize with the reading of the will that my father's life with Edith had been one of frustration. He bequeathed his son Thomas Jr. only five hundred dollars, and to Edith twenty-five hundred. My father wasn't satisfied to leave his former wife with only the minimum one-third of his estate, as required by law. He felt it necessary to add:

It is my desire and request, and I direct for reasons fully known to her, that Edith Waller shall receive only the minimum portion of my estate to which the law provides she is entitled and which I am compelled to leave her by law. If, after the execution of this Will and at the time of my decease, the law of the State of New York be altered or amended so that I shall have the right to disinherit the said Edith Waller, in whole or in part, then and in that event, I do revoke and annul in whole or in part all such bequests to her, and I do specifically disinherit the said Edith Waller, in whole or in part, and I direct that she shall then be entitled to receive only what the law specifically provided for, and the bequest herein, in whole or in part, shall be added to and divided between [Anita, Maurice, and Ronald Waller.]

Bernard Miller, an attorney, was appointed trustee of the estate, as directed in father's will. The income from royalties was supposed to be invested, and expenses of the trustee were to be paid out of their interest and income. In 1946 Edith Waller surprised our family when she relinquished all rights in the will. Her share was supposed to revert to my mother, my brother, and me. This full one-third share remained undistributed for quite some while. The difficulties and complications were only beginning.

Bernard Miller appointed his brother and law partner, Morton Miller, as the counsel for the trusteeship. Unknown to the family, Morton Miller and Ed Kirkeby had formed the C. R. Publishing Company and, as Dad's copyrights expired with Robbins, Leeds, or any of the original publishers, they were transferred to C. R. Publishing. Under the law, these copyrights should have been renewed by members of the immediate family, who would then designate a publisher. The renewals and reassignments to C. R. Publishing were concealed from us. Also unknown to us, Miller and Kirkeby had directed RCA to pay Edith Waller one-ninth of all royalties. She collected that money until her death in 1954. The balance of her share, which was two ninths, was given by the Miller brothers to Ed Kirkeby. Under the terms and conditions of the will, it should have been paid to us. Kirkeby demanded this share on the basis that he was Dad's personal manager and had written my father's songs with him. This assertion seemed ridiculous to me. Kirkeby wasn't even around when Dad and Andy wrote "Honeysuckle Rose," "Ain't Misbehavin'," and "What Did I Do to Be So Black and Blue?" My father wrote his broadway show, *Early to Bed,* and *London Suite* without Kirkeby's assistance.

In February of 1950 Bernard Miller stepped down as the trustee because Ronnie and I were of age, and, under the conditions of the will, we were to be successors. Unaware of the actions of Kirkeby and Morton Miller, and the fact that Miller was a partner of and attorney for Kirkeby, we retained Miller as the attorney for the estate. My mother, Ronnie, and I were induced to sign a document ordering RCA to pay royalties directly to Kirkeby.

Ronnie and I eventually became suspicious and, as trustees, demanded to see a copy of all the records, books, and accounts. Morton Miller claimed there were no such records, so we had to bring a civil action to the courts. Miller countersued, claiming we owed him legal fees. It was a mess that dragged on for years, and was still in litigation in 1977. But the courts ruled that the agreement signed in 1950 by our family and Kirkeby is null and void. All of his life my father felt he was cheated by greedy publishers, and now in death he was being cheated again.

Dad's reputation as a musician and personality has grown to legendary proportions. In April of 1944 a group of his friends held a memorial concert for him at Town Hall. The entire Waller Band was reunited for the occasion and played his biggest hits. Jazz greats including Count Basie, Lena Horne, and Hazel Scott entertained and shared with the audience their remembrances of Fats Waller. Since his death, usually on the anniversary of his birthday, there have been several memorial concerts at the Overseas Press Club, performed by surviving members of the band. In recent years I have sat in on piano with the group. We play Dad's hits and the audience is always receptive.

It has been well over thirty years since my father died, but his records continue to be big sellers for RCA Victor. In Europe he is treated as a jazz immortal—particularly in France, where his recordings and sheet music do a phenomenal amount of business. Easily one-third of all the royalties received by the estate come from Europe. In 1976 *Reader's Digest* issued a special Fats Waller record, and again I was surprised by the large number of sales it generated.

In recent years there has been a revival of black-oriented material, and with it has come a renewed interest in Fats Waller. His music is heard in the hit show *Bubblin' Brown Sugar,* and his life story has become of interest to several film companies and Broadway producers.

Over the years several members of Dad's old groups have tried to form their own bands and capitalize on his style. But none of them has succeeded—because Fats Waller's style went beyond his piano playing. He was able to incorporate his comic sense, his irony, and his infectious personality into his music. When he sat down to a piano he wasn't playing just music, he was playing Fats Waller.

It seems like every day that I run into people who knew the man, or worked with him, or at least crossed his path at one time or another. They talk about his drinking, his generosity, his sense of humor. I must have heard, "Hey Maurice, did I ever tell you about the time. . . ." a million times over. Sometimes I pass music shops and in the window I see his photograph on the cover of a music book or a record. There he is, looking back at me, like some kind of mischievous cherub with that impish grin on his face. That knowing twinkle in his eye. That beat-up derby at any moment ready to fall off his head.

All I have to do is play one of his records and I can see him there, rocking in time to the music. As part of the music. As long as I have the memories and the music, I still have my father.

One of Fats' last appearances—New York City, late 1943.
Courtesy of Michael Lipskin.

Recording Dates and Personnel

Date and Place	Songs	Personnel	Instruments
October, 1922	MUSCLE SHOALS BLUES BIRMINGHAM BLUES	Fats Waller	piano
Late 1922	'TAINT NOBODY'S BIZNESS IF I DO YOU GOT EVERYTHING A SWEET MAMA NEEDS BUT ME MAMA'S GOT THE BLUES LAST GO ROUND BLUES	Sara Martin Fats Waller	vocal piano
	I'M CERT'NLY GONNA SEE 'BOUT THAT SQUABBLIN' BLUES	Sara Martin Clarence Williams Fats Waller	vocal vocal piano
1923	SISTER KATE YOU CAN'T DO WHAT MY LAST MAN DID TRIXIE BLUES (2 takes)	Anna Jones Fats Waller	vocal piano
Early 1924	YOU DON'T KNOW MY MIND BLUES WEST INDIES BLUES	Justin Ring Clarence Todd Clarence Williams Fats Waller	wood block kazoo kazoo piano
1925	STINGAREE BLUES	Albert Hunter Fats Waller	vocal piano
1925	MAYBE SOMEDAY WHEN YOUR TROUBLES ARE JUST LIKE MINE	Hazel Meyers Fats Waller	vocal piano
Late 1925	HATEFUL BLUES I AIN'T GONNA PLAY NO SECOND FIDDLE LUCY LONG	Perry Bradford Louis Armstrong Don Redman Fats Waller James P. Johnson Charlie Allen	vocal cornet alto sax piano piano trumpet

Continued

Date and Place	Songs	Personnel	Instruments
1926	MAMA'S LOSING A MIGHTY GOOD CHANCE AIN'T GOT NOBODY TO GRIND MY COFFEE	Caroline Johnson Fats Waller	vocal piano
1926	NOBODY KNOWS THE TROUBLE I SEE I'VE GOT THE JOOGIE BLUES BLACK SNAKE BLUES	Alta Brown Bertha Powell Fats Waller	vocal vocal piano
November 3, 1926	HENDERSON STOMP	Fletcher Henderson Fats Waller Tommy Ladnier Russel Smith Joe Smith Charlie Green Buster Bailey Don Redman Coleman Hawkins Charlie Dixon June Cole Kaiser Marshall	piano piano trumpet trumpet trumpet trombone clarinet alto sax tenor sax banjo bass drums
	THE CHANT	Same personnel as above except: Fats Waller	organ
November 17, 1926	ST. LOUIS BLUES LENNOX AVENUE BLUES	Fats Waller	organ
November 19, 1926	SWEET THING I NEED LOVIN'	Same personnel as November 3, 1926	
January 12, 1927	SOOTHIN' SYRUP STOMP SLOPPY WATER BLUES LOVELESS LOVE MESSIN' AROUND WITH THE BLUES RUSTY PAIL	Fats Waller	organ

Date	Titles	Personnel	Instrument
		Same personnel as November 3, 1926	
January 22, 1927	HAVE IT READY	Fats Waller	organ
February 16, 1927	STOMPIN' THE BUG HOG MAW STOMP	Fats Waller	piano
March 11, 1927	SHUFFLIN' SADIE	Same personnel as November 3, 1926 except:	
April 27, 1927	ST. LOUIS SHUFFLE VARIETY STOMP WHITEMAN STOMP I'M COMING VIRGINIA	Jimmy Harrison Bob Escudero	tuba bass
May 20, 1927	FATS WALLER STOMP SAVANNAH BLUES WON'T YOU TAKE ME HOME?	Thomas Morris Charlie Irvis Fats Waller unknown unknown	cornet trombone organ guitar drums
May 20, 1927	SUGAR BEALE STREET BLUES	Fats Waller	organ
	SUGAR BEALE STREET BLUES	Alberta Hunter Fats Waller	vocal organ
November 14, 1927	FLORENCE	Juanita Stinette Chappelle Fats Waller	vocal organ
	BYE BYE FLORENCE MEMORIES OF FLORENCE	Bert Howell Fats Waller	vocal organ
December 1, 1927 Camden, N.J.	HE'S GONE AWAY RED HOT DAN GEECHEE PLEASE TAKE ME OUT	Thomas Morris Jimmy Archey Fats Waller unknown unknown	cornet trombone organ guitar drums
	I AIN'T GOT NOBODY THE DIGAH'S STOMP	Fats Waller	organ

Continued

Date and Place	Songs	Personnel	Instruments
January 17, 1928	NOBODY KNOWS HOW MUCH I LOVE YOU	Johnny Thompson	vocal
		Fats Waller	piano
		Howard Nelson	violin
November, 1928	YOU DONT UNDERSTAND	James P. Johnson	piano
	YOU'VE GOT TO BE MODERNISTIC	Fats Waller	piano
		King Oliver	cornet
		Dave Nelson	cornet
		Jimmy Archey	trombone
		Charlie Frazier	sax
		Teddy Bunn	guitar
		Harry Hall	bass
March 1, 1929 New York City	THE MINOR DRAG HARLEM FUSS	Fats Waller	piano
		Charlie Gains	trumpet
		Charlie Irvis	trombone
		Arville Harris	clarinet and alto sax
	HANDFUL OF KEYS NUMB FUMBLING	Eddie Condon	banjo
		Fats Waller	piano
March 27, 1929	WILLOW TREE 'SIPPI THOU SWELL PERSIAN RUG	Fats Waller	organ
		Jabbo Smith	trumpet
		Garvin Bushell	clarinet, alto sax, and bassoon
		James P. Johnson	piano
August 2, 1929 Camden, N.J.	AINT MISBEHAVIN' SWEET SAVANNAH SUE I'VE GOT A FEELING I'M FALLING LOVE ME OR LEAVE ME GLADYSE VALENTINE STOMP	Fats Waller	piano

Date	Titles	Personnel	Instrument
August 24, 1929	WAITING AT THE END OF THE ROAD BABY OH WHERE CAN YOU BE (3 takes) TANGLEFOOT (2 takes) THAT'S ALL (2 takes)	Fats Waller	organ
August 29, 1929	WAITIN' AT THE END OF THE ROAD BABY WHERE CAN YOU BE	Fats Waller	piano
September, 1929	THAT'S ALL	Fats Waller	organ
September 11, 1929 New York City	GOIN' ABOUT MY FEELINGS ARE HURT	Fats Waller	piano
September 12, 1929	THAT'S HOW I FEEL TODAY	Rex Stewart Claude Jones Don Redman Benny Carter Coleman Hawkins FatsWaller unknown unknown unknown	trumpet trombone sax and vocal alto sax tenor sax piano tuba drums banjo
	SIX OR SEVEN TIMES	Personnel same as above with the addition of: a vocal trio	unknown
September 24, 1929	SMASHING THIRDS	Fats Waller	piano
September 30, 1929	LOOKIN' GOOD BUT FEELIN' BAD I NEED SOMEONE LIKE YOU	Fats Waller Charlie Gains Jack Teagarden Otto Hardwick Eddie Condon Al Morgan Gene Krupa The Wanderers	piano trumpet trombone alto clarinet banjo bass drums vocal

Continued

Date and Place	Songs	Personnel	Instruments
October, 1929	MUSCLE SHOALS BLUES GEE AIN'T I GOOD TO YOU	Fats Waller Joe Smith Len Davis Claude Jones Benny Carter Don Redman Coleman Hawkins Ted McCord Lonnie Johnson Fats Waller Bill Taylor Dave Wilborn	piano trumpet trumpet trombone sax sax sax sax guitar piano bass banjo
November 6, 1929	I'D LOVE IT THE WAY I FEEL TODAY MISS HANNAH	Same personnel as November 5, 1929	
November 14, 1929	PEGGY WHEREVER THERE'S A WILL	Same personnel as November 5, 1929	
November 25, 1929	MY FATE IS IN YOUR HANDS	Gene Austin Fats Waller	vocal piano
December 4, 1929	MY FATE IS IN YOUR HANDS TURN ON THE HEAT	Fats Waller	piano
December 18, 1929 New York City	RIDIN' BUT WALKIN'	Len Davis Jack Teagarden Otto Hardwick Happy Cauldwell Fats Waller Eddie Condon Al Morgan Kaiser Marshall	trumpet trombone alto sax and clarinet tenor sax piano banjo bass drums

WON'T YOU GET OFF IT PLEASE

Same personnel as above
with the substitution of:
Jay C. Higginbotham — trombone

WHEN I'M ALONE
LOOKING FOR ANOTHER SWEETIE

Same personnel as above
with the addition of:
Orlando Robeson — vocal

March 21, 1930
New York City
ST. LOUIS BLUES
AFTER YOU'VE GONE

Fats Waller — piano
Bennie Paine — piano

March 5, 1931
EGYPTIAN ELLA

Muggsy Spanier — cornet
Dave Klein — trumpet
George Brunies — trombone
Benny Goodman — clarinet
Ted Lewis — clarinet and vocal
Don Murray — saxes
Bud Freeman — tenor sax
Sam Shapiro — violin
Sol Klein — violin
unknown — accordion
Fats Waller — piano
Tony Gerardi — guitar
Harry Barth — bass
John Lucas — drums

DALLAS BLUES

Same personnel as above
with the addition of:
Fats Waller — vocal

I'M CRAZY 'BOUT MY BABY
ROYAL GARDEN BLUES

Same personnel as above
with the substitution of:
Fats Waller — vocal

March 13, 1931
I'M CRAZY 'BOUT MY BABY
DRAGGIN' MY HEART AROUND

Fats Waller — piano

Continued

191

Date and Place	Songs	Personnel	Instruments
October 13, 1931	THAT'S WHAT I LIKE ABOUT YOU	Charlie Teagarden	trumpet
		Sterling Bose	trumpet
		Jack Teagarden	trombone and vocal
		Tommy Dorsey	trombone
		Artie Shaw	clarinet and alto sax
		Bud Freeman	tenor sax
		Fats Waller	piano
		Dick McDonough	guitar
		Artie Bernstein	bass
		Stan King	drums
		Max Farley	baritone sax
	YOU RASCAL YOU	Same personnel as above with the substitution of:	
		Fats Waller	vocal
November, 1931	CHANCES ARE	Same personnel as	
	CAROLINA'S CALLING ME	October 14, 1931	
July 26, 1932 New York City	I WOULD DO ANYTHING FOR YOU	Henry Allen	trumpet
	YELLOW DOG BLUES	Jimmy Lord	clarinet
	YES SUH!	Pee Wee Russell	tenor sax
		Fats Waller	piano
		Eddie Condon	banjo
		Jack Bland	guitar
		Pops Foster	bass
		Zutty Singleton	drums
		Billy Banks	vocal
	MEAN OLD BED BUG BLUES	Same personnel as above with the addition of:	
		Una Mae Carlisle	vocal

Date	Titles	Personnel	Instrument
May 16, 1934	I WISH I WERE TWINS ARMFUL OF SWEETNESS DO ME A FAVOR A PORTER'S LOVE SONG TO A CHAMBERMAID	Fats Waller Herman Autrey Ben Whittet Al Casey Bill Taylor Harry Dial	piano and vocal trumpet clarinet and alto sax guitar bass drums
August 17, 1934	GEORGIA MAY THEN I'LL BE TIRED OF YOU DON'T LET IT BOTHER YOU HAVE A LITTLE DREAM ON ME	Same personnel as May 16, 1934 with the substitution of: Eugene Sedric	clarinet and alto sax
September 28, 1934 New York City	SERENADE FOR A WEALTHY WIDOW HOW CAN YOU FACE ME SWEETIE PIE MANDY LET'S PRETEND THERE'S A MOON YOU'RE NOT THE ONLY OYSTER IN THE STEW	Same personnel as May 16, 1934 with the addition of: Floyd O'Brien and the substitution of: Mezz Mezzrow	trombone clarinet and alto sax
November 7, 1934	HONEYSUCKLE ROSE BREAKIN' THE ICE	Fats Waller	piano
	BELIEVE IT BELOVED DREAM MAN I'M GROWING FONDER OF YOU IF IT ISN'T LOVE	Fats Waller Bill Coleman Eugene Sedric Al Casey Bill Taylor Harry Dial	piano and vocal trumpet clarinet and alto sax guitar bass drums
November 16, 1934	AFRICAN RIPPLES CLOTHES LINE BALLET ALLIGATOR CRAWL VIPER'S DRAG	Fats Waller	piano

Continued

Date and Place	Songs	Personnel	Instruments
January 5, 1935 Camden, N.J.	I'M A HUNDRED PER CENT FOR YOU BABY BROWN NIGHT WIND BECAUSE OF ONCE UPON A TIME I BELIEVE IN MIRACLES YOU FIT INTO THE PICTURE	Fats Waller Herman Autrey Ben Whittet Al Casey Charles Turner Harry Dial	piano or organ and vocal trumpet clarinet and alto sax guitar bass drums
March 6, 1935 New York City	LOUISIANA FAIRY TALE I AIN'T GOT NOBODY (2 takes, vocal and non-vocal) WHOSE HONEY ARE YOU ROSETTA PARDON MY LOVE WHAT'S THE REASON CINDERS OH, SUZANNA! DUST OFF THAT OLD PIANNA	Fats Waller Herman Autrey Rudy Powell Al Casey Charles Turner Harry Dial	piano, celeste, and vocal trumpet clarinet and alto sax guitar bass drums
March 11, 1935	BABY BROWN VIPER'S DRAG HOW CAN YOU FACE ME DOWN HOME BLUES DINAH HANDFUL OF KEYS SOLITUDE I'M CRAZY 'BOUT MY BABY BELIEVE IT BELOVED TEA FOR TWO SWEET SUE SOMEBODY STOLE MY GAL HONEYSUCKLE ROSE WHERE WERE YOU ON THE NIGHT OF JUNE 3RD? CLOTHESLINE BALLET	Fats Waller Rudy Powell	piano clarinet and sax

DON'T LET IT BOTHER YOU
E FLAT BLUES
ALLIGATOR CRAWL
ZONKY
HALLELUJAH!
DO ME A FAVOR
CALIFORNIA, HERE I COME
AIN'T MISBEHAVIN'
YOU'RE THE TOP
BLUE TURNING GREY OVER YOU
RUSSIAN FANTASY

May 8, 1935   LULU'S BACK IN TOWN   Same personnel as
New York City   SWEET AND SLOW   March 6, 1935
YOU'VE BEEN TAKING LESSONS IN LOVE
YOU'RE THE CUTEST ONE
I'M GONNA SIT RIGHT DOWN AND WRITE MYSELF A LETTER
I HATE TO TALK ABOUT MYSELF

June 24, 1935   DINAH   Fats Waller   piano and vocal
New York City   TAKE IT EASY   Herman Autrey   trumpet
YOU'RE THE PICTURE, I'M THE FRAME   Eugene Sedric   clarinet and
MY VERY GOOD FRIEND THE MILKMAN   alto sax
BLUE BECAUSE OF YOU   James Smith   guitar
THERE'S GONNA BE THE DEVIL TO PAY   Charles Turner   bass
TWELFTH STREET RAG   Arnold Bolden   drums
THERE'LL BE SOME CHANGES MADE
SOMEBODY STOLE MY GAL
SWEET SUE

August 2, 1935   TRUCKIN'   Same personnel as above
New York City   SUGAR BLUES   with the substitution of:
AS LONG AS THE WORLD GOES ROUND   Rudy Powell   clarinet and
GEORGIA ROCKIN' CHAIR   alto sax
BROTHER, SEEK AND YE SHALL FIND   Harry Dial   drums
THE GIRL I LEFT BEHIND ME

Continued

Date and Place	Songs	Personnel	Instruments
August 20, 1935 New York City	YOU'RE SO DARN CHARMING WOE IS ME RHYTHM AND ROMANCE LOAFIN' TIME A SWEET BEGINNING LIKE THIS GOT A BRAN' NEW SUIT I'M ON A SEE-SAW THIEF IN THE NIGHT	Same personnel as August 2, 1935	
November 29, 1935	SWEET THING WHEN SOMEBODY THINKS YOU'RE WONDERFUL I'VE GOT MY FINGERS CROSSED SPREADIN' RHYTHM AROUND A LITTLE BIT INDEPENDENT YOU STAYED AWAY TOO LONG	Fats Waller Herman Autrey Eugene Sedric James Smith Charles Turner Yank Porter	piano, vocal and celeste trumpet clarinet and alto sax guitar bass drums
December 4, 1935	FAT AND GREASY FUNCTIONIZIN' I GOT RHYTHM	Fats Waller Hank Duncan Herman Autrey Sidney DeParis Benny Morton Edward Inge Rudy Powell Don Redman Eugene Sedric Bob Carroll James Smith Charles Turner Yank Porter	piano trumpet trumpet trumpet trombone clarinet clarinet and sax alto sax tenor sax tenor sax guitar bass drums
February 1, 1936	THE PANIC IS ON SUGAR ROSE OOOH! LOOK-A-THERE MOON ROSE	Same personnel as November 29, 1935	

WEST WIND
THAT NEVER-TO-BE-FORGOTTEN NIGHT
SING AN OLD FASHIONED LOVE SONG
GARBO GREEN

April 8, 1936

ALL OF MY LIFE
CHRISTOPHER COLUMBUS
CROSS PATCH
IT'S NO FUN
CABIN IN THE SKY
US ON A BUS

Same personnel as
November 29, 1935
with the substitution of:
Al Casey   guitar

June 5, 1936

IT'S A SIN TO TELL A LIE
THE MORE I KNOW YOU
YOU'RE NOT THE KIND
WHY DO I LIE TO MYSELF ABOUT YOU
LET'S SING AGAIN
BIG CHIEF DE SOTA

Same personnel as
April 8, 1936

June 8, 1936
New York City

BLACK RASPBERRY JAM
FRACTIOUS FINGERING
PASWONKY
LOUNGING AT THE WALDORF
LATCH ON
BACH UP TO ME

Same personnel as
April 8, 1936

August 1, 1936

I'M CRAZY 'BOUT MY BABY
I JUST MADE UP WITH THAT GIRL OF MINE
UNTIL THE REAL THING COMES ALONG
THERE GOES MY ATTRACTION
THE CURSE OF AN ACHING HEART
BYE BYE BABY

Same personnel as
April 8, 1936

September 9, 1936
New York City

S'POSIN'
COPPER COLORED GAL OF MINE
I'M AT THE MERCY OF LOVE
FLOATIN' DOWN TO COTTON TOWN
LA-DE-DE, LA-DE-DA

Same personnel as
April 8, 1936
with the substitution of:
Wilmore "Slick" Jones   drums

Continued

Date and Place	Songs	Personnel	Instruments
November 29, 1936 Chicago	HALLELUJAH! THINGS LOOK ROSY NOW (2 takes, with and without vocals) 'TAIN'T GOOD (2 takes, with and without vocals) SWINGIN' THEM JINGLE BELLS (2 takes, with and without vocals) A THOUSAND DREAMS OF YOU (2 takes, with and without vocals) A RHYME FOR LOVE I ADORE YOU	Same personnel as September 9, 1936	
December 24, 1936	HAVIN' A BALL I'M SORRY I MADE YOU CRY WHO'S AFRAID OF LOVE PLEASE KEEP ME IN YOUR DREAMS ONE IN A MILLION NERO	Same personnel as September 9, 1939	
February 22, 1937	YOU'RE LAUGHING AT ME I CAN'T BREAK THE HABIT OF YOU DID ANYONE EVER TELL YOU WHEN LOVE IS YOUNG THE MEANEST THING YOU EVER DID	Same personnel as September 9, 1939	
March 18, 1937	CRYIN' MOOD WHERE IS THE SUN YOU'VE BEEN READING MY MAIL TO A SWEET AND PRETTY THING OLD PLANTATION SPRING CLEANING	Same personnel as September 9, 1939	

Date / Location	Titles	Personnel	Instruments
March 27, 1937 New York City	HONEYSUCKLE ROSE BLUES	Bunny Berigan Tommy Dorsey Fats Waller Dick McDonough George Wettling	trumpet trombone piano guitar drums

April 9, 1937
New York City
	YOU SHOWED ME THE WAY
	  (2 takes, with and without vocals)
	BOO-HOO
	THE LOVE BUG'LL BITE YOU
	SAN ANTON'
	I'VE GOT A NEW LEASE ON LOVE
	SWEET HEARTACHE
	HONEYSUCKLE ROSE
		Fats Waller
		
		Herman Autrey
		Al Casey
		Charles Turner
		Eugene Sedric
		
		Slick Jones
			piano and vocal
			
			trumpet
			guitar
			bass
			clarinet and
			  alto sax
			drums and vibes

June 9, 1937	SMARTY DON'T YOU KNOW OR DON'T YOU CARE LOST LOVE I'M GONNA PUT YOU IN YOUR PLACE BLUE TURNING GREY OVER YOU	Same personnel as April 9, 1937	
June 11, 1937	KEEPIN' OUT OF MISCHIEF NOW STARDUST BASIN STREET BLUES TEA FOR TWO I AIN'T GOT NOBODY	Fats Waller	piano
September 7, 1937 New York City	YOU'VE GOT ME UNDER YOUR THUMB BEAT IT OUT OUR LOVE WAS MEANT TO BE I'D RATHER CALL YOU BABY I'M ALWAYS IN THE MOOD SHE'S TALL, SHE'S TAN YOU'RE MY DISH MORE POWER TO YOU	Same personnel as April 9, 1937	

Continued

Date and Place	Songs	Personnel	Instruments
October 7, 1937 New York City	HOW CAN I WITH YOU IN MY HEART THE JOINT IS JUMPING A HOPELESS LOVE AFFAIR WHAT WILL I DO IN THE MORNING HOW YA BABY JEALOUS OF ME	Same personnel as April 9, 1937	
December 16, 1937 Hollywood	EVERY DAY'S A HOLIDAY NEGLECTED MY WINDOW FACES SOUTH AM I IN ANOTHER WORLD WHY DO HAWAIIANS SING ALOHA MY FIRST IMPRESSION OF YOU	Fats Waller Paul Campbell Caughey Roberts Ceele Burke Al Morgan Lee Young	piano and vocal trumpet clarinet and alto sax guitar bass drums
January, 1938	BLUE TURNING GREY OVER YOU HONEYSUCKLE ROSE	Fats Waller Herman Autrey Eugene Sedric Al Casey Cedric Wallace Slick Jones	piano and vocal trumpet clarinet and alto sax guitar bass drums
March 11, 1938	SOMETHING TELLS ME I LOVE TO WHISTLE YOU WENT TO MY HEAD FLORIDA FLO LOST AND FOUND DON'T TRY TO CRY YOUR WAY	Same personnel as January, 1938	
April 12, 1938	IN THE GLOAMING YOU HAD AN EVENING TO SPARE LET'S BREAK THE GOOD NEWS SKRONTCH I SIMPLY ADORE YOU THE SHEIK OF ARABY	Fats Waller Herman Autrey John Hamilton Nathaniel Williams George Robinson John Haughton	piano and vocal trumpet trumpet trumpet trombone trombone

	HOLD MY HAND	Eugene Sedric — sax
	INSIDE	Samuel Simmons — sax
		William Alsop — sax
		James Powell — sax
		Alfred Skerritt — sax
		Al Casey — guitar
		Cedric Wallace — bass
		Slick Jones — drums
July 1, 1938 New York City	THERE'S HONEY IN THE MOON TONIGHT	Fats Waller — piano and vocal
	IF I WERE YOU	Herman Autrey — trumpet
	WIDE OPEN SPACES	Al Casey — guitar
	ON THE BUMPY ROAD TO LOVE	Cedric Wallace — bass
	FAIR AND SQUARE	Slick Jones — drums
	WE, THE PEOPLE	Eugene Sedric — clarinet and alto sax
August 21, 1938 London, England	DON'T TRY YOUR JIVE ON ME	Fats Waller — organ and vocal
	FLAT FOOT FLOOGIE	Dave Wilkins — trumpet
	PENT UP IN A PENTHOUSE	George Chisholm — trombone
	MUSIC MAESTRO PLEASE	Alfie Kahn — clarinet and tenor sax
	A-TISKET-A-TASKET	Ian Sheppard — tenor sax and violin
	ANITA	Alan Ferguson — guitar
		Len Harrison — bass
		Harry Schneider — drums
	AIN'T MISBEHAVIN'	Same personnel as above with the substitution of: Edmundo Ross — drums
	SWING LOW SWEET CHARIOT	Fats Waller — organ
	ALL GOD'S CHILLUN GOT WINGS	
	GO DOWN MOSES	
	DEEP RIVER	
	WATER BOY	
	LONESOME ROAD	

Continued

201

Date and Place	Songs	Personnel	Instruments
August 21, 1938	THAT OLD FEELING I CAN'T GIVE YOU ANYTHING BUT LOVE	Adelaide Hall Fats Waller	vocal organ and vocal
September, 1938 London, England	SMOKE DREAMS OF YOU YOU CAN'T HAVE YOUR CAKE AND EAT IT	Fats Waller	organ and vocal
October 13, 1938	TWO SLEEPY PEOPLE I'LL NEVER FORGIVE MYSELF YOU LOOK GOOD TO ME TELL ME WITH YOUR KISSES YACHT CLUB SWING SHAME! SHAME!	Fats Waller Herman Autrey Al Casey Cedric Wallace Slick Jones Eugene Sedric	piano and vocal trumpet guitar bass drums clarinet and alto sax
December 7, 1938	LOVE, I'D GIVE MY LIFE FOR YOU I WISH I HAD YOU I'LL DANCE AT YOUR WEDDING IMAGINE MY SURPRISE I WON'T BELIEVE IT THE SPIDER AND THE FLY PATTY CAKE	Same personnel as October 13, 1938	
January 19, 1939	A GOOD MAN IS HARD TO FIND YOU OUT-SMARTED YOURSELF LAST NIGHT A MIRACLE HAPPENED GOOD FOR NOTHING BUT LOVE HOLD TIGHT KISS ME WITH YOUR EYES	Same personnel as October 13, 1938	
March 6, 1939	SWEET SUE I CAN'T GIVE YOU ANYTHING BUT LOVE	Gene Austin Fats Waller	vocal piano
March 9, 1939	YOU ASKED FOR IT—YOU GOT IT SOME RAINY DAY 'TAIN'T WHAT YOU DO GOT NO TIME STEP UP AND SHAKE MY HAND UNDECIDED	Same personnel as October 13, 1938	

REMEMBER WHO YOU PROMISED

Date	Title	Personnel	Instrument
April 3, 1939	LONDON SUITE	Fats Waller	piano
		Max Lewin	drums
June 13, 1939 London, England	LONDON SUITE	Fats Waller	piano
		Max Lewin	drums
Summer, 1939	HONEY HUSH	Fats Waller	piano and vocal
	I USED TO LOVE YOU	Herman Autrey	trumpet
	WAIT AND SEE	Chauncey Graham	tenor sax
	YOU MEET THE NICEST PEOPLE IN YOUR DREAMS	John Smith	guitar
	ANITA	Cedric Wallace	bass
	WHAT A PRETTY MISS	Larry Hinton	drums
August 2, 1939	THE MOON IS LOW	Fats Waller	piano and vocal
	HONEYSUCKLE ROSE	John Hamilton	trumpet
	SHEIK OF ARABY	John Smith	guitar
	B FLAT BLUES	Cedric Wallace	bass
	AIN'T MISBEHAVIN'	Slick Jones	drums
	NAGASAKI	Eugene Sedric	clarinet and tenor sax
	SWEET SUE		
	CRAZY 'BOUT MY BABY		
	SPIDER AND THE FLY		
	AFTER YOU'VE GONE		
	TEA FOR TWO	Fats Waller	piano
	POOR BUTTERFLY		
	ST. LOUIS BLUES		
	HANDFUL OF KEYS		
	HALLELUJAH!		
September, 1939	SQUEEZE ME	Fats Waller	piano and vocal
	BLESS YOU	John Hamilton	trumpet
	IT'S THE TUNE THAT COUNTS	John Smith	guitar
	ABDULLAH	Cedric Wallace	bass
	WHO'LL TAKE MY PLACE	Slick Jones	drums
	BOND STREET	Eugene Sedric	clarinet and tenor sax

Continued

Date and Place	Songs	Personnel	Instruments
November 3, 1939	IT'S YOU WHO TAUGHT IT TO ME SUITCASE SUSIE YOUR FEET'S TOO BIG YOU'RE LETTIN' THE GRASS GROW UNDER YOUR FEET DARKTOWN STRUTTERS' BALL	Same personnel as September, 1939	
	I CAN'T GIVE YOU ANYTHING BUT LOVE	Same personnel as September, 1939 with the addition of: Una Mae Carlisle	vocal
November 15, 1939 New York City	I'VE GOT A CRUSH ON YOU HOW LONG HAS THIS BEEN GOING ON? BUT NOT FOR ME	Max Kaminsky Pee Wee Russell Fats Waller Eddie Condon Artie Shapiro George Wettling Lee Wiley Brad Gowans (arranger)	cornet clarinet piano and celeste guitar bass drums vocal
	SOMEONE TO WATCH OVER ME	Lee Wiley Fats Waller	vocal organ
January 12, 1940	SWINGA DILLA STREET AT TWILIGHT OH FRENCHY CHEATIN' ON ME BLACK MARIA MIGHTY FINE THE MOON IS LOW (PART 1) THE MOON IS LOW (PART 2)	Fats Waller John Hamilton John Smith Charles Turner Slick Jones Eugene Sedirc	piano, organ, and vocal trumpet guitar bass drums clarinet and tenor sax

March 24, 1940
New York City

GEORGIA GRIND
OH SISTER! AIN'T THAT HOT?
DANCING FOOL
YOU'RE SOME PRETTY DOLL

Marty Marsala	cornet
George Brunis	trombone
Pee Wee Russell	clarinet
Fats Waller	piano
Eddie Condon	guitar
Artie Shapiro	bass
George Wettling	drums

April 11, 1940

OLD GRAN'DAD
FAT AND GREASY
LITTLE CURLY HAIR IN A HIGH CHAIR
SQUARE FROM DELAWARE
YOU RUN YOUR MOUTH
TOO TIRED
SEND ME JACKSON
EEP, IPE, WANNA PIECE OF PIE

Same personnel as
January 12, 1940

June 12, 1940

AT TWILIGHT

Same personnel as
January 12, 1940

July 16, 1940

STOP PRETENDING
I'LL NEVER SMILE AGAIN
MY MOMMIE SENT ME TO THE STORE
DRY BONES
"FATS" WALLER'S ORIGINAL E FLAT BLUES
STAYING AT HOME
HEY! STOP KISSING MY SISTER

Same personnel as
January 12, 1940

November 6, 1940
New York City

EVERYBODY LOVES MY BABY
I'M GONNA SALT AWAY SOME SUGAR
'TAINT NOBODY'S BIZNESS
ABERCROMBIE HAD A ZOMBIE
BLUE EYES
SCRAM

Same personnel as
January 12, 1940
with the addition of:

Fats Waller	celeste

and the substitution of:

Al Casey	guitar

Continued

Date and Place	Songs	Personnel	Instruments
January 2, 1941 Chicago	MAMACITA LIVER LIP JONES BUCKIN' THE DICE PANTIN' IN THE PANTHER ROOM CAME DOWN TO EARTH SHORTNIN' BREAD I REPENT	Fats Waller (remainder of personnel unknown)	piano and vocal remainder of personnel
March 20, 1941	DO YOU HAVE TO GO PAN-PAN THAT GETS IT MR. JOE YOU'RE GONNA BE SORRY ALL THAT MEAT AND NO POTATOES LET'S GET AWAY	Fats Waller John Hamilton Al Casey Cedric Wallace Slick Jones Eugene Sedric	piano and vocal trumpet guitar bass drums clarinet and alto sax
May 13, 1941	GEORGIA ON MY MIND ROCKIN' CHAIR CAROLINA SHOUT HONEYSUCKLE ROSE RING DEM BELLS	Fats Waller	piano
May 13, 1941	TWENTY-FOUR ROBBERS I UNDERSTAND SAD SAP SUCKER AM I HEADLINES IN THE NEWS	Same personnel as January 12, 1940	
July 1, 1941 Hollywood	CHANT OF THE GROOVE COME AND GET IT RUMP STEAK SERENADE GETTIN' MUCH LATELY? (AIN'T NOTHIN' TO IT)	Fats Waller (remainder of personnel unknown)	piano and vocal remainder of personnel
October 1, 1941 New York City	OH BABY, SWEET BABY BUCK JUMPING I WANNA HEAR SWING SONGS THE BELLS OF SAN RAQUEL	Fats Waller John Hamilton Al Casey	piano, vocal, and organ trumpet guitar

BESSIE, BESSIE, BESSIE
CLARINET MARMALADE

unknown	bass
Slick Jones	drums
Eugene Sedric	clarinet and tenor sax

December 26, 1941
New York City

WINTER WEATHER
CASH FOR YOUR TRASH
DON'T GIVE ME THAT JIVE
YOUR SOCKS DON'T MATCH

Fats Waller	piano and vocal
Herman Autrey	trumpet
Al Casey	guitar
Charles Turner	bass
Arthur Trappier	drums
Eugene Sedric	clarinet and tenor sax

March 16, 1942
New York City

WE NEED A LITTLE LOVE
YOU MUST BE LOSING YOUR MIND
REALLY FINE (TWO BITS)
JITTERBUG WALTZ

Fats Waller	piano and vocal
Courtney Williams	trumpet
John Hamilton	trumpet
Joe Thomas	trumpet
Herb Fleming	trombone
Bob Carrol	tenor sax
Al Casey	guitar
Cedric Wallace	bass
Arthur Trappier	drums
Eugene Sedric	clarinet and tenor sax
George Wilson	trombone
Lawrence Fields	tenor sax
G. R. James	tenor sax

July 13, 1942

BY THE LIGHT OF THE SILVERY MOON
SWING OUT TO VICTORY
UP JUMPED YOU WITH LOVE
ROMANCE A LA MODE

Fats Waller	piano
John Hamilton	trumpet
Deep River Boys	vocal
Arthur Trappier	drums
Cedric Wallace	bass
Al Casey	guitar
Eugene Sedric	saxes

Continued

Date and Place	Songs	Personnel	Instruments
January 23, 1943 from sound track of *Stormy Weather*	AIN'T MISBEHAVIN' MOPPIN' AND BOPPIN' THAT AIN'T RIGHT	Fats Waller Benny Carter Alton Moore Gene Porter Irving Ashby Slam Stewart Zutty Singleton Ada Brown	piano and vocal trumpet trombone clarinet and sax guitar bass drums vocal
September 23, 1943 Hollywood	AIN'T MISBEHAVIN'/TWO SLEEPY PEOPLE SLIGHTLY LESS THAN WONDERFUL/THERE'S A GAL IN MY LIFE THIS IS SO NICE IT MUST BE ILLEGAL MARTINIQUE—JIVE WALLER JIVE HALLELUJAH REEFER SONG THAT'S WHAT THE BIRD SAID TO ME	Fats Waller	piano and vocal
	SOLITUDE BOUNCIN' ON A V-DISC SOMETIMES I FEEL LIKE A MOTHERLESS CHILD	Fats Waller	organ

Fats Waller's Published Songs

Year and Title of Composition	Collaborators
1924	
HOME ALONE BLUES	John Holmes
PLEASE TELL ME WHY	Ed Adams
FLAT TIRE PAPA, MAMA'S GONNA GIVE YOU THE AIR	Spencer Williams
IN HARLEM'S ARABY	Joseph Trent
STRIVERS ROW	Jack Moore
WHAT CAN BE WRONG WITH ME	Joseph Trent
1925	
THE HEART THAT ONCE BELONGED TO ME BELONGS TO SOMEONE ELSE	Clarence Williams
ANYBODY HERE WANT TO TRY MY CABBAGE	Andy Razaf
KISS MA AGAIN	Clarence Williams
AN AWFUL LOT MY GAL AIN'T GOT	Spencer Williams
SQUEEZE ME	Clarence Williams
1926	
SEÑORITA MINE	Spencer Williams, Clarence Williams, and Eddie Rector
GEORGIA BO-BO	Joseph Trent
THAT FLORIDA LOW DOWN	J. Fred Coots and Joseph Trent
OLD FOLKS SHUFFLE	Clarence Williams
MIDNIGHT STOMP	Clarence Williams
CHARLESTON HOUND	Clarence Williams, Eddie Rector, and Spencer Williams
1927	
I'M MORE THAN SATISFIED	Raymond Klages
ST. LOUIS SHUFFLE	Jack Pettis
MEDITATION	
COME ON AND STOMP, STOMP, STOMP	Chris Smith and Irving Mills
I'M GOIN' HUNTIN'	J. C. Johnson
SHAKE YOUR FEET	Irving Mills
NOBODY KNOWS	Bennett Carter and B. Allen
A DARKIE'S LAMENT	
FAT MAN BLUES	
ALLIGATOR CRAWL	
1928	
CANDIED SWEETS	Jack Pettis
WILLOW TREE	Andy Razaf
GOT MYSELF ANOTHER JOCKEY NOW	Andy Razaf
LOVIE LEE	Andy Razaf
WHITEMAN STOMP	Clarence Williams
HOW JAZZ WAS BORN	Andy Razaf
1929	
MY MAN IS GOOD FOR NOTHIN' BUT LOVE	Andy Razaf and Harry Brooks
IF YOU LIKE ME LIKE I LIKE YOU	Clarence Williams and Spencer Williams
AIN'T MISBEHAVIN'	Andy Razaf and Harry Brooks
I'VE GOT A FEELING I'M FALLING	Billy Rose and Harry Link
MY FATE IS IN YOUR HANDS	Andy Razaf
ZONKY	Andy Razaf
HONEYSUCKLE ROSE	Andy Razaf
WHAT DID I DO TO BE SO BLACK AND BLUE	H. Brooks and Andy Razaf
SWEET SAVANNAH SUE	H. Brooks and Andy Razaf
CAN'T WE GET TOGETHER	H. Brooks and Andy Razaf
SNAKE HIP DANCE	H. Brooks and Andy Razaf
THAT RHYTHM MAN	H. Brooks and Andy Razaf

Continued

Year and Title of Composition	Collaborators
OFF-TIME	H. Brooks and Andy Razaf
WHY AM I ALONE WITH NO ONE TO LOVE	Spencer Williams and Andy Razaf
I'M NOT WORRYING	Clarence Williams
SAY IT WITH YOUR FEET	H. Brooks and Andy Razaf
DIXIE CINDERELLA	H. Brooks and Andy Razaf
SIX OR SEVEN TIMES	Irving Mills

1930

GONE	Harry Link and Andy Razaf
ROLLIN' DOWN THE RIVER	Stanley Adams
BLUE TURNING GRAY OVER YOU	Andy Razaf
KEEP A SONG IN YOUR SOUL	Alex Hill
PRISONER OF LOVE	Andy Razaf

1931

LITTLE BROWN BETTY	Alex Hill
I'M CRAZY ABOUT MY BABY, AND MY BABY'S CRAZY 'BOUT ME	Alex Hill
HEART OF STONE	Alex Hill
TAKE IT FROM ME, I'M TAKIN' TO YOU	Stanley Adams
CONCENTRATIN' ON YOU	Andy Razaf
THE ICE MAN LIVES IN AN ICE HOUSE	R. Duromo and Elmer S. Hughes
AFRICAN RIPPLES	
RIDIN' BUT WALKIN'	

1932

KEEPIN' OUT OF MISCHIEF NOW	Andy Razaf
BUDDIE	Andy Razaf
IF IT AIN'T LOVE	Donald Redman and Andy Razaf
RADIO PAPA, BROADCASTIN' MAMA	Andy Razaf
WHEN GABRIEL BLOWS HIS HORN	Andy Razaf
LONESOME ME	Con Conrad and Andy Razaf
GOTTA BE, GONNA BE MINE	Andy Razaf
OH! YOU SWEET THING	Andy Razaf
STRANGE AS IT SEEMS	Andy Razaf
THAT'S WHERE THE SOUTH BEGINS	George Brown
ANGELINE	George Brown
MY HEART'S AT EASE	Joe Young
SHELTERED BY THE STARS, CRADLED BY THE MOON, COVERED BY THE NIGHT	Joe Young
I DIDN'T DREAM IT WAS LOVE	Elliot Grennard and Con Conrad
OLD YAZOO	
HOW CAN YOU FACE ME	Andy Razaf
THE APPLE OF MY EYE	Joe Young
I'M NOW PREPARED TO TELL THE WORLD IT'S YOU!	Andy Razaf
BLOWING OF THE BREEZE BLEW YOU INTO MY ARMS	Spencer Williams
WHERE THE DEW DROPS KISS THE MORNING	Spencer Williams
GLORIES GOOD MORNIN'	

1933

AIN'T-CHA GLAD	Andy Razaf
TALL TIMBER	Andy Razaf
SITTIN' UP WAITIN' FOR YOU	Andy Razaf
DOIN' WHAT I PLEASE	Andy Razaf
HANDFUL OF KEYS	Andy Razaf

1934

SWING ON MISSISSIPPI	Ned Washington
CLOTHES LINE BALLET	

Continued

VIPERS DRAG
EFFERVESCENT
ACE IN THE HOLE — Frank Crumit and Bartley Costello

1935
NUMB FUMBLIN'
THE PANIC IS ON — George and Bert Clarke and Winston Tharp
FUNCTIONIZIN' — Irving Mills

1936
SMASHING THIRDS
STEALIN' APPLES — Andy Razaf
I CAN SEE YOU ALL OVER THE PLACE — Clarence Williams
SUGAR ROSE — Phil Ponce
WAIT AND SEE — Andy Razaf

1937
OUR LOVE WAS MEANT TO BE — Alex Hill and Joe Davis
LOST LOVE — Andy Razaf

1938
I HAD TO DO IT — Andy Razaf
YOU'RE MY IDEAL — Spencer Williams
INSIDE THIS HEART OF MINE — J. C. Johnson
ON RAINY DAYS — Andy Razaf
HOLD MY HAND — J. C. Johnson
I GOT LOVE — Spencer Williams
COTTAGE IN THE RAIN — Spencer Williams
WHAT A PRETTY MISS — Spencer Williams
NOW THERE, RIGHT HERE — Spencer Williams
MOONLIGHT MOOD — J. C. Johnson
THE SPIDER AND THE FLY, POOR FLY, BYE-BYE — Andy Razaf and J. C. Johnson
PATTY CAKE, PATTY CAKE — Andy Razaf and J. C. Johnson
I CAN'T FORGIVE YOU — J. C. Johnson
UNDERCURRENT

SWINCOPATIONS

BACH UP TO ME
BLACK RASPBERRY JAM
FRACTIOUS FINGERING
LATCH ON
LOUNGING AT THE WALDORF
PASWONKY

1939
HONEY HUSH — Ed Kirkeby
SAY YES — J. C. Johnson and Andy Razaf
CHOO CHOO — Eugene Seebic and Andy Razaf
ANITA

1940
HAPPY FEELING
STAYIN' AT HOME — Andy Razaf
MIGHTY FINE — Andy Razaf
BOND STREET

1941
ALL THAT MEAT AND NO POTATOES — Ed Kirkeby
BLUE VELVET — Spencer Williams

Continued

211

PIANO ANTICS

CHINA JUMPS
SNEAKIN' HOME
PALM GARDEN
WAN'RIN AROUN'
FALLING CASTLE

1942
THE JITTERBUG WALTZ
CASH FOR YOUR TRASH   Ed Kirkeby
FATS WALLER ET LE SWING

1943
WHEN THE NYLONS BLOOM AGAIN   George Marion

EARLY TO BED

THE LADIES WHO SING WITH A BAND   George Marion
THERE'S A MAN IN MY LIFE   George Marion
THIS IS SO NICE   George Marion
SLIGHTLY LESS THAN WONDERFUL   George Marion
HI DE HI HO IN HARLEM   George Marion

1945
YACHT CLUB SWING   J. C. Johnson and Herman Autrey

BOOGIE WOOGIE (SUITE FOR PIANO)

BOOGIE WOOGIE BLUES
BOOGIE WOOGIE STOMP
BOOGIE WOOGIE RAG
BOOGIE WOOGIE JUMP

1946
MOPPIN' AND BOPPIN'   Benny Carter and Ed Kirkeby

1947
MINOR DRAG

LONDON SUITE

WHITECHAPEL
LIMEHOUSE
SOHO
PICCADILLY
CHELSEA
BOND STREET

Fats Waller's Unpublished Songs

Year and Title of Composition	Collaborators
1923	
ALL ALONE	
BLUES NEVER DIE	
DONE GONE MAD	
DON'T WANT YOU NO MORE	
WILD CAT BLUES	Clarence Williams
IT SEEMS TO ME	
1924	
MY BABY'S COMIN' BACK HOME	Joseph Trent
MY JAMAICA LOVE	Andy Razaf
MY MAN CURES THE BLUES	Joseph Trent
SWEET BABY	Clarence Williams
SWEETIE DON'T GROW SOUR ON ME	Charles O'Flynn
THE BLUE STRAIN	Spencer Williams
THAT'S MY MAN	Joseph Trent
MY SWEET BABY IRENE	Andy Razaf and Spencer Williams
PLEASE TAKE ME BACK	Joseph Trent
ROCK ME JUST AS A SWEET DADDY SHOULD	Andy Razaf
STROLLIN' ROUN THE TOWN	Joseph Trent
SHUT YO' MOUF	Andy Razaf
ICE COLD PAPA, MAMA'S GONNA MELT YOU DOWN	Andy Razaf
I MAY BE A LITTLE GREEN, BUT I AIN'T NO FOOL	Spencer Williams
I'M GOING RIGHT ALONG	Joseph Trent
IN HARLEM	Joseph Trent
IN MY BABY'S EYES	Joseph Trent
IN THE SPRINGTIME	Joseph Trent
MANDY, I'M JUST WILD ABOUT YOU	Joseph Trent and Clarence Williams
HELLO ATLANTA TOWN	Joseph Trent and Clarence Williams
THE SHORT TRAIL BECAME A LONG TRAIL	Andy Razaf
ANY DAY THE SUN DON'T SHINE	Andy Razaf
ORIENTAL TONES	
CALL THE PLUMBER IN	Andy Razaf
WHEN YOU'RE TIRED OF ME, JUST LET ME KNOW	Andy Razaf
OLD FASHIONED SUSIE'S BLUES	Clarence Williams and Andy Razaf
RAMBLIN' PAPA BLUES	Spencer Williams
SLAVING	Clarence Williams
WHAT CAN BE WRONG WITH ME	Joseph Trent
BLOODY RAZOR BLUES	Spencer Williams
BULLET WOUND BLUES	Spencer Williams
FRIENDLESS BLUES	
1925	
CAMP MEETIN' STOMP	
BROTHER BEN	Spencer Williams
HOUSE PARTY STOMP	
WORKIN' WOMAN BLUES	Spencer Williams
BALL AND CHAIN BLUES	Andy Razaf
WALLER-ING AROUND	
1926	
THAT STRUTTIN' EDDIE OF MINE	Eddie Rector and Clarence Williams
GREAT SCOTT	Henry Troy
BEETHOVEN'S SANGWATTNI	
CRAZY 'BOUT THAT MAN I LOVE	Spencer Williams and Clarence Williams
CONGO LOU	
LONESOME ONE	Clarence Williams and Andy Razaf
LEVEE LAND	

Continued

Year and Title of Composition	Collaborators
1927	
RUSTY PAIL BLUES	
WRINGIN' AND TWISTIN'	Frank Trumbauer and Joseph Trent
LONG, DEEP AND WIDE	
FATS WALLER STOMP	T. Morris and C. Irvis
LENOX AVENUE BLUES	
SAVANNAH BLUES	Thomas Morris
MESSIN' AROUND WITH THE BLUES	Phil Worde
SOOTHIN' SYRUP STOMP	
SLOPPY WATER BLUES	
1928	
MONKEY TALK	
DIGAH'S STOMP	
ONE O'CLOCK BLUES	Bud Allen and Walter Bishop
HOG MAN STOMP	
I HOPE YOU'RE SATISFIED	Clarence Williams
LION'S ROAR	
PLEASE TAKE ME OUT OF JAIL	Thomas Morris
1929	
LAUGHING WATER	Harry Brooks and Andy Razaf
GODDESS OF RAIN	Harry Brooks and Andy Razaf
TOUCHDOWN	
FIND OUT WHAT THEY LIKE	Andy Razaf
WALTZ DIVINE	Harry Brooks and Andy Razaf
THAT WAS MY OWN IDEA	Billy Moll
HEAVY SUGAR	Andy Razaf
VALENTINE STOMP	
TROUBLE	
THAT JUNGLE JAMBOREE	Harry Brooks and Andy Razaf
GLADYSE	
I NEED SOMEONE LIKE YOU	
LOOKIN' GOOD BUT FEELIN' BAD	Lester A. Santly
NO WONDER	Morey Davidson
1930	
HARLEM FUSS	
WON'T YOU GET OFF IT, PLEASE	
BE MODERN, THERE'S HAPPINESS IN STORE FOR YOU	Alexander Hill
JO JO JOSEPHINE	Billy Moll
1931	
MY FEELIN'S ARE HURT	
THAT'S ALL	
CRUMBS OF YOUR LOVE	Minto Cato and Andy Razaf
1932	
HUNGRY	Andy Razaf and Joe Young
SINCE WON LONG HOP TOOK ONE LONG HOP TO CHINA	Jack Meskill
ONLY SOMETIMES	Joe Young
BREAKIN' MY HEART	Spencer Williams
MY GIFT OF DREAMS	Edgar Dowell and Andy Razaf
DOWN ON THE DELTA	Sam H. Stept and Spencer Williams
DO ME A FAVOR, LEND ME A KISS	Spencer Williams and Andy Razaf
1933	
ON SUNDAY, WHEN WE GATHERED 'ROUND THE ORGAN	Alexander Hill and Andy Razaf

Continued

Year and Title of Composition	Collaborators
SLOWER THAN MOLASSES	Andy Razaf
I'VE GOT YOU WHERE I WANT YOU	Spencer Williams
1935	
RUSSIAN FANTASY	
1936	
SHAKIN' IT ALL NIGHT LONG	Spencer Williams
BENNY SENT ME	Spencer Williams
1937	
JOHN HENRY	Andy Razaf
SWINGIN' HOUND	Eddie Rector, Clarence Williams, and Spencer Williams
1938	
BLUER THAN THE OCEAN BLUES	Spencer Williams and Tommie Connor
I'M GONNA FALL IN LOVE	Spencer Williams
IF I MEANT SOMETHING TO YOU	J. C. Johnson
SOLID ECLIPSE	J. C. Johnson
WHAT'S YOUR NAME	J. C. Johnson
JEALOUS OF ME	Andy Razaf
HOW CAN I, WITH YOU IN MY HEART	J. C. Johnson
HOW YA BABY	J. C. Johnson
WHAT WILL I DO IN THE MORNING	J. C. Johnson
THE JOINT IS JUMPIN'	Andy Razaf and J. C. Johnson
HOPELESS LOVE AFFAIR	Andy Razaf
I'M SAVIN' UP MY PENNIES	
1939	
WALKIN' THE FLOOR	Andy Razaf
SMOTHER ME WITH YOUR LOVE	
1940	
OLD GRAND DAD	
1941	
I REPENT	
1942	
MY SONG OF HATE	Andy Razaf
YOU GOTTA SWING IT	
IT PAYS TO ADVERTISE	
SING OUT	Manny Kurtz
1943	
SCRAM, SCOUNDREL, SCRAM	Ned Washington
ON YOUR MARK	George Marion
A GIRL SHOULD NEVER RIPPLE WHEN SHE BENDS	George Marion
THERE'S YES IN THE AIR	George Marion
GET AWAY YOUNG MAN	George Marion
SUPPLE COUPLE	George Marion
ME AND MY OLD WORLD CHARM	George Marion
LONG TIME NO SONG	George Marion
1944	
AT TWILIGHT	Anita Waller
SWING OUT TO VICTORY	Ed Kirkeby
UP JUMPED YOU WITH LOVE	Ed Kirkeby
YOU MUST BE LOSIN' YOUR MIND	Ed Kirkeby
WE NEED A LITTLE LOVE, THAT'S ALL	Ed Kirkeby

Continued

Year and Title of Composition	Collaborators
DON'T GIVE ME THAT JIVE,	
COME ON WITH THE COME ON	Ed Kirkeby
DO YOU HAVE TO GO	Ed Kirkeby
BESSIE, BESSIE, BESSIE	Ed Kirkeby
COME AND GET IT	Ed Kirkeby
DEAR LITTLE MOUNTAIN SWEETHEART	Ed Kirkeby
WALLER'S ORIGINAL E FLAT BLUES	Ed Kirkeby
RUMP STEAK SERENADE	Ed Kirkeby
SAD SAPSUCKER	Ed Kirkeby
1945	
YOU CAN'T HAVE YOUR CAKE AND EAT IT	Spencer Williams
BLUES IDIOM	
FUSSIN' AROUND	
I'M LOOKING FOR A RAINBOW	
LOOK-A-HERE	
MARCH OF THE SPADES	
ONION TIME	
PARAPHERNALIA	
PEEKIN' IN SEEK	
ASBESTOS	
1946	
IN THE EVENING BY THE MOONLIGHT	Spencer Williams
MY LOVE GETS HUNGRY TOO	Ed Kirkeby
DID-JA	Ed Kirkeby
1947	
CHOCOLATE BAR	
BLACK CAT RAG	
1949	
I HATE TO LEAVE YOU NOW	Harry Link and Dorothy Dick
1953	
WHERE THE HONEYSUCKLE GROWS	George Thorne
1954	
BREEZIN'	
AM ARMFUL OF YOU	

FATS WALLER'S PIANO ROLLS
(Recorded Circa 1923–1927)

GOT TO COOL MY DOGGIES NOW
LAUGHIN' CRYIN' BLUES
YOUR TIME NOW
SNAKE HIPS
'TAIN'T NOBODY'S BIZNESS IF I DO
PAPA BETTER WATCH YOUR STEP
THE HAITIAN BLUES
MAMA'S GOT THE BLUES
LAST GO ROUND BLUES
CLEARING HOUSE BLUES
JAIL HOUSE BLUES
SQUEEZE ME
18TH STREET STRUT
WILDCAT BLUES
DO IT MR. SO AND SO
DON'T TRY TO TAKE MY MAN AWAY
IF I COULD BE WITH YOU (played with James P. Johnson)
A NEW KIND OF MAN WITH A NEW KIND OF LOVE FOR ME
I'M CRAZY 'BOUT MY BABY
I'M COMIN' VIRGINIA
NOBODY BUT MY BABY
YOU CAN'T DO WHAT MY LAST MAN DID

"Ain't Misbehavin'"

Fats Waller's version of one of his most famous songs.

AIN'T MISBEHAVIN'

("FATS" WALLER'S CONCEPTION)

Ain't Misbehavin'

"Anita"

Fats Waller's manuscript of the song he wrote for his second wife, Anita.

— ANITA —

Thomas "Fats" Waller

"Got Religion in My Soul"

A previously unpublished song by Fats Waller in his manuscript.

GOT RELIGION IN MY SOUL

MUSIC THOS. WALLER

229

Index

Note: Only Fats Waller's major compositions—those cited extensively—are listed herein. See the end-of-book sections for a complete accounting. *Index prepared by Astor Indexers, N.Y., N.Y.*

Abyssinian Baptist Church, 2, 3, 177–178
Adams, Cedric, 154
Adrian's Tap Room, New York, 111–112
"Ain't Misbehavin'," xvi, 84, 85–87, 93, 181
Allen, Buddy, xvi, 42, 52, 101
Anderson, Eddie "Rochester," xv, 151
Anderson, Murray, 158
Andrew, Dope, 40
Apollo Theatre, 115, 124, 137, 150, 156, 163–164
Armstrong, Louis "Satchmo," 52, 61–62, 70, 71, 85, 87, 93, 127, 130, 177
Asmussen, Sven, 135
Austin, Gene, 77–78, 90
Autrey, Herman, 112, 114, 118, 136, 142

Bailey, Buster, 71
Banner Records, 107
Barron's, New York, 29
Basie, William "Count," 36–37, 41, 60, 147, 169, 182
Baskette, James, 85
Baxter, Warner, 120
Beachcomber, Omaha, 158, 159
Beardslee, Harry, 137
Bechet, Sidney, 49
Benford, Tommy, 40
Berlin, Irving, 18, 56, 75, 164
Berigan, Bunny, 127
Blake, Eubie, xii, xiv, xvi, 25, 28, 31, 45, 64
Block, Martin, 130, 145, 168, 169
Bloom, Marty, 101, 106
Blythe, Jimmy, 30

Bolden, Arnold, 127, 128
Bolling, Pat, 6
Boogie woogie, x, 126, 136
Bornstein, Saul, 100–101
Boyette, Raymond "Lippy," 37, 38, 97
Bradford, Perry, xiv, 43, 59, 61
Brecher, Leo, 42
Brooks, Russell, 17, 26–28, 37–38, 40, 41
Brooks, Wilson, 26, 27
Brown, James, 169
Bryant, Freddy "Harmony King," xii, 18, 25
Buck, Gene, 179
Burgess, Charley, 52
Bushell, Garvin, 74, 96

Calloway, Blanche, 74
Calloway, Cab, 85
Capitol club, New York, 41
Capone, Al, 62–63
Carle, Frankie, 146
Carlisle, Una Mae, 108–110, 138
Carnegie Hall, 7, 75–76, 152–153
Carroll, Bob, 114
Carter, Benny, 88, 155, 160
Casey, Al, 112, 125, 130, 136, 146, 168
Chapman, Louis, 151
Charlie Turner Band, 113, 114
Cole, Cozy, 130
Coll, Vincent "Mad Dog," 105
Columbia Records, 74, 95–96, 101
Condon, Eddie, 84–85, 90, 101, 106, 107, 120–121, 127
Connie's Inn, 55, 81, 88–89, 105–106

Conrad, Con, 73
Cook, J. Lawrence, 45–46, 52
Coots, Fred, 145, 168, 169
Costello, Frank, 73
Crawford, Jesse, 88, 95
Creamer, Henry, 73

Daisy Chain, New York, 60–61
Davis, Joe, 89, 95, 96, 101, 109
Desmond, Florence, 133
Dewey, Thomas E., 60
Dial, Harry, 112
Diamond, Jack "Legs," 73
Donaldson, Don, 130, 131, 142, 152
Dorsey, Tommy, 101, 112, 127
Down Beat Room, Chicago, 153, 154
Downes, Marie, 19–20, 36
Drew, Drusilla, 96
Driver, Bobby, 119, 141
Duncan, Hank, 113, 114, 115

Early to Bed, 156–158, 181
Ellington, Duke, xi, xii, xiii, 31, 56, 101
Elliot, Ernest, 40

Fats Waller and His Buddies, 85, 88, 90
Fats Waller and His Rhythm, 112, 113,
    116–119, 126–131, 141–147, 182
Faye, Alice, 120
Foster, Pops, 107
Freeman, Bud, 96, 101

Gains, Charlie, 88
Gant, Willie, xii, 31
Garlund, Nils T., 56, 86–87, 158, 159
Gershwin, George, xiii, 18, 30, 65, 75, 106,
    110–111, 136, 144, 150, 153, 165
Godowsky, Leopold, 65, 74
Goodman, Benny, 95, 127
Gould, Walter, xii
Green, Eddie, 85
Guinan, Texas, 136

Hager, Fred, 43–45
Hall, Adelaide, 96, 97, 133, 134
Handy, Katharine, 76
Handy, W. C., xiv, 44, 75–76
Hardin, Lil, 70
Hardwick, Otto, 88, 90, 96
Harper, Leonard, 65, 85, 86, 88–89
Harris, Fats, xii
Harris, Reuben, 20, 97
Haughton, Jimmy, 130, 131
Hawkins, Coleman, 52, 65, 70, 88, 90, 144
Henderson, Fletcher, 51–52, 65–66, 70, 164
Henderson, Stephen "Beetle," xii, 30, 31

Heywood, Donald, 178
Higgenbotham, J. C., 90
Hill, Alex, 96
Hines, Earl "Fatha," 71, 144
Hines, Jimmy, 77, 84
His Master's Voice, 133, 134, 139
"Honeysuckle Rose," xvi, 82–83, 181
Hooray for Love, 116, 120
Hopkins, Claude, 178
Horne, Lena, 155, 169, 182
Hot Chocolates, 85–87, 93, 156
Hotfeet Club, New York, 96
Howell, Bert, 73
Hunter, Alberta, 61, 70, 76, 96

"I'm Gonna Sit Right Down and Write Myself
    a Letter," 117
Immerman, Connie, 13, 55, 81, 83, 85, 93,
    105–106
Immerman, George, 13, 55, 81, 83, 93,
    105–106

Jackson, Cliff, xii, 31
Jam Session at Victor, 127
Jimmy Johnson Orchestra, 90
Jimmy Ryan's, New York, 136
Johnson, J. C. (James), 58, 129, 146, 178
Johnson, James, Jr., 168
Johnson, James P., x–xvi, 12, 17, 26–31,
    33, 35, 39–40, 45–46, 51, 64, 72–76,
    90, 97–98, 101, 106, 168, 178
Johnson, Lil, 29, 168
Johnson, Myra, 118–119, 130
Johnson, Oceola, 168
"Joint Is Jumping, The," 129
Jones, Anna, 61
Jones, "Slick," 128
Joplin, Scott, 25
Joseph, "One Leg" Willie, xii
Junior Blackbirds, 65

Keep Shufflin', 72–76, 156
Kentucky Club, New York, 56–57
King of Burlesque, The, 120, 125
Kirk, Andy, 178
Kirkeby, Wallace "Ed," 128–139, 141–142,
    146, 149, 152, 153, 155–158,
    175–178, 181, 182
Kollmar, Richard, 156, 175, 179
Kortlander, Max, 45–46
Krupa, Gene, 88, 90
Kyle, Billy, 136–137

La Guardia, Fiorello, 60
Lafayette Theatre, New York, 42, 55, 58, 59
Lambert, Donald, xii

Leroy's, New York, 29, 39–40
Lewin, Max, 139
Lewis, Bert, 56–57
Lewis, Katharine Handy, 61, 62
Lewis, Ted, 95–96
Lincoln Theatre, New York, 18–21, 30, 36–37, 42, 55, 58
Load of Coal, 81–84, 85
Logan, Ella, 112
London Suite, 139, 181
Louis, Joe, 170
Luciano, Lucky, 73, 94
Lyles, Aubrey, 64, 72, 74

Macomber, Ken, 59, 65
Maines, George H., 55–58, 61, 63–64, 66, 69, 70, 84, 85, 87, 106, 147
Major, Addie, 40
Marks, John, 139
Martin, Sara, xi, 43–44, 45
McDonough, Dick, 127
McHugh, Jimmy, 164
McKinney's Cotton Pickers, 90
McLean, Richard "Abba Labba," xii, 25, 28
McManus, George, 77
Meyers, Hazel, 61
Miley, Bubber, 89
Miller, Bernard, 181
Miller, Flournoy, 12, 64, 72, 74
Miller, Glenn, 127
Miller, Max, 133
Miller, Morton, 181
Mills, Florence, 73
Mills, Irving, 87, 155
Mills Music, 87, 108
Mitroupolos, Dimitri, 152, 154
Monk, Thelonius, xiii
Moore, Alton, 155
Morgan, Helen, 136
Morris, Thomas, 70, 73
Morton, Jelly Roll, 66, 94
Mullins, Mazie, 18, 19
Murray, Kitty, 146

Nicholas, Anne, 72–73

Oakie, Jack, 120
Oberstein, Eli, 127
Official Films, 149
Okeh Records, xi, xiv, 43–44, 49, 88
Oliver, King, 90
Owens, Jesse, 135

Paderewski, Ignace, 7
Paine, Bennie, 94
Paley, William, 110–111

Panassie, Hughes, 100
Panther Room, Chicago, 144, 153
"Paramount on Parade," 95
Paramount Theatre, New York, 88
Parker, Leroy, 40
Payton, Phillip, 3
Peer, Ralph, xiv, 43–45, 65, 69, 73, 74, 84, 106
Piano rolls, xiv, 27, 45–46
Pickett, "Old Man," xii
Ponce, Phil, 106–107, 109, 110, 112–115, 117, 119, 120, 124, 127–128, 141–142
Porter, Gene, 155
Powell, Adam Clayton, Jr., 69, 178–179
Powell, Adam Clayton, Sr., 179
Powell, Rudy, 114, 116
Prime, Albert, 96
Pyle, Harry, 39, 40

QRS, 45–46

"Radio Roundup," 96
Raye, Martha, 112
Raymond, Gene, 116
Razaf, Andy, xvi, 50–51, 53, 58, 59, 72, 73, 75, 81–83, 85, 86, 89, 96, 126, 129, 178, 179
Redman, Don, 51, 52, 61, 65, 70, 88, 90, 105, 114, 152, 178
Regal Theatre, Chicago, 88, 94–95
Reisenfeld, Hugo, 57
Rent parties, 5, 30–31, 37–38, 40, 42
RKO, 115–116, 120
Robbins, Jack, 154
Roberts, Luckey, xii, xiv, xvi, 12, 28, 29, 31, 45
Robinson, Bill "Bojangles," 56, 116, 155
Robinson, Jackie, 169
Rollini, Adrian, 111
Ross, Edmundo, 133
Rothstein, Arnold, 72–73, 75–77
Runyon, Damon, 72
Russell, Pee Wee, 101, 107

Sampson, Edgar, 7
Saunders, Gertrude, 64
Schiffman, Frank, 42, 59–60, 65, 115, 124
Schultz, Arthur "Dutch," 105
Schumach, Murray, 12, 98
Scott, Hazel, 182
Scott, James, 25
Sedric, Eugene, 112, 113, 114, 136, 142, 145
Sewell, Willie "Egghead," xii
Shaw, Artie, 101
Shepherd, Caroline, 166
Shepherd, George, 170

Shepherd, Herman "Buster," 128, 131, 137, 141–147, 150, 155, 168
Shepherd, Mother, 61, 63, 76, 145, 167
Shuffle Along, 64
Siders, Irving, 124–125
Singleton, Zutty, 89, 106, 107, 130, 155
Sissle, Noble, 64
Smith, Bessie, xiii, 44, 115, 124
Smith, Jabbo, 74, 85
Smith, Mamie, xiv, 43
Smith, One Leg Willie, 18, 25
Smith, Willie "The Lion," xii, xvi, xvii, 17, 25–26, 30–33, 35, 39–41, 51, 97–98, 101–102, 106, 111–112, 168, 169, 180
Sothern, Anne, 116
Spanier, Muggsy, 96
Stewart, Slam, 155
Stinette, Juanita, 73
Stormy Weather, 155–156
Stride piano, xi, xiii, 25–26
Styne, Jule, 116

Tan Topics, 65
Tate, Erskine, 70–71
Tatum, Art, 96–98, 127
Taylor, Billy, 112
Taylor, Eva, 43, 49, 51, 90, 168
Teagarden, Jack, 88, 90, 101, 127, 130
Ted Lewis Band, 95
Thompson, Johnny, 74
Tibbs, Leroy, xii
Todd, Clarence, 58, 73
Trinity Church, 13, 69
Turk, William, xii
Turner, Charlie, 145
Turpin, Tom, 25
Twentieth Century Fox, 120, 125, 155

Valentine, Hazel, 60
Victor Talking Machine Company, 65–66, 69–70, 84, 87–90, 93–94, 112, 114–118, 127, 149, 152

WABC Radio Station, 111
Walker, Frank, 95
Walker, Jimmy, 96
Wallace, Cedric, 130
Waller, Adeline Lockett (mother), 1–8, 11–14, 17–18, 21–22, 134
Waller, Adolph (grandfather), 13
Waller, Alfred Winslow (brother), 2
Waller, Anita Rutherford (second wife), 61, 63–64, 70–73, 76–78, 93–95, 99, 101, 106, 108–109, 131–134, 144, 150–151, 156, 157, 167, 171, 177, 181
Waller, Charles A. (brother), 2

Waller, Edith Hatchett (first wife), 20–21, 35–41, 44, 51, 58–59, 71, 76, 87, 117, 178, 180–181
Waller, Edith Salome (sister), 2, 22, 145, 166
Waller, Edward Lawrence (brother), 2, 12, 22, 124, 137, 166
Waller, Edward Martin (father), 1–2, 4–7, 12–14, 18, 21–22, 26, 27, 35, 61, 71, 77
Waller, Esther (sister), 2
Waller, Mary Naomi (sister), 2, 3–6, 8, 11, 13, 22, 35, 61, 77, 131, 178; *see also* Washington, (May) Naomi Waller
Waller, Ronald (son), 81, 88, 109, 110, 116, 119, 123, 131, 165, 166, 168, 170–172, 177, 180, 181
Waller, Ruth Adeline (sister), 2
Waller, Samuel (brother), 2
Waller, Thomas, Jr. (son), 40, 45, 178, 180
Waller, Thomas "Fats"
  at Apollo Theatre, 115, 124, 137, 150, 156, 163–164
  Armstrong, Louis and, 52, 62, 70, 71
  Basie, Count and, 36–37, 169
  Berlin, Irving and, 56
  birth, 2
  on boogie woogie, x, 126, 136
  in Britain, 132–134, 138–139
  Brooks, Russell and, 26–27, 38
  Capone, Al and, 62–63
  Carlisle, Una Mae and, 108–110
  Carnegie Hall concert, 152–153
  childhood, 3–8, 11–14
  as composer, xvi, 49–51, 53, 65, 72–74, 81–87, 129, 146, 156
  Condon, Eddie and, 84–85, 120–121
  at Connie's Inn, 55, 105–106
  death, 176–177
  discrimination against, 11, 78, 159, 169
  drinking, 40, 42, 100, 124, 128, 129, 143, 151, 160, 165
  Early to Bed, 156–158, 181
  early piano playing, xi, 5–7
  education, 7
  finances, 52–53, 58–59, 76–77, 87, 117, 123–124
  in France, 99–101, 134–135
  funeral, 178–180
  Gershwin, George and, 30, 110–111, 144, 150
  Henderson, Fletcher and, 51–52, 65
  Hot Chocolates, 85–87, 93
  in jail, 59, 76–77
  Johnson, James P. and, xiii, 26–30, 33, 39–40, 45–46
  Keep Shufflin', 72–76

at Kentucky Club, 56–57
at Lafayette Theatre, 42, 55, 58, 59
at Leroy's, 39–40
at Lincoln Theatre, 18–21, 30, 36–37, 42, 55, 58
Load of Coal, 81–84, 85
London Suite, 139, 181
Maines, George and, 55–58, 63–64, 70, 106
memorial concert for, 182
movies of, x, 116, 120, 125, 155–156
nickname, 8
parents, relationship with, 13, 14, 21–22, 26, 27, 36, 61
physical appearance, 8
radio broadcasts, 51, 56, 95–96, 106–113, 124
Razaf, Andy and, 50–51, 53, 72, 73, 75, 81–83, 85, 86, 89
recordings, xv–xvi, 45–46, 58, 61, 65–66, 69–70, 73–74, 84–85, 87–90, 93–96, 107, 112–118, 133–134, 137, 139, 149
at Regal Theatre, 94–95
rent parties, 37–38, 40, 42
in Scandinavia, 135
Shepherd, Buster and, 141–147
as singer, 53, 74, 95–96, 107
Smith, Willie The Lion and, 32–33, 40
sons, relationship with, 61, 163–173
Tatum, Art and, 96–98
on television, 135
theories on music, 125–126
at WABC, 111–113
Waller, Anita and, 63–64
Waller, Edith and, 20–21, 35–41, 44, 51, 58–59, 71, 76–78, 87

will, 180–181
Williams, Clarence and, 42–46, 49, 50
at WWL, 106–110
at Yacht Club, 136–137
Waller, William Robert (brother), 2, 5–6, 22, 166
Walsh, Paul, 96
Walters, Tiny, 96
Washington, Dinah, 154
Washington, (May) Naomi Waller (sister), xix
Waters, Ethel, 44, 96
Watson, Loren, 89
Wettling, George, 127
"What Did I Do to Be So Black and Blue?," 85–87, 181
Whitby Grill, New York, 111
Whiteman, Paul, 30, 65, 75, 106
Whittet, Ben, 112
Wiley, Lee, 149
Wilkins, Barron, 29
Wilkins, Leroy, 29
Williams, Clarence, 42–46, 49–50, 58, 59, 123, 168, 178
Williams, Corky, 30, 31, 37–38, 40, 41
Williams, Mary Lou, 88–89
Williams, Spencer, 58, 59, 65, 98–101, 133, 134
Wilson, Edith, 86, 87
Wilson, Jack "The Bear," xii
Winchell, Walter, 86, 125, 126
WWL Radio Station, 106–110

Yacht Club, New York, 136–137
Yancy, Jimmy, 30

Zanzibar Room, Hollywood, 158, 159